ABOVE THE BEST

Published by Mindstir Media, LLC
1931 Woodbury Ave. #182 | Portsmouth, New Hampshire 03801 | USA
1.800.767.0531 | www.mindstirmedia.com

Printed in the United States of America
ISBN-13: 978-0-9962872-8-9
Library of Congress Control Number: 2016900799

ABOVE THE BEST

281st ASSAULT HELICOPTER COMPANY
FIRST US ARMY SPECIAL OPERATIONS
HELICOPTER COMPANY

William McDaniel McCollum

MINDSTIR MEDIA

To the Members of the 281st AHC:

Throughout my 38 years of service, and to this day, my assignment to Detachment B-52 (Project Della), 5th Special Forces Group in Vietnam remains one of my fondest memories. The professionalism, courage and dedication of Project Delta NCOs and the pilots and crew members of the 281st made it that way. Training as one team, the operators in Delta knew that the crews of the 281st could always be counted on when the chips were down. Foul weather, enemy fire nor rugged terrain would not preclude the 281st from inserting us or coming to our rescue.

To this day, I owe my life to the 281st AHC crew, led by Captain Bob Moberg, who came to my rescue and that of SFC Robinette and our team along the Laotian border in the fall of 1967. Captain Moberg lowered the jungle penetrator into the triple canopy jungle and lifted out our team in spite of having to nestle the Huey into the trees until he was literally getting blade strikes. As General Sherman said to President Grant, while lamenting the fact that Grant was no longer in the field beside him, "I always knew you would come when I called, if alive," or words to that affect. That was how I always viewed the men of the 281st AHC.

Thanks to each of you for your service to our nation.

General Henry Hugh Shelton
US Army Retired,
14th Chairman, Joint Chiefs of Staff.

Dear Intruders:

The 281st arrived in Vietnam in June 1966, was assigned to the 10th Combat Aviation Battalion on 1 July 1966 and was placed under the Operational Control of the 5th Special Forces Group two days later. It never occurred to me to seek a change in the operational status of the 281st. Indeed, from the very start, I was proud of your mission and the way you went about your demanding tasks. Besides, having the 281st working for the 5th SF Group gave me a chance to fly and visit them all over the country. Flying as a crew member on one of your cross-border operations certainly gave me a different perspective on our normal 10th Battalion operations. In looking over my files, I found this note from Captain William D. Harris of 281st AHC Project Delta, who wrote [The 281st is] "the most lonesome helicopter company in the war." The 281st AHC Intruders developed the tactics and techniques and set the standards for the kind of operations now performed by the 160th Special operations Aviation Regiment. The 281st was very much a part of the Vagabonds of Vietnam, and each of you can be very proud of your legacy.

Intruders, I salute you!

Major General Ben L. Harrison
US Army Retired,
Former Commander,
10th Combat Aviation Battalion

BEYOND BRAVERY

Our team had been performing reconnaissance duties, which required that we stay out of contact with the North Vietnamese soldiers (NVA). However, they had spotted us, and now we were in mortal danger. The brush and the wait-a-minute vines were slowing us down. We were completely exhausted, and we only had a few rounds of ammo left. We were being chased through the dense jungle by a large number of battle-tested, tough, hard core North Vietnamese soldiers. I called on my radio for an emergency extraction. The response was that the 281st was on the way. We had been on the run for hours. I could not imagine how they were going to get us out. The jungle was triple canopied. My map indicated that if we went down a steep hill, there was a river, which I figured we could get across. The North Vietnamese soldiers were gaining on us. It would take a miracle to save us.

I could hear the choppers above us, but could not see them and did not think they could see us. There was no way for a rope ladder or McGuire rig to penetrate the jungle canopy. Suddenly I heard the whop, whop, whop sound of a helicopter getting closer and closer. We had made it to the river, and I could not believe my eyes when I saw the Huey hovering up river under the tree canopy. It was so low that the rotor blades were clipping low-hanging branches. The skids of the helicopter were under water. How did the pilot and crew get that helicopter down under the trees, and how could they control the Huey when there were only inches to spare on each side? This was unbelievable; this was beyond bravery. I knew the real action was about to take place as I hurried my men out into the water. I stayed on shore until the last minute, continuing to fire at the enemy. The crew chief and gunner were also firing their machine guns while helping my wet, tired, and scared men to board the chopper. Then I made a mad dash into the water and was pulled to safety. With a fully loaded helicopter and the North Vietnamese soldiers on the bank shooting at us, the pilots and the crew had to get the Huey turned around to get us out. The problem was there was not enough room to make the turn. Somehow they made it happen, and we got out safely.

Jerry Nelson
Sergeant First Class
5th Special Forces

DEDICATION

It is with humility and a deep sense of honor this book is dedicated to the men, as well as to the wives and families, of America's first Special Operations Helicopter Unit, the 281st Assault Helicopter Company.

Especially recognized and remembered are our fifty-two brothers who died in service to their country. At the time of this writing, ten of those individuals are still unaccounted for. All have been presumed dead. However, each of these men continues to live in the hearts and minds of those who proudly served with them.

As a result of its special operations missions, the unit suffered a higher casualty rate than most aviation units serving in the Vietnam War. Even worse, of the great number of wounded, many continue today to struggle physically and emotionally. We honor them all. We hope that this book will in some way ease their pain.

"No man is dead until he is forgotten"

INTRODUCTION

The 281st Assault Helicopter Company (AHC) has a rich history and involvement in Special Forces Operations. From the first UH-1 helicopter that was operational with the unit in Vietnam until the day the colors were retired, the 281st AHC, as well as the 6th and the 145th Airlift Platoons which preceded it, were instrumental in the strategic reconnaissance missions that were the mainstay of the 5th Special Forces Group Airborne (ABN), Special Projects and Special Operations units. The 281st is considered by the U.S. Army historians to be the legacy unit for today's Special Operations Aviation units, and it was the only assault helicopter company that was directly attached to the 5th Special Forces Group during the Vietnam War.

The following pages are not a history in the true sense of the word; that is not this book's intent. It is a personal story of this special combat assault helicopter unit, from its conception to its conclusion as a combat unit, told by those who served in the 281st. It is a history compiled both from official journals and from the personal experiences of the soldiers who made up its flight crews and support elements.

Why have you never heard of this unit before? As with all Special Operations units, its missions and locations were classified until 1996, and its members were reluctant and unable to describe their combat accomplishments. This history can never be told in complete detail. For each of the incidents related here, members can remember and recount numerous others that are not found in these pages. The accounts of the missions and incidents related here represent the experiences of the majority of the members of the unit. At any given time in its short life span, the 281st and its support elements were comprised of approximately 300 men. They were America's best. They put their lives on the line every day of their tour of duty. These individuals went far beyond doing their job to aid and rescue the Special Forces soldiers they supported. The 281st won its share of awards and honors, receiving twenty battle streamers and numerous national, international and combat accolades, but it paid dearly for all the honors it won. In addition to the ten missing in action, forty-two others lost their lives in the war.

This history highlights the helicopter crews, which include aircraft commanders, co-pilots, crew chiefs and the door gunners. The crew chief and door gunner manned machine guns in flight and as such they had the most dangerous jobs in the unit, no one can deny that. But every member of the 281st served with distinction and honor to make the 281st the outstanding unit it was. Each man performed his duty, often around the clock, to ensure each mission was successful.

There is enough glory in the records and accomplishments of this unique unit to be shared by all. For each name mentioned in this book, countless others could be inserted, for the Vietnam War had as many different views, faces and outcomes as there were individuals serving, and every man has a similar story to describe his view of a particular incident in this book. All the men who served with the 281st in any capacity added their worth to its success; therefore, there is no major character in this book. The real heroes are the men who gave their lives to save their fellow-men. No more can be asked. The purpose of the following pages is simply to record as much of the history of the 281st as possible, while it is still comparatively fresh in the minds of those who served. In years to come, the families of the men who served in this distinguished unit may ask, "What did my relative do in the Vietnam War, and where did he serve?" The honorable veteran or his family can hand them this book and reply, "He served with the 281st." It is an honor to have served with the 281st Assault Helicopter Company and to play a part in recording its history for future generations.

PREFACE

Gathering information and intelligence is of vital importance during a war. The more you know about your opponent or enemy, the better you can plan a surprise and successful attack. Getting good information is the guiding force of any mission. Without intelligence it is only a guessing game. No military leader worth his rank would ever risk the lives of his men by acting on blind chance. At its onset, the mission seemed to be impossible. However, the 281st Assault Helicopter Company was a special helicopter company with good leadership, the right equipment, and brave men with a "can do attitude."

Finding the enemy scattered across a wide area which was hidden underneath the trees of a triple canopy jungle would require foot soldiers on the ground. This first part of the paradox was solved by assigning Special Forces men who had special training, and who were willing and able to accomplish the mission. The second part fell upon the 281st Assault Helicopter Company. The "Intruders" would answer the call. It would be complicated, but the company, as a whole, had a can-do attitude. The problem was how would the Special Forces soldiers get on the ground and then get back out without being detected.

Coordinates of a map do not provide the needed information regarding the small pinholes in the thick jungle canopy in which to set down a helicopter heavily loaded with Special Forces soldiers and their equipment. Nor do the coordinates on a military map pinpoint a hole in the jungle floor for an extraction under heavy fire and, in most cases, different from the location of the insertion. Consequently, the first step was to fly over an area at a high altitude in a small, light, single-engine, fixed-wing aircraft with a US Air Force pilot known as the Forward Air Controller (FAC).

Next was to scout out the potential sites by a helicopter platoon and develop disguising tactics that would give the insertion team a reasonable chance of touching down on the ground without being detected. The extraction was often completed under extremely hostile conditions and in areas where there was no place to land.

The extraction was by ladders, slings hoist and rope tactics that later evolved into the better-suited McGuire rig. These methods left the Special Forces insertion team hanging dangerously in the air under the helicopter while receiving intense enemy fire, holding on for their lives at speeds of more than fifty knots until they were clear of danger.

A great many of those Green Berets did not survive their mission, nor did numerous helicopter crews who flew the insertions and extractions. Some of America's best died while supporting and helping one another. We were brothers and so young.

Jack Green
Captain

Years later, one former 281st warrant officer reminded another of their tour of duty by informing him that he must remember, "We were only summer help."

So goes the story of the 281st Assault Helicopter Company.

CREATION OF PROJECT DELTA

In the mid to late 1950's, Charles (Charlie) Beckwith had gone through significant training with other countries and had learned the need for and significance of covert, top secret missions for reconnaissance and counterinsurgency operations. When the Vietnam War came around he had honed his skills and knowledge for this type of operation and convinced the Army of the need of such a project. Hence, Project Delta was created.

Beckwith, Charles A. (Charlie)
(1983) Delta Force.
New York: Harper Collins.

With trial and error, he was finally able to fine tune his "Project" and began to run an ad for volunteers. "Wanted Volunteers…will guarantee you a medal, a body bag, or both." This no doubt set the stage for the quality of men who would work in his "Project Delta." Early on, Beckwith learned in order to run his Project properly he needed his own helicopter unit and pressed Special Forces and The Army for such a unit. The orders were cut and so began the creation of the 281st Assault Helicopter unit. While running his operations in the south, he was using two aviation units: the 6th platoon and the 145th. They worked individually and collectively giving Charlie and Project Delta support. The Delta missions became more demanding and a whole new kind of flying had to be developed to support these demands; rappelling, rope ladders, McGuire rigs, impossible landing zones, special flight maneuvers such as the "high overhead approach" flight formations," gunship support and much more. The 281st used a Delta or "V" flight formation: hole ships on the left and recovery aircraft on the right. Wolf Pack was right behind. With itchy trigger fingers and sweaty palms, the guys were drooling for action. To the good guys on the ground it was salvation. To the bad guys, the thunderous whop, whop of the incoming flight was the fear of God.

Since Delta was a part of the 5th Special Forces Group, a compound was established at the Group Headquarters in Nha Trang. Delta moved into its compound and along with the Project came the 6th and 145th. These two units were combined into the 2nd Platoon of the 171st Assault Helicopter Company and Beckwith had the seed for his autonomous aviation unit. The men of these two units learned and honed the skills required for Delta missions and were ready to pass on their knowledge to the 281st guys when they got there. While they were "holding down the fort," the 281st was on its way for deployment to South Vietnam.

FOREWORD

A 281st BANDIT PLATOON LEADER REMEMBERS

In my judgment, the pilots and crews of the 281st Assault Helicopter Company were like the knights of old. They went out day after day, singly or in twos and threes, to hold the battlefield against all comers and to do battle in defense of the Fifth Special Forces and its long range reconnaissance unit, Detachment B-52, Project Delta. Pilots and air-crews felt they were invincible; "6 Feet Tall and Bullet proof."

Single-ship missions were done without support. The life of each man depended on his own skill while working in harmony with the skills of the rest of the crew against the enemy. A single-ship insertion into a jungle hole was a result of collective mission planning between the Project Delta Long Range Reconnaissance Patrol (LRRP) team leader and the aircrews. The teamwork for the organizing, planning, equipping, operations, rehearsals, briefings and execution of this precision mission made the difference between failure and success. This process drove a bond of close relationships, cohesion, accountability and ownership for a Project Delta LRRP team during its various stages of operation.

Pilots and aircrews followed the daily movement of their inserted LRRP team and were prepared to extract the assigned team under any conditions, day or night. In the process of an emergency extraction, a few sets of rotor blades might be lost, but the LRRP teams came home safely, ready for another day of work. In summary, I did not find this bond of cohesion and trust between the foot soldiers and Army aviation in other units in which I served. Each act of valor I witnessed went so far beyond human comprehension that no one could really explain it, not even those who had served in battle and were involved in the events.

Today, 47 years later, I find these acts of sacrifice so profound that I am somewhat uneasy with the commonness of my own humanity. The 281st certainly did personify the ideals and virtues of Army Values: Loyalty, Duty, Respect, Selfless Service, Honor, Integrity and Personal Courage. The battlefield and the strategic environment changed as the 281st moved into the Delta, Central Delta, Central Highlands and A Shau Valley, but the character of the unit did not. On many occasions the 281st displayed immeasurable loyalty and courage under the most harrowing conditions. As I recall, when the 281st was fighting in the A Shau Valley, aircrews risked their lives repeatedly during insertions, extractions, combat assaults and evacuation of the wounded and dead. The 281st became the LRRP's and reaction forces' only connection to the world outside the bloody battleground.

During one particular tactical emergency, many aircrews flew again and again through a barrage of antiaircraft and small arms fire to support Project Delta. "I was there as a Platoon Leader. I witnessed the events that unfolded while flying helicopter tail number 113, with Ken Smith as co-pilot, Jay Hays as crew chief and Ron De Leon as gunner."

Those twin sixties fabricated by Jay Hays saved us. They barked with distinction, providing suppressive fire time and again. I never did ask Jay where he had obtained the extra M-60 machine guns. Someday I will. The modification and neat floor mike switches that Jay fabricated allowed Jay and Ron to keep those machine guns firing while talking to the pilots about the grave situation. Other aircrews and number 113 went many times into this single-ship, hot-landing zone (LZ) while withstanding a gauntlet of automatic weapons fire. Ship 113 went out, again and again, to assist an aircraft that had been shot down or shot up with wounded on board. We sucked it in and went to deliver ground forces or extract wounded, downed crews or to rescue a maintenance rigging crew. Unfortunately, some made the ultimate sacrifice, and others were wounded. Heroism was reflected in physical courage, deep moral conviction, and the stamina to continue the fight.

Indeed, the legacy of the 281st is a story of a remarkable, unyielding spirit and uncompromisingly fierce defiance in the face of death and a determined enemy. I clearly remember the many acts of valor of this unit and the courage and sacrifice of the pilots and crews who fought and served with a one-of-a-kind aviation unit in Vietnam, the 281st. Today and always, my heart, mind and soul are with the 281st because this Army Aviation Unit was the best of the best and flew above the best. There were no "we can't" words spoken by the pilots and aircrews of the 281st Assault Helicopter Company.

Colonel John Wehr
U.S. Army, Retired

CONTENTS

1966

IN THE BEGINNING

The major said, "Captain, welcome aboard. You are going to be the service platoon leader. You have a big job ahead of you, and there is no time to waste." The way he kept saying "you" left a lump in my stomach. I was wondering if I could talk myself out of this job. I had been a pilot for a few years flying the Bird Dog and the Beaver. I had just recently completed training in the UH-1 helicopter. I knew the importance of a good pre-flight check but had never been a maintenance type person. In fact, I had never been much of a mechanic, even with my own car. I said, "Sir, I think you have the wrong man for this job as I would do a much better job as a gunship platoon leader." He stood up, looked at me, and said, "You come here well recommended, and I have all the confidence in the world in you." Then he walked out and left me standing there with that lump. Of course, he was the company commander, and I have learned that it is very hard to change a major's mind. The one good thing about the situation was that we had no helicopters, yet.

Captain Lynn Coleman,
Fort Benning, Georgia
January, 1966

Fort Benning, Georgia was a busy place on a cold January morning. The Army Airborne School, with its jump tower for training purposes, was just up the road. The Army Infantry Officers Training School was just up the street. The shoulder patch said, "Follow me." Their shoulder patch was round with the letters OCS on their left shoulder. Everything there was spit and shine. The students were pushed to the limits. Everything was "dress right dress." Each company was going its own way, each singing its own cadence song. For the most part, this was where the infantry's "Queen of Battle" started. Soldiers were becoming a part of the lean, mean, green machine. Some would say this was the real army; this is what it was all about.

Just three years earlier, the 11th Air Assault was organized and began its training with the new workhorse of aviation, the UH-1 Bell helicopter known as the "Huey." Lawson Army Airfield was a busy place. Later the 11th Air Assault became the 1st Cavalry Division (Airmobile.)

The Army was in the process of forming a special helicopter company with a mission unlike anything the Army had ever had before. Usually, when a new outfit was formed, it consisted of personnel and equipment that no one else wanted. But the 281st was not that kind of unit. Officers and enlisted men were of the highest caliber, well trained and well qualified. From its beginning, the 281st operated with highly-trained men with new equipment.

281st AIR MOBILE LIGHT

The 281st was organized on paper and first placed on the rolls of the army on 6 October 1965, per general order 318, para. 1, Third U.S. Army. It was comprised of a Headquarters element, a Service Platoon, the 483rd Transportation Detachment and the 499th Signal Detachment. (The 499th Signal Detachment history dates back to April 1945.) It was designated as the 281st (-) Air Mobile Light. The (-) indicated that it was missing some of its elements.

There was no big painted sign out front to indicate that this was the new company, just a building with a number. It did not stand out; there was nothing fancy about the place. When something like this starts up, there is usually chaos, with people running around not knowing what is going on. However, everyone knew that this was a special kind of army outfit, and right from the start it was well organized.

SIGNING IN

Officers and enlisted men were signing in; the company headquarters was a very busy place. Each man came well qualified to do his assigned job. There were no loose ends. The company was coming together rather quickly. Officers and enlisted men were working side by side, getting to know one another, becoming a team and a band of brothers.

Equipment was arriving and was logged and packed in containers in preparation for being shipped overseas. Nothing was packed away haphazardly. Each item and container was numbered. The organizational skills of the officers and enlisted men were outstanding.

The men in the new company knew where they were going. Each man knew he was heading off to war. All knew that they had to work as a team. The news on TV and in the newspapers carried daily stories of how things were going in South Vietnam. The war was real and was going to become personal in a few months. Some men were anxious, and others were excited; some were looking forward to their assignment, and others dreaded leaving. After a few months the company was ready to go. The men had been briefed on what lie ahead and what would be expected of them. However, at this early date they had no idea how important a role this new organization, the 281st Aviation Company, would play in this one-of-a-kind mission.

To put the final touch on all of this, there were immunizations, record checks, personal effects, legal forms to fill out, and most important - family. The hardest part for everyone was saying goodbye to loved ones. Going off to war is a sad thing for families, a very sad thing.

Company picture taken at Lawson Army Air Field, Fort Benning, Georgia.

SHIPPING OUT

The containers were full, locked and sealed. Each had a number, and a complete inventory had been made. The company was ready to go. Moving 200 plus men and equipment would be a nightmare, but the Army was good at this sort of thing, and the Navy would help with the use of its steel "transporters," conex containers. It was easy.

The conex containers were a rigid, steel, reusable container capable of carrying 9,000 pounds. They were 8'6" long, 6'3" wide, and 6'10" high. On one end there

Two connexes converted to a field house.

was a double-door that could be locked and secured. Each container was mounted on elevated skids and had lifting rings on the top four corners.

These containers became the backbone of logistics support for Vietnam, and nearly every major Army unit moving into the theater carried their spare parts and supplies in these containers.

Many containers never made it back from the theater; they were employed as command posts, dispensaries, portable stores, and bunkers, whatever was needed. The containers provided millions of square feet of covered storage that the theater lacked. These containers were life savers for the shipment of supplies from one place to another.

In some ways this was the easy part. The list had been checked, checked again and then again one last time. It was time to move out. With bag and baggage each soldier was ready to go. The service platoon leader with eight men and six UH-1 helicopters went aboard an old but pretty good navy ship. Or was it?

USNS BRETON

The Breton had been commissioned in 1943, and it had seen a lot of action during WW II as an aviation transport ship. In 1946 the ship had been docked and put out of commission. In early 1958, the Breton had been refurbished and was back in service. This was definitely an old ship, but she served her purpose. The Navy and the Army were working together to make this a good ride. The tugboats pushed her out into the Pacific and turned her loose. The big engines slowly turned as the captain took her from the pier and under the Golden Gate Bridge to start her voyage to the Philippine Islands.

The belly of the Breton was full of all kinds of aircraft; six of the UH-1s were brand new and assigned to the 281st. The old ship was fully loaded with men, spare parts, all kinds of equipment and soldiers. General Westmoreland had ordered the U.S. Navy not to waste any time; the aircraft were needed as soon as possible.

The captain and his crew had the engines churning at good speed, moving at about 30 knots. The Breton was on course and on time. With warm weather and rough seas, the heavy ship was rocking and rolling.

Without any warning, the ship made an unusual noise and then slowed to a crawl. Everyone aboard knew something was wrong. Out in the Pacific Ocean, following the sun, the old ship had broken down, just north of 30 degrees latitude and west of 130 degrees longitude, a long way from the Philippine Islands. The USNS Breton was barely moving. Now what?

The captain announced over the ship's intercom that there was a mechanical problem. He would have to make a change in direction, taking a slight turn to the left, and to try to make it to an island called Hawaii.

"I made sure my men knew what I knew and passed on the information about the mechanical problems. I informed them the captain was going to try to make it to Hawaii; there was not one complaint or grumbling about the detour."
Lynn Coleman

While docked at this sunny paradise, it took twelve days and nights to fix the problem. On the thirteenth day, with all the repairs completed and everyone back aboard, it was time to return to the Pacific. Each night the crew listened

USNS Breton

to news reports about how the war was going in that small country called Vietnam.

Sixteen days later the captain made his way through the channels and docked at the southern tip of Vietnam at a city called Vung Tau. There the 281st mechanics installed the blades, checked each aircraft and made sure the "Hueys" were ready to take to the air. It had been a long trip. The pilots and crews loaded up and rose from the decks of a Navy ship for their first flight. They headed north along the shores of the South China Sea to Nha Trang, South Vietnam. Captain Lynn Coleman, Captain Stanley (Rudy) Morud, and PFC Gary Stagman, Crew Chief, led the flight of aircrafts to their new home.

USNS GORDON

Another old ship, the USNS Gordon, was also brought out of mothballs and was making its first voyage since 1955. This type of ship, first known as a liberty ship, was being used as a troop transport carrier. The main body of the 281st was aboard, with 321 men sectioned off in the belly of this beast. The canvas bunks were arranged one on top of the other and stacked five high.

This voyage was a first for most of the men, and when the old ship began to rock and roll in the swells of the Pacific, you could see that sick look on some faces as men hurriedly made their way up to the deck. There is no need for the details. Navy food is not bad until you start to feel that rumbling feeling deep down in your stomach. It has a way of coming back up at the worst time.

A slow journey to a foreign land is not a good thing for soldiers. The general sentiment was to get over there, get the job done and get back home.

"I was thinking that if our service was needed so badly then why not let the U.S. Air Force get us there. That would only take hours, not days. But hey, I am only a low ranking enlisted man. What do I know? It is what it is." Larry Hubbard, Private First Class

The old ship was doing pretty well, and what a good thing it was to see land. A straight line from California to the Philippine Islands is about 6,975 miles. It takes a lot of fuel and supplies to keep a large ship like the Gordon out on the high seas. Nineteen days of riding in the belly of the ship was a long time and a rough ride. It was good to be docked, but that only lasted for a short eighteen hours.

USNS Gordon

Naturally, no one was allowed to go ashore. Before the sun had cast its morning rays on the waters, the tugboats pushed the big ship back out into the deep waters and headed her east. Three more days.

USNS Gordon docked, but that only lasted for a short eighteen hours. Naturally, no one was allowed to go ashore. Before the sun had cast its morning rays on the waters, the tugboats pushed the big ship back out into the deep waters and headed her east. Another three days of sailing lay ahead.

NHA TRANG BAY

Saturday, 4 June 1966, the old ship was moving ever so slowly as she entered the Bay of Nha Trang. All the troops were out on deck. The beach looked inviting, the weather was hot, and the humidity was high. All at once the old boat came to a sudden stop. She was a sitting duck out in the Bay. She had run aground on a sand bar. The sun was beating down while this big USNS waited until the tugs pushed her free. Welcome to South Vietnam.

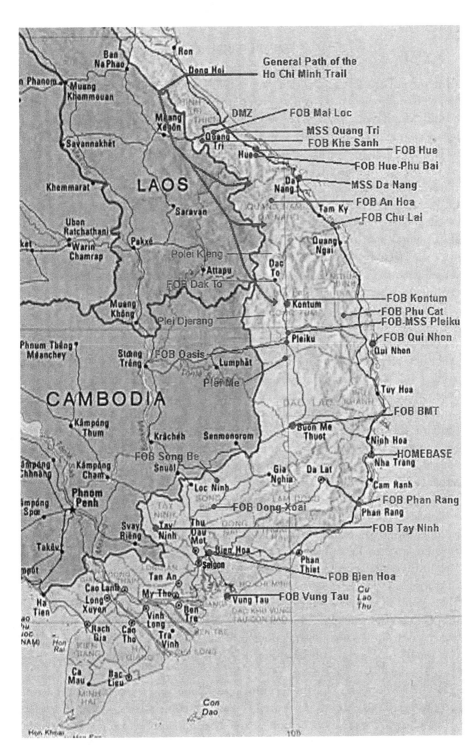

Map of South Vietnam – Courtesy of Bob Mitchell

23

THE BLENDING

The men of the 281st AHC had arrived "in country" and were ready for action although none of them had any idea what kind of action they were in for. The men of the 145th lift platoon supported by the gunships of the 6th had accepted every challenge thrown at them from Beckwith and his "Project Delta." Men like Jack Green who flew the first McGuire rig extraction in combat with his underpowered "B" model Huey, Kevin Murphy, the CO of the 145th, John Hyatt, Cpt. Gary Steele CO of the 6th along with Jerry Stanfield, Daniel Bishop, Josef Thorne and many others all helped set the stage for final merging of the units. All the knowledge and experience of these men had to be passed on and absorbed by the newly arriving men of the 281st.

It is important that the story of the men who built the foundation and paved the way for the 281st. be told. These men of the 6th guns and the 145th Air Lift Platoon had the experience; they had been tested, scarred, wounded and some had lost their lives while serving their country. These stories belong to them.

****

Families, organizations and military units all have a "family history;" a starting point. Some are just more colorful than others. The 281st originated from a more unusual background than most modern military organizations. It was the blending, mending, and mentoring of three of the most unlikely candidates for the first Special Operations Helicopter unit the Army would not admit to. Each of the three elements; the 6th, the 145th, and the 281st Air Mobile Light, had its own unique story of how and why they were merged together in June of 1966 to become the 281st Assault Helicopter Company.

The 145th was a holdover from the early days of the Vietnam conflict before the Air Mobile became a reality. The resultant change in aviation support saw large assault helicopter companies performing a greater role in troop transport, and no one knew quite what to do with these small, ten-aircraft units. By mid-1965 the mission of this unit gradually changed toward increased support of the 5th Special Forces headquartered in Nha Trang, and a new classified mission known as Project Delta.

The second in country element of the unit in this master plan involved the 6th Airlift Platoon gunships known as the "Fangs." Both units had similar beginnings and were given similar mission assignments. These were typical assignments handed out to small units in the early stages of the Vietnam conflict, which included supporting Special Forces operations.

The change of mission for the two units came about as a result of an after action report by the Commander of 5th Special Forces Detachment B-52, known as Project Delta. The report was highly critical of the aviation support being received from the various army aviation units that supported the highly classified "Project Delta." The report stated that U.S. helicopter pilots needed to be permanently assigned to

Project Delta for training and operations.

On Christmas Day 1965, the 145th and the 6th were reassigned to support the 5th Special Forces by the Commander, United States Army Vietnam (USARV), and specialized unit training was begun with Project Delta. The stage was now set to combine the initial in country assets to form the core of what was to become the first Special Operations Helicopter Unit in the United States Army. The two units were combined and based in Nha Trang with the 5th Special Forces Group Headquarters.

If anyone thought that being assigned to the newly-formed Aviation Company was going to be a cake walk, they were wrong! During one of the first support missions in An Lao Valley in February 1966, all hell broke loose. Excerpts from the memoirs of individual crew members who were involved in that first full-blown mission reveal how bad it was:

I remember the Bong Song mission. It seemed as if they had decided to put every Recon team that Delta had into the AO at the same time, and every team made contact with Charlie at the same time, plus the weather closed in on us. The Delta Commander wouldn't listen to us about not inserting ALL of Delta's teams at the same time. We didn't have enough Hueys for one thing. Oh yeah, if we needed more, we were told that the 1st Cav. would send some up from their blocking position on the river and in the valley farther south. When it all hit the fan, we never did see any of them. I made four or five trips up that damned valley to where the Recon teams were getting shot up. This was also when one of the Special Forces Team Leaders was MIA. He walked southeast for days until he arrived at Nha Trang. Then we had to hover over an LZ to extract the only survivor of one of the teams, and we had to use a rope ladder to extract him. The rotor rpm was falling, and we did this wild 180 degree turn DOWN the hillside with the ladder hanging out the open cargo door. I was expending as much ammo as I could, while at the same time I was checking the upcoming tree line trying to judge distance and rate of climb. Yeah, I know that's "the pilot's job," but you are forgetting that I was on the bird too. I immediately handed the Recon Sergeant an axe designed to cut the rope ladder. He must have finally cut the rope because we made it out with tree branches in the skids and busted chin bubbles. After refueling and rearming, soiling my pants, puking my guts out and pumping JP4, all at the same time, there was still room for me to think, "God, do I really have to go back up that damned valley AGAIN!" I was not scared, I was TERRIFIED! Upon arrival in the north of that valley, the loudest sound I ever heard went through the cabin of our Huey. The pilot, co-pilot, crew chief and door gunner all looked at each other and never said a word. I have no idea what made the noise. I do remember thinking, "David, you have to get a Bigger Gun!" Right after that I informed Company HQ that I was really a trained helicopter crew chief and the infantryman thing was secondary.

Sergeant David L. Bitle
Door Gunner, Crew Chief and Platoon Sergeant
Wolf Pack 36 Yankee

"My God, Bitle, you've gotta be talking about pulling in Wylie Gray, the only really quiet southerner I've ever met. He was from West Virginia if my memory serves me correctly! Wylie had been running solo for three or four days with the locals in hot pursuit. Desperate to find him, I put search teams out, and he flashed a panel. We had one gunship and one slick flying at 500 feet to let the survivors know we were there for them and could drop in quick. I was flying the slick and Joe Thurston was in trail with the lone gunship. We'd just taken some serious ground fire. It was so serious that five rounds hit my seat pan and threw me against the harness so hard I was black and blue from shoulder blades to my belly button. All I remember is the radio call from the pilot they had a flashing panel and were going to check it out. About two or three lifetimes later, the pilot answered my 4th or 5th radio call with the words, "We have one SF on board, and I think we're gonna make it." God, how did I ever get involved with you crazy bastards?"

Major Kevin Murphy
Platoon Commander

This photo was taken right after the 145th Aviation Platoon became OPCON to the 5th SFG in 1966. The crews were issued new camouflage fatigues (tiger stripes) including a bush hat. The uniforms were "sterile" in that they had no rank or other identification. The uniforms appear to be new and the helicopter had no markings.

AN LAO VALLEY

It was 1966, and the 145th Airlift Platoon had been working for several days out of Bong Son Special Forces Camp in support of Project Delta, which was conducting recon missions in the An Lao Valley, located in Binh Dinh Province in South Vietnam. I was the crew chief of a troop carrying "slick" tail number 22045, and "Mardi Gras 6" was our call sign. The gunner was a Californian named Russell Isaacs. Nine of the ten helicopters in the platoon were on the mission: six slicks, two gunships, and a "Hog Frog." Our tenth helicopter was undergoing maintenance back at our home base in Nha Trang. Our mission, as I understood it, was to quietly insert the Delta teams into the valley, provide air cover with our gunships, and pick them up on demand. The Delta Team was to locate a large Viet Cong and North Vietnamese Army force in the An Lao Valley. As soon as it was located, a brigade of the 1st Cavalry Division, which was operating nearby in the Bong Son Plain, would destroy the force as quickly as possible. This was part of the early stages of Operation Masher.

The Delta teams in the valley were compromised almost from the start. On the morning of January 29, most of the platoon was out flying direct support or combat assault missions in or around the An Lao Valley. Major Kevin Murphy, the platoon commander, had gone off to the Special Forces Camp to meet with Major Charlie Beckwith and other Project Delta operations staff. Our helicopter, tail number 045, was parked nearby in an adjacent graveyard where we had bivouacked the last few nights. Isaacs and I were doing routine maintenance on the ship and our weapons when Major Murphy came running out and told us to saddle up. One of the recon teams was in contact and needed immediate pickup. Major Beckwith arrived with three other Delta people, a first sergeant, a radioman, and another officer. We immediately started the engine, and Major Murphy made radio contact with the rest of the platoon. However, the men had either just landed or were on their way back to refuel and rearm at the camp airstrip and could not join up with us right away. A quick decision was made for 045 to leave immediately, in advance of the rest of the platoon, and to quickly locate the team. We would then act as the Command & Control aircraft while the others made the pickup and delivered any required aerial gun support. We took off with our crew of four, which included Aircraft Commander Major Murphy, Co-pilot Chief Warrant Officer Southwell, Isaacs and me, as well as the four Delta members. The weather was awful. It was cold, there was low-level cloud cover with a ceiling below 1,000 feet, and rain was falling in a constant drizzle that could lighten to a mist or fall more heavily. Fog and drizzle drifted down from slate-gray clouds seldom higher than 3,000 feet. Visibility usually extended no more than three miles. In the early morning hours, low stratus clouds dropped below a 1,000 foot ceiling, and the fog that resulted lifted slowly, dissipating by mid-to-late morning. Fog frequently persisted in the valleys, obscuring mountain ridges and peaks and creating perilous flying conditions.

Since the ceiling was so low, we flew at an altitude of 300 to 400 feet over the area just outside of the Special Forces camp and then over some farms, picking up speed as we flew. Sitting in the open cargo door on the pilot's side, I wore my field jacket under my flak jacket and chicken plate, and I had the visor down on my helmet in an attempt to stay warm and shield myself from the rain. Each drop of rain that hit was painful. Even with protection, the rain was still impacting on my hands and chin, while the water running down my helmet visor and neck soaked me under my jacket. The visibility was not good, but I could see fairly well along the ground from our low altitude. Few people were in view, but those I could see looked like farmers moving about. Not far from the Bong Son Airfield, and before we had gotten to the narrow part of the valley, we suddenly broke into the open over some rice paddies. Our altitude was still only a few hundred feet, and in front of us and slightly to the left was a paddy dike lined with tall palm trees and another dike off to the far left. I saw no people.

Almost immediately, I heard the sharp, sub-sonic cracking of small arms and automatic weapons, and I realized that we were taking fire from the tree line along the paddy dike, which we were flying toward at about a 30 degree angle from my side of the helicopter. I started to deliver some suppressive fire from my M-60 into the tree line, working from the right to the left. Major Beckwith, who was sitting next to me, began firing his M-16 over my right shoulder, and the first sergeant, who was sitting on the floor in front of me, also began firing. I was leaning forward in my seat, holding the 60 with both hands, my right elbow resting on my right knee and my left hand under the weapon to steady it as I fired. I only got off about 20 or 30 rounds when WHAM! My right hand was literally blown off the M-60's pistol grip, and I felt an almost equal impact on my right thigh. The world seemed full of red dots, and the pain was beyond description. At that moment, time seemed to slip into slow motion.

I looked down at my hand, and I could see smoke coming out of the hole in the top. I glanced at Major Beckwith, and I knew immediately that he had a gut wound and was hurt much worse than I was. I looked up at the first sergeant. The look of total surprise on his face, combined with red spots of blood all over his face and head, made me start laughing, more in pain than in mirth. I held out my arm to him because I wanted him to stop the bleeding. I'm sure that he had no idea why I was doing this, but eventually he clamped down on my arm and slowed the blood loss.

I was not able to process everything that was happening. There was a lot of smoke and confusion in the helicopter, and a very active radio net was assessing the situation. I thought that Warrant Officer Southwell got hit in the butt with shrapnel when something came up through the floor, but I'm not exactly sure what happened after I was hit. The helicopter was shaking furiously as we continued on, banking somewhat to the right. I could hear Isaac's M-60 working, and the pain in my hand and the fear of getting hit again or, even worse, of crashing, made me decide to keep at it. I took my weapon in my left hand and starting firing again, one-handed, toward the base of the tree line, which was now very close to us. As we banked over the tree line along the paddy dike, I could see people in uniform tracking us with their weapons. All of us were firing furiously, aiming at anything that moved. Beckwith was half lying on the seat and in a lot more pain than I was, and I could hear his staff telling him to hold on. The Special Forces officer told him, "Hold on, Boss. You're hit pretty bad. We're going to have to get you back." He then got on the radio, and he and Major Murphy decided to abort and go directly back to the Special Forces compound.

The fight had seemed to last a very long time, but I'm sure that it was only seconds. We flew back to Bong Son and landed just outside the perimeter wire of the Special Forces camp. Major Beckwith was unloaded, and Isaacs came over to my side of the helicopter to hold me up, putting my left arm over his shoulders. He carried me over to the narrow path leading through the wire, where we encountered a journalist who was blocking the way. Isaacs started yelling at him to get out of the way, but the guy just stood there with his mouth open, fumbling with his camera equipment, trying to get it out and take a picture. When we got to him, Isaacs shoved him over the roll of barbed wire, where he landed on his back on top of more wire and fell to the ground. I don't think that he ever said a word to us.

Isaacs then took me into the aid station and stayed with me for a bit while a medic gave me some morphine. Things began to get hazy for me, but I remember that they were working furiously on Major Beckwith. After a while I heard Major Murphy start yelling. It sounded like he was getting really angry because they were not working on me and also because the dustoff chopper had not arrived yet. I also remember someone trying to calm him down. Eventually, a dustoff chopper picked me up and took me to the Hospital in Qui Nhon.

When I woke up from my surgery, Colonel McKean, the Commander of 5th Special Forces, was sitting on the bed next to mine while members of his staff circled in the background. I was pretty groggy, but what I remember of the conversation was that the 145th had done a good job and had recovered the survivors of the team that we were after. Overall casualties among the teams inserted into the valley were heavy, but they had found a large number of Viet Cong, and Colonel McKean had requested that a B-52 strike take place before the enemy had time to flee. When I asked him what had happened to the backup that we were promised, he told me that the 1st Cavalry was unable to carry out their end of the mission because they were bogged down in a fight elsewhere. I also remember asking him about certain Delta members and expressing a great deal of anger over our losses to find an enemy who was then allowed to get away.

Later on, I decided that I really appreciated his visit. He made me feel like I had contributed to an important mission and that I had the respect of people that I thought of as some of the bravest people that I had ever met. It was also the only time in that war that anyone ever took the time to give me an explanation of how our efforts fit into the larger campaign picture and why it was worth it. To this day, I still do not know what I was hit with! While I was in the hospital, Russell Isaacs told me that it was a .30 caliber armor piercing round and that it had also hit Major Beckwith. Because the Major was sitting right next to me firing over my shoulder, the round went through my hand, nicked my right leg, and then hit him in the stomach. We were both hit at exactly the same time. The round made an M-16 sized hole in the back of my hand and a larger exit wound in my wrist. If it had been a .51 caliber, I would have lost my entire hand.

I spent a year at Madigan Army Hospital in Tacoma, Washington, getting my hand repaired. I then went back to college, graduated, went to work, got married and had kids. Life has been good for me, but every day I remember the men I served with in the 145th Airlift Platoon. Even though it has been a long while since this incident, I still think about it often.

Duane D. Vincent
Private First Class

In early February 1966, the new UH-1D helicopter arrived, and all the personnel from the 6th Airlift Platoon started transition training. In early April the initial Company Headquarters folks from the 281st arrived in Nha Trang.

By the end of March all of the assets were consolidated at Nha Trang and placed under complete Operational Control of the Commander, 5th Special Forces. The mission was to provide helicopter aviation support, as directed by the 5th Special Forces Group. It was OFFICIAL, and the unit was becoming pretty good at the task.

Now the dance began. In mid to late March the 281st was supporting "Delta" at Hue Phu Bai. This mission placed it in the unenviable position of "hunting for Charlie" in the A Shau Valley, which was like flying up the Grand Canyon with a jungle clinging to the walls. The weather and location combined to create some nearly impossible situations to operate in. Often the visibility and power to climb ran out at the same time. The Recon teams didn't fare much better, but with combined teamwork the job got done. Returning to Nha Trang from this mission, two aircraft were lost and had one seriously injured crew chief in the following incident:

My luck ran out on me today, 30 March 1966. To explain why, I'll have to go back to yesterday at Phu Bai. We had been supporting a brutal Long Range Reconnaissance Patrol (LRRP) mission in the A Shau Valley. We were returning to our home base in Nha Trang. Our formation formed up after a refuel stop at Qui Nhon. I had changed aircraft there because one of the gunship pilots stated that his bird was acting up, and I wanted to see for myself just what the problem was. I left my personal gear aboard the first aircraft since this was to be the last leg of a routine flight back to Nha Trang. Our flight was at 4,500 feet, just south and west of Tuy Hoa on the central coast, when Joe Thurston, the pilot of the lead gun ship which had all my personal gear, called over the radio, "My God, Witch Doctor," (my maintenance call sign) "Our engine just exploded, I'm going into autorotation." He made a wide, descending turn toward the paved highway below and began his autorotation. The remainder of the flight began to orbit while the recovery ship that I was in and another gun ship started to follow the downed helicopter for what we all thought was going to be a routine recovery. The first ship had been hit by the equivalent of 50 caliber anti-aircraft gunfire. Joe T. and his crew made a beautiful approach to the road staring at only to find themselves a VC (Viet Cong) road block. Joe set the ship down on the road, and his entire crew immediately began drawing fire. He called on the FM radio and said, "My crew chief has just been hit and we're taking heavy fire from all sides." The gunship flying cover then began a gun run to suppress the enemy fire, and Jim Jackson and I in the recovery ship began a low fast approach to the downed aircraft. Our recovery ship was about to touch down in a rice paddy next to the helicopter that had auto-rotated when a number of guys in the other green uniforms began to run away in all directions. Suddenly, it appeared to be hailing lead all around our Huey as we attempted to complete the recovery. Our crew chief shouted, "Look out!" as Jim J. started to bring our ship to a hover. Just then our Huey seemed to literally explode. The head, mast, rotor blades and transmission left the aircraft, and then there were nine people on the ground with Charlie instead of four. At this point, time seemed to go into suspended animation as we waited for additional helicopter gunship support from Tuy Hoa to arrive on site to help neutralize Charlie. The following ordeal actually took 27 minutes from autorotation to our final recovery, but it seemed like several years. When our recovery aircraft crashed into the rice paddy, both crews were evacuated under heavy fire from an estimated platoon of Viet Cong, (later revised to nearly thirty-five), from a hillside about 250 feet to the west of our position. Because of the extreme heavy fire, neither of our flight crews was able to move to a more suitable location for evacuation. Two helicopters attempting to rescue us were forced to abort. My first response mentally was, "My God, this is it. We're going home in a box." Once I regained my composure, I realized that the enemy positions had to be taken under fire by aircraft before another rescue attempt could be made. The only way this was going to happen was for someone to go back inside one of the downed Huey's, turn on the radios, put on the flight helmet and start talking with the ship assigned as command and control (C&C). Ignoring enemy fire from as close as 150 feet, I began to advise the C&C of our situation. As additional gunships arrived on scene, I called fire direction for them in order to neutralize the situation. By this time the VC had selected more strategic positions and was becoming harder to spot. After we substantially reduced the enemy fire, the first recovery ship was directed into the landing zone, and we ensured that the first six crew members were on board the recovery ship. They made it out okay, but once again the small arms fire seemed to intensify. The C&C aircraft crew instructed the first recovery ship to immediately head for the medical facilities at Tuy Hoa to attend to the wounded crew chief. I called in another round of ARA (Aerial Rocket Artillery) before directing the second recovery ship in to pick up the remaining crew members

on the ground." Everyone was recovered, and the wounded crew chief was evacuated to 8th field hospital in Nha Trang where he recovered. The next day after the 339th Aircraft Maintenance Company went in and recovered the downed helicopters, they counted 200 bullet holes, nearly equally divided between the two recovered Hueys.

The 101st Airborne secured the area and helped with the recovery of the aircraft along with what gear Charlie saw fit to leave behind, which in this case was darn little.

What we did not know until 35 years later after much of the information was declassified, was that our flight had been tracked from Phu Bai to Qui Nhon by the North Vietnamese and Viet Cong. We had been specifically targeted to be ambushed south of Tuy Hoa. The 5th Special Forces LRRP missions had disrupted a significant NVA military operation in I Corps and retribution was in order.

April began slowly, but by the end of the month, we were in the Tra Bong Valley, basing our aircraft at the Marine Base in Chu Lai. The word was out that if anything happened to you on any of these flights, you were pretty much on your own. We were operating near the Laotian Border where one of the exits from the Ho Chi Minh Trail traveled to a point just south of Da Nang. At this point the 6th Airlift Platoon and the 145th Airlift Platoon were officially combined into an organization known as the 2nd Platoon of the 171st Assault Helicopter Company. This was a result of the first "blending" in preparation for the final combining of the three elements that would create the 281st. We had endured this "blending" process five months prior when the 6thand 145th joined forces to officially support the Fifth Special Forces Group and "Project Delta." The two units were just getting comfortable with each other when we received word of the "Stateside Element" that was due somewhere around the first of June. We knew that these new guys had no idea about the units real mission or what experience would be needed for the task they were about to undertake.

The following is an excerpt from a letter dated 16 May 1966 that our aircraft maintenance officer sent to his wife:

It is now 11:40 pm, and I'm just getting a chance to write to you. We finally finished processing the last of our old birds today and got them transferred to their new owners. This evening we had a safety and maintenance meeting on our new UH-1Cs and then had a gun platoon meeting about the same aircraft. In a few weeks things will be in a state of total confusion around here again when the last element of people and equipment finally arrives from the States, and we become the 281st Assault Helicopter Company. If all goes according to plan, we'll have 28 new aircraft at that point and no one with any serious experience to keep them flying. Most of our Old Guys will have passed their DEROS (Date of Expected Rotation from Over Seas assignment), and God only knows if the New Guys have any idea of the mission and maintenance requirements that lie ahead of them.   Lou

On 19 May we were supporting Project Delta for an operation out of Tay Ninh. During this action, in a firefight north of Tay Ninh, Sergeant Mahlon Buckalew, the first Wolf Pack (gunship) Platoon Sergeant, was awarded the Silver Star for Gallantry in Action, making him the first member of the 281st Assault Helicopter Company and the 10th Combat Aviation Battalion to receive such an honor. It was another mission where during the extraction of a Delta Team. The helicopter crews came under intense ground fire while leaving the LZ. Sergeant Buckalew dismounted his M-60 machine gun, secured himself to the aft cargo wall of the Huey, stepped out onto the skids, and proceeded to fire his M-60 machine gun "John Wayne Style" providing covering fire to the rear of the flight, suppressing the enemy fire and allowing a safe departure for his unit comrades. You really had to be there to believe it, and even if you were there, you still had difficulty believing it!

On 23 May 1966 the major part of the 281st Assault Helicopter Company arrived in Nha Trang. The last portion of the "blending process" began, and it did not start well. The New Guys from the States, Officers and Non Commissioned Officers alike, were used to the "spit and polish" of the stateside bases, not the rough and tumble, devil may care attitude of the seasoned combat troops. The veterans knew that to accomplish the mission EVERYONE had to pull their weight; there were no slackers. The main body of the 281st Aviation Company (AML) along with its attached

Captain Lou

units, 483rd Transportation Detachment and 499th Signal Detachment, debarked from the USNS W.H. Gordon, docked in Nha Trang Bay. Everything and everyone was in place as of 9 June 1966. The 281st Aviation Company (AML) had arrived.

Captain Lou Lerda

The new men were settling in, getting used to the smell, the heat and the living conditions in Nha Trang, South Vietnam. It had been a long trip from Fort Benning, Georgia to Vietnam. The officers and their men were as prepared as they could be for what lay ahead. All had been trained well and all were looking forward to getting the job done, accomplishing the mission, making their mark in the history books and then getting back home to their families.

The company headquarters and enlisted men's barracks were just tents placed over a wooden frame with sandbags stacked about four feet high all around them. This was home base and it certainly could have been a lot worse. The officers' quarters were about the same. This was all within the 5th Special Forces compound area, just a few hundred yards from the flight line and the Nha Trang airfield.

The 6th and the 145 airlift platoons had been in country for well over eighteen months and knew the area of operation (AO). Their pilots and crews were well oriented and had been tested under fire supporting the 5th SFG. The incoming 281st Assault Helicopter Company (AHC) would rely heavily on these experienced men as the blending process of the three units came together to form one very outstanding Assault Helicopter Company. The 5th Special Forces Group had come to depend on these platoons, and the Green Berets could always count on them to come and retrieve them no matter what the situation, to always be there if and when they needed help. Without the experience of the officers and their crew of the 6th and the 145th, the outcome of the 281st would have been a very different story. It was a Godsend to have these experienced men as mentors.

The 281st personnel became well trained, well qualified and well led. Most of the New Guys had not seen any combat, but with the help of these seasoned air and ground crews they were checked out, briefed and put to work flying missions with experienced crews in a matter of days.

War is a dangerous and serious game, very exciting but very deadly. No matter what you have been taught in training, the real thing is always different, sometimes extremely different. Flying anywhere and anytime in Vietnam was hazardous business, and you would often hear someone say, "Forget what you learned in training; this is how it works here!" The jungles, the country side and the whole northern area of Vietnam is beautiful from above, but experienced aviators knew that death was lurking under the jungle canopy, at the edge of a rice paddy or just over the next ridge. Being introduced to "Project Delta," the entire unit of the 281st was assuming a mission like no other unit in the history of the United States Army. The 6th and the 145th airlift platoons were the forerunners; they had battle scars and combat experience. Their knowledge was now passed on to the new pilots and crews.

The 281st had to work together as a whole, no single area or individual was more important than the other. Each had to perform in an excellent manner at all times. The blending of the three units made it better for the maintenance personnel by providing more aircraft mechanics, more spare parts, and more available aircraft. Captain Lou Lerda, the first maintenance officer, and his maintenance crew set the example for others to follow. Eighty percent of all the aircraft were always fully mission-capable, an unheard record in a war zone.

The foundation was built, and the records tell the story of the many brave men who went above and beyond. Our thanks and appreciation goes far beyond words to the men of the 6th and 145th.

This was the real beginning. The 281st Assault Helicopter Company was prepared for its unique mission.

Six good men had already paid the ultimate price. On the 5 April 1965, Specialist Five Joseph R. Foss was killed in action. The 19th of April 1965 was an especially tragic day. Specialist Four Terry W. Mills, Specialist Five Charles F. Millary, Warrant Officer Daniel E. Bishop, First Lieutenant Josef L. Thorne and Captain Gary L. Steele were shot down by enemy fire, and all were lost. They were part of the crew that paved the way for the 281st; they are our brothers and will never be forgotten.

On 17 June 1966, at a Special Forces camp, we lost Lieutenant Leon Flanders in a mortar attack.

On 24 June 1966, Major William "Bill" Griffin assumed command of the Company. Major Hackett, the first commander, and Major Wilson, the executive officer, were both promoted to the rank of lieutenant colonel and were transferred to staff positions.

On 7 July 1966, Private G. W. Whitaker, a communication specialist, died from complications from a heart attack.

On 25 September 1966, First Lieutenant William R. Beasley, aircraft commander, and Specialist Four Lawrence Williams Jr., door gunner, died in a non-hostile helicopter crash.

On 26 October 1966 Private First Class Gary B. Flabbi died from non-hostile causes.

281st ASSAULT HELICOPTER COMPANY

An Assault Helicopter Company, when fully operational, was comprised of several components or sub units. Lift Platoons (AKA the slicks), a gunship platoon, maintenance, avionics, motor pool, POL (the gas station), flight operations,

and orderly room or Company headquarters. Although each of these units had their own unique responsibilities, it goes without saying; they all had to work together in unison to make things work. At full strength the 281st was comprised of three flight platoons...two lift or slick platoons (12 aircraft each) and one gun platoon with 10 aircraft. The lift ships or slicks were the troop or cargo carriers. They were called slicks because of the noticeable absence of weapons. On each side were mounted M-60 machine guns. In the beginning, the company headquarters and enlisted men's barracks were just tents placed over a wooden frame with sandbags stacked about four feet high all around them. This was home base and it certainly could have been a lot worse. The officers' quarters were about the same. This was all within the 5th Special Forces compound area, just a few hundred yards from the flight line and the Nha Trang Airfield. With the passage of time, the living quarters improved to nearly the quality of home in the states...not hardly but with better comforts than tent living.

Main Street 281st AHC

Officers' Quarters

35

RAT PACK

The 1st Flight Platoon of the 281st Assault Helicopter Company was organized as a Lift Platoon. It was originally assigned 12 UH-1D aircraft, which were later upgraded to the more powerful UH-1H. Each aircraft was equipped with two M-60D 7.62 caliber machine guns that were mounted in the rear cabin area and manned by the crew chief and door gunner. The personnel in this platoon consisted of pilots, crew chiefs and door gunners, as well as the leadership positions of platoon sergeant and captain, who served as the platoon leaders. Initially, the assigned mission of the 1st Platoon was to provide support for the lettered companies and A Teams and C Detachments of the 5th Special Forces Group (Airborne). These A Teams and C Detachments were strategically located in the II Corps Tactical Zone, which was a very large flying area. The platoon call sign, Rat Pack, came into existence when Platoon Leader Captain John "Hoppy" Hopper named the platoon in mid-1967.

BANDITS

The 2nd Flight Platoon of the 281st AHC was also organized as a Lift Platoon and also initially assigned 12 UH-1D aircraft, which were later upgraded to the more powerful UH-1H, in the same fashion as its sister platoon. It was like the 1st Flight Platoon in weapons, crew and leadership. However, the missions of the two platoons were different. Initially, the assigned mission of the 2nd Platoon was to support the B Detachments and Special Operations. At that time the Special Operations units consisted of Special Projects: Delta, Gamma, Omega and Sigma. In 1967 all Special Operations entities were absorbed by MACV Studies and Observations Group with the exception of Project Delta, which remained under the command of the 5th SFG (ABN). The command relationship of the 281st AHC and 5th SFG (ABN) changed in 1967, causing the 281st to come under the command and control of the 10th Combat Aviation Battalion (CAB). The 2nd Platoon was attached under Operational Control (OPCON) of Project Delta and located at Forward Operating Bases (FOB) with Project Delta. Both the 2nd Platoon and the 1st Platoon also supported the MACV RECONDO School in Nha Trang which provided an ideal training environment for new 281st crew members. Starting in 1967 the first and second platoons rotated supporting Project Delta operations. The 2nd Platoon call sign, Bandit, also came into existence in 1967 when Platoon Leader, Captain Robert (Mo) Moberg named the platoon.

RIGGING SYSTEMS AND WEAPONS FOR 281st AHC SLICKS

When operational for Special Operations missions, the aircraft were configured with specific mission equipment. The equipment was principally related to extraction methods, but could include other equipment, as well:

McGuire Rigs
Rope Ladders
Rappelling Rigs
Rescue Hoist

McGuire Rigs inside the Griswold bags with sand bags sitting on the ends for deployment. The teak yoke can be seen in the background. Once the McGuire Rigs were placed the ladders were fastened on top of them. (Courtesy Norm Doney)

McGuire rigs and rope ladders (Courtesy Norm Doney Project Delta)

Crew chief's Mike Olsen and John Ware sitting in front of a hoist

The role a specific aircraft played in the mission determined, in most cases, the rigging of special equipment. Normally the "Hole Ship" or aircraft designated to insert the team would be rigged with rope ladders, rappelling lines or McGuire rigs, which allowed the team to exit the aircraft into the LZ during insertions and, if required, to extract them immediately. Usually, half of the LZs were nothing but holes in the triple canopy jungle, holes that could be as deep as 300 feet. Typically, the holes had been blown out by a 10,000-pound bomb well in advance of the operation. Many times this would leave tree stumps that were 25-50 feet tall, making it impossible to maneuver the aircraft to the ground. The proximity of the aircraft to the ground rested solely on the skill level of the pilots and crew. A natural opening in the jungle or an outcropping of rock also served as LZs. They were strictly one-ship LZs. The "Recovery Aircraft" was rigged with McGuire rigs to provide quick and timely extractions when the team was in trouble. The team members typically carried 80-pound ruck sacks which made it difficult if not impossible to climb up a rope ladder. Again, the skill level of the crew would come into play in negotiating the LZ or hole. In some cases the rescue hoist would be installed on one of the aircraft to pull out Recon Team members or air crewmen if the need arose. The hoist was not reliable and difficult to use.

In addition to the two M-60D machine guns mounted on the aircraft, many pilots and crewmen had a variety of weapons in addition to their issued weapon. The crew chief and gunner were issued M-16, .223 caliber carbines. The pilots were issued .45 caliber automatic pistols in the early days. By 1969 the Army, in its infinite wisdom, elected to arm pilots with a .38 caliber revolver, which was limited to five rounds in the cylinder in order to keep the cylinder in front of the firing pin clear. The standard joke was if you got shot down, you should shoot yourself in the head with the .38 since it would be of no use in any fire fight. Besides what was issued, there were many weapons of choice:

CAR-15, .223 caliber, a shortened version of the M-16
M-1 carbine, .30 caliber, M-2 full automatic paratrooper variant preferred
M-14 rifle, 7.62x51
AK-47, 7.62x39, folding stock variant preferred
Swedish K SMG, 9mm
M-3 SMG or "Grease Gun," .45 caliber
M-1928A1 SMG, .45 caliber "Thompson" M-79 grenade launchers, 40mm, with the stock and barrel shortened considerably by a hacksaw, probably army model M1A1

The crew members also kept a good supply of hand grenades and smoke grenades on board.

In the later years, the pilots were issued a survival vest and survival radios. Some of these appeared in the unit prior to the Army issuing them; they were obtained by barter or appropriated from a United States Marine Corps or a United States Air Force unattended aircraft. It is important to understand that these items were not stolen; they were simply moved from one service to the other. They all still belonged to Uncle Sam and to the men who served.

Colonel Robert (Bob) Mitchell
U.S. Army Retired

WOLF PACK

Wolf Pack was the call sign for our Armed Platoon, also commanded by a captain. The first armed aircraft in the unit were UH-1B's which were grossly underpowered for the missions. The UH-1C came later and was called simply the "Charlie Model." It was a faster, more-maneuverable version of the B Model. The Charlie Model had the new "540 Rotor System," which made it considerably more maneuverable in flight. However, the power was still somewhat limited and it was typically overloaded, which made it difficult to hover. There were ten helicopters in the Wolf Pack platoon. Two of these gunships were called "Frogs." They were equipped with a 40 mm cannon on a turret that was mounted on the nose of the Huey. The 40 mm high-explosive (HE) projectile looked like a big over-sized bullet, about one inch long and one and a half inches wide. The 40mm round was low velocity, so the pilot could actually see the stream of projectiles and walk them to the target. Exploding on impact, it was a deadly round. Because of the relatively slow rate of fire and the boom, boom, boom noise as it fired, the Frog was also nicknamed "Thumper." Frog gunships were usually loaded with oversized-rocket pods that carried nineteen rockets on each side. The combination of a 40 mm grenade launcher and nineteen-shot rocket pods was called a Hog-Frog. Although very heavy, the aircraft carried a lot of firepower for its day. The same style "2.75" folding fin rockets are still used on the Apache gunships today.

The other six Wolf Pack gunships were equipped with fourteen rockets (two seven-shot pods) and two mini-guns (similar to the Gatling guns seen in some of the old west cowboy movies). These guns each had six spinning barrels and two electric motors. One motor pulled the ammo into the gun while the other spun the barrel mechanism. The configuration of the armament on a gunship was often limited only to the crews' imagination. The mini-guns fired up to 6,000 rounds per minute, but at that rate of fire they would quickly expend the ammo. They were typically fired one side at a time and at 2400 rounds per minute. This allowed much more time on station and provided deadly firepower. They did not sound like a regular machine gun; it was more like a loud growling noise. It must have terrified the enemy on the ground. The recoil of these guns would actually slow the aircraft down by as much as 20 knots.

The UH-1Cs carried a crew of four: pilot, co-pilot, crew chief and gunner. The pilot fired the rockets, and the copilot fired the 40mm cannon on the Frogs or the mini-guns. The copilot aimed the mini-guns or Frog grenade system up, down, left and right with a hanging gun sight, which could be snapped to an upright position, out of the copilot's face when not in use. Crew chiefs and door gunners each had an M-60 machine gun. Unlike the machine guns on slicks, these M-60s were not mounted to the aircraft, which allowed the men to lean outside and shoot under the aircraft when breaking away from the target. The crew chief and gunner were an integral part of the team and critical to the mission.

Ammunition fired in the mini-guns was standard issue 7.62 mm in linked belts; with a tracer every fifth round. The guns fired so fast that at night it looked like a continuous stream of fire from the helicopter to the ground. At times the door gunners used straight tracer rounds, which looked as though the aircraft were firing four mini-guns.

The relationship between the lift platoons (slicks) and the gunship pilots and crew included a lot of good-natured kidding and occasional bad mouthing between the groups. The gunship men walked with a kind of a swagger; each one thinking he was kin to the gunslingers of the old west. The lift platoon was always proud to have them on their side, especially when they were flying into a hole in the jungle for insertions and extractions. They appreciated them even more when being shot at while unloading and loading. It was comforting to look up and see those loud mouths bring hell from above down on the enemy.

Platoon Sergeant David L. Bitle was apparently responsible for the call sign "Wolf Pack." Sometime in late 1966, according to Fred Phillips, Bitle painted a cartoon-like caricature of a Wolf with a cigar in its mouth and the words WOLF PACK painted under it. Everyone liked it and the armed platoon became the Wolf Pack.

Each soldier's life depended on every other soldier; we always worked as a team. One of the gunners from Wolf Pack was heard to say, "Death was our business, and business was good."

RIGHT, RIGHT

Arriving in Vietnam at Cam Ranh Bay, I quickly discovered my first big mistake as I changed from my khaki uniform to fatigues. I had packed two right boots but no left ones. Managing to put a right boot on a left foot, I hobbled to the salvage pile of jungle boots that had been tossed behind supply. I hoped that this was not an omen of what my year would be like. I rummaged through the pile until I found right and left boots, size12. Sheepishly making my way back to my bunk, I put on my new heavily-used jungle boots. This footwear put me ahead of the other new arrivals, for I had authentic jungle boots, and they did not! However, I immediately wrote to my wife and asked her to mail me my two left boots as soon as she could.

First Sergeant Bob Ohmes

Intruder maintenance shed…note the connexes beside the building

OUR MAINTENANCE TEAM

I had received my orders to the 483rd Maintenance Detachment, attached to the 281st AHC. After arriving at the 483rd, I realized I was joining a well-organized group, and my job would be to ensure that our aircraft would be flyable whenever needed. During my first few days in the unit, I was briefed on the mission. My next priority was to get acquainted with the other enlisted members of the 483rd. There were aircraft and engine mechanics, as well as personnel from sheet metal, avionics, armament, motor pool, rotor head and some I have forgotten. I soon realized that this was going to be a 24/7 responsibility and job. I literally prayed to God to give me strength to accomplish my part of the mission. After meeting with my maintenance personnel, I knew I had a great team to help me accomplish the mission, and my real responsibility was to keep this well-oiled machine going in the right direction. Our maintenance area consisted of maintenance tents on top of connexes with PSP flooring. Old Mother Nature sent the winds and rains right through the maintenance tents, so a lot of our work was done in the revetment area or outside our three maintenance tents. Before long, a new hangar was built, constructed with five bays and enclosed on three sides with only one side open to the wind and rain. When it was completed, we were able to have five aircraft in it with electronics and armament sections included. It was like going from night into day when we moved to the new hangar. Working with the 97 personnel of the 483rd, I quickly realized that there were 97 different personalities to deal with. I knew there would be things I would have to ask my men to do, but also things I myself had not formerly done. Many times during that year, I asked them to work eighteen to twenty hours a day, as the Mission of the 281st was to support the 5th Special Forces, which was a 24-hour mission. During my year as the 483rd first sergeant, working with the 281st Maintenance NCO, we replaced more aircraft than we were assigned. Out of necessity, we had to work longer hours to keep the aircraft we had available. When the mechanics were in the hangar working, I was there with them. There was no grumbling about the long hours; we were there to do a job, and we did it. Ninety-five percent of the personnel worked well both as individuals and as a team.

Parts for the 281st were very easy to come by, so we were able to stock engines, transmissions, rotor heads, tail rotors, and tail booms and install them in the shortest time possible. We never had a set test to check how fast something could be replaced on a Huey because it was a daily race to replace an item on an aircraft as soon as possible to maintain availability. There were times I had to decide to cannibalize one aircraft to ready another, but I did this as rarely as possible because every aircraft was needed to accomplish the mission. For example, when we were installing the new L13 engines, we found that the "hot ends" on the rear of the engines required a special tool that we could not obtain through battalion supply routes. A short time later, needing something else, I went to the local "hardware" store in Nha Trang. While going through some small boxes, I found an oddly-shaped tool which had "Lycoming Engine" engraved on the back. It was the very tool we needed for the inspections of the L13 hot ends. Needless to say, I bought all six tools for about 50 cents each and returned to the engine shop. The mechanics wanted to know where I got them, and I told them at the local hardware store. From that day on, we had no trouble removing and inspecting the hot ends. I was very curious as to by whom and when they had been sold to the store, but I NEVER FOUND OUT. I was happy to have them.

Another time, main rotor blades were cracking at the tip of the first laminate; we had several crack in the same place. A Bell Helicopter Representative arrived to figure out the problem. He took pictures and statements and said he would get back to us with answers. For some time after his departure, we continued to have problems resulting in extra man hours replacing/repairing the blades. We were finally told the problem occurred during manufacture. The factory workers were using a grease pencil to indicate where on the blades the laminate should start. When the blades were heated, the grease made a hot spot on the aluminum, causing it to crack under stress. As soon as this practice was eliminated during the manufacturing process, we had no more problems with cracking blades.

MY KIDS

They weren't able to come home and tell about their own "Glory days" unless they had very active imaginations or could pass off, as theirs, wild stories that had been told to them by someone else. These were the men who worked in the engine shop and repacked short shafts. Imagine how many thousands of hours a unit flies in a year's time and then divide that by 25 to get the approximate number of short shafts the typical E-4 or E-5 had to repack for his tour in Vietnam. Consider how many times he had to inspect the hot end of an engine, realign a rotor head, repair the radios, buck the rivets, repack the bearings on push-pull tubes, and perform the other hundreds of small jobs that needed to be done by the maintenance

Bob Ohmes, Command Sergeant Major

people to keep the aircraft flying. Moreover, the maintenance officer was constantly yelling to get the aircraft ready in order to keep availability up to 80%. These guys did not have great stories to tell their kids or grandkids but I believe that their jobs were just as important to the overall success of the mission as the work of the pilots, crew chiefs and gunners. I know that I yelled a lot at these kids to get things done because some days they didn't feel like working, and neither did I. However, I was and am very proud of the work they accomplished. Many of you are here now because of their dedicated work. Guess I will get off my soapbox; I have preached enough today.

Bob Ohmes

UNSUNG HEROES

I believe we should do more for the men who served behind the scenes, but I would like to carry the pride one step further. The need for all of us to reach out and find all the unsung heroes is absolutely priority one. I knew quite a few of the maintenance and operations people, but not all of them. It was easy to fly back to Nha Trang, get out, file the after action paperwork and head to the house. Many hours of hard work followed, accomplished by those people who worked long into the night, without much chance of an air medal or even tales of danger and intrigue to tell their grandchildren. I hope we can get some of these names onboard, so we can all express our gratitude for the job they did. I didn't get to thank them then, so maybe I can do so at some future event.

Bob Green

Field operations created a completely different environment for the maintenance team. The first thing to be done was to get all the needed spare parts; extra rotor blades, engines, transmissions, gear boxes, all the nuts, bolts, lubricants and anything else that could be forgotten. It was like Christmas. They made their list and checked it twice and probably a third or fourth time. It was inevitable the pilots would break the aircraft.

The maintenance team was ready for anything the pilots could throw at them. They could fix things as fast as the pilots would break them. As a pilot, you would look over at the maintenance area; see an aircraft torn apart and put back together right in front of your eyes. There was no doubt in your mind the aircraft would perform perfectly, as if it was new.

COMPANY HEADQUARTERS

Company headquarters, also known as the orderly room, was the office of the company commander, the executive officer, the first sergeant and a very busy company clerk. A good company clerk was worth his weight in gold. He alone was the one who kept track of all our men. He did the morning report, sick call, typed up letters of recommendation, letters for promotion and a hundred other reports. He typed the missing or killed in action letters that were sent to the next of kin back home. Back then we had no computers, and most of the typewriters were manual. He was always busy, and since there were no safe places in Vietnam, he knew how to load and fire a number of weapons. We were most fortunate to have two company clerks: one who worked in the orderly room and the other in flight operations.

Company Headquarters

The orderly room was a place of official business, so when someone was ordered to report to the company headquarters, he had better have his ducks in line. The first sergeant sometimes called the first sheriff or top, was the top enlisted man in our company. He set the example, made things happen and generally made sure that all the enlisted men were informed of what was going on within the company. Most of our first sergeants had been in the army for about twenty years. You could say that they had been there and done that. The company commander and his executive officer, who was second-in-command, had their hands full with the normal operations of the whole company. One or the other, sometimes both, would be at the forward operating base, flying command and control. Their greatest concern was that the missions went well. They were responsible for the operations of the whole company. It was more than a full time job. It was their life.

THE MOTOR POOL

So much importance is placed on the aircraft, crew, maintenance and communication in an aviation company, but when all is said and done, it takes the effort of every available man to keep the whole operation running smoothly. This fact will be repeated over and over again throughout this book. It must be stated that the motor pool was a very important part of the 281st Assault Helicopter Company. Without the motorized vehicles, we would not have operated.

The motor pool was just a small space adjacent to the airfield. There wasn't a shop or a tent; everything was lined up side by side in the dirt. There was no office for the motor sergeant and no place to perform scheduled maintenance. The only structure was a steel conex container. This was our motor pool. And believe it or not, our men made this work and made it work very well.

The mechanics worked outside in all weather, rain or shine, performing the necessary work to keep 43 vehicles running. We had quarter-ton jeeps, three-quarter-ton trucks, two-and-a-half-ton trucks and a five-ton wrecker. It was the responsibility of the motor sergeant and his men to keep them all in top-notch shape by keeping track of each vehicle and making sure the maintenance was performed at the proper time. With little or no fanfare, they did an excellent job.

Needless to say, they had their hands full. At times there were more vehicles than we were authorized to have, particularly with quarter-ton-jeeps. At one time, there were five more jeeps than were assigned. The motor sergeant did not ask any questions; he just made sure each was operating at its best. What he did at inspections no one knew. This was a war zone, and for the most part there were no questions asked. These men deserved much more than just a pat on the back. They were the "unsung heroes." We were a fortunate helicopter company with some very good equipment and good men in each section who knew how to make things work. This story is not about helicopters, vehicles, or equipment; it is about these special men.

Our motor pool

As if the guys with the motor pool didn't have enough work to do keeping a fleet of vehicles fully operational, they were tasked with having vehicles available and in good working order in the field. Jeeps, trucks, wrecker, were all needed at the FOB. They had to get there and back and ready for use. Occasionally, they were thrown a curve just to keep them on their toes and keep their creativity and skills honed.

Sometimes it's not a good idea to trust young warrant officers, whose favorite saying is "hold my beer and watch this."

Truck extraction…Motor pool got the last laugh…the pilot had to sign a statement of charges and was taken off flight status until he got the truck running again

POL

Petroleum, Oils, and Lubricants
The Gas Station

In the 281st we were fortunate to have a great team of individuals who did their jobs without the fanfare or thrills associated with fighting off the NVA or recovering a recon team on the run. One of these groups was the POL teams. Over the years they did their job in the sweltering heat and did it well. They took care of petroleum, oil and lubrication. There were no medals and little recognition at the time for any of them. However, over the years we have come to realize how important these men were to our success and safety. Whether it was, the Oasis, Polei Kleng, or Nha Trang, our POL teams kept the JP-4 flowing, and I doubt that anyone can recall a time when we were short of POL at one of the refueling points that these outstanding young men operated for us on a 24/7 basis. It's not easy to put a gas station in the middle of a jungle. Even the great army officer Lieutenant General George Patton was forced to recognize the importance of the POL team. He informed his troops in his famous prewar speech he did not ever want to hear anyone say that they were holding their position; he wanted to hear they were advancing, moving towards the enemy. What he meant was that they were not to stop for anything.

Basic warfare maintains the army must be able to shoot, move and communicate. Thousands of Patton's tanks ran out of fuel. They could shoot and communicate, but they were sitting ducks when they could not move.

Ask any pilot or crew member about the pucker factor associated with a low fuel warning light or a sucking sound, both indications that he was almost out of fuel, and he will tell you how important POL is.

Every person in each section of the 281st Assault Helicopter Company had an important job; there was not one position more special than any other. Our POL team was always there. The POL specialists were also truck drivers, performing the very dangerous job of hauling thousands of gallons of explosive fuel from one point to another. They knew and practiced safety continuously. They had to, for their lives and the lives of others depended on them, performing their job perfectly every time. There was no room for even one mistake. It was a very dangerous job, to say the least. No matter where and what time of day or night, our POL team was there. Our helicopters used JP-4 mixture. When fuel was needed, a simple call was all that was needed. They were always ready, always on call. They always delivered what was needed, and they were taken for granted. There is no doubt they were the best. They played a very important part in the overall success of the missions.

Now, looking back after so many years, one of our commanders stated: "If this book does nothing else, it made me think of the many guys on the ground that kept us flying and received little or no recognition for their hard work." If any member of our POL team is reading this, the least I can say is, "Thanks, guys. We would have been in deep trouble without your attention to detail and hard work."

POL truck

Gas station in the field

AVIONICS

We had 34 helicopters, 24 UH-1 slicks and 10 UH-1 gunships. Each one had at least three radios. The platoon leaders had four; the command and control had even more. There were large, enclosed, self-contained radios in the back of three-quarter-ton trucks, single-side band radios, radios in flight operations and one experimental jeep equipped with special radios that could be moved to forward operating bases to act as air traffic control. Radios were everywhere. At one point, a stereo system was set up in the maintenance hangar.

One would think with so many aircraft with so many radios, keeping them all operational would be a real problem. The vibrations, the moisture, and war took its toll on just about everything. Yet, in the 281st, our avionics men made sure each radio in every helicopter was operating at its very best. Never was a mission or flight cancelled because of radio problems. When the avionics men had some free time, they would ride along on missions, sometimes as a door gunner if qualified. These men were well trained and highly motivated. Communications was top-notch in the 281st Assault Helicopter Company and was provided by the skilled avionics men of the 499th Signal Detachment.

SUPPLY

The supply room was always one busy place; just about anything you needed could be found in the supply room. You would think this would have been a great place to work because you were inside most of the time. However, that was not the case in Vietnam. The supply men had the very important job of keeping track of all the items the company needed to perform its mission. It was a never ending job. Everything, from the extra-large tents to toilet paper, came from our supply room. How our supply men knew what 291 men needed was something most of us took for granted. The company armorer worked in the supply room and at the forward operating base. What a demanding job he had keeping each weapon in good shape and ready to go at a moment's notice. All the individual weapons were stored in the supply room when not in use, and every item had to be accounted for.

It was a war zone. No matter what your job was, you had to be prepared to defend yourself and put your life on the line. This included the supply men. We were all in this together.

NHA TRANG

281st Home Base

As you flew into Nha Trang, you were struck by the beauty of the crystal blue waters with miles and miles of sandy beaches along the coast of the South China Sea. Flying in on an airplane or in a helicopter, the sight was truly magnificent! A massive mountain range called the Grand Summit extended from the southern tip to the northern end of the city. Thick, lush vegetation covered the mountains. Although not a jungle nor treacherous, there was no doubt the mountains were deadly. From time to time, jet fighters dropped bombs along the top of the highest mountain. White billows of smoke rose from the mountaintop as the bombs hit the ground and exploded. There was a stark contrast in the two views: a beautiful coastal city that resembled a peaceful resort town, and a deadly battle against the North Vietnamese Army taking place in the mountains overlooking it. The mountain was honey combed with caves for the NVA to hide in. At one point the Korean Army painted numbers on the cave entrances for identification for air strikes. Fuel bladders were dropped from altitude and would burst on impact with the resulting spilled fuel being set ablaze. The mountain was a dangerous war zone just outside compound wires.

The attire for the native men ranged from western shirts, pants and boots that did not fit, to black silk pajamas, bare feet and coolie hats. Whatever clothing they could find was the dress of the day. Vietnamese women dressed more uniformly and most wore coolie hats. Bicycles were the preferred mode of transportation. Children played on the streets, people relaxed on the palm-fringed beach, rickshaws roamed the streets and boats covered the water. It was, however, the large, white, gleaming statue of Buddha atop a hill overlooking the city that got your attention when you flew into this seaside city.

The city of Nha Trang, in South Vietnam was not as large as Saigon; not as crowded and much easier to navigate from one side to the other. The South Vietnamese people of Nha Trang were, for the most part, a peaceful people. Our relationship with them was usually cordial. Hundreds of them worked on the military base and performed their duties very well. We were fortunate to have our home base along the South China Sea. What more could a GI ask for than a duty in the garden spot of Vietnam. Added to this perfect location was the security of countless Green Berets!

BUDDHA

The Buddha of Nha Trang
Unquestionably the best known landmark in all of Vietnam

5th SPECIAL FORCES GROUP (ABN)

5th Special Forces Group deployed to South Vietnam in February of 1965. Although new to this war zone, the group deployed throughout the four military regions of South Vietnam. Its operational teams established and manned camps at 270 different locations, where it trained and led indigenous forces of the civilian irregular defense groups, as well as other units of the Armed Forces of the Republic of South Vietnam.

Even though they were one of the smallest units engaged in this armed conflict, the 5th Special Forces Group colors flew twenty campaign streamers, and its soldiers were among the most highly decorated in the history of our nation with seventeen Medals of Honor awarded; eight given posthumously.

Special Forces had its own motto: De Oppresso Liber (It is United States Army tradition that this Latin phrase means "to free from oppression" or "to liberate the oppressed") It never failed to live up to its motto.

At our home base in Nha Trang, South Vietnam, we were right next door to the impressive white building that housed the 5th Special Forces headquarters. To observe and work daily with the best of the US Army was our privilege. These professional soldiers, the Green Berets, were our neighbors and our brothers in arms. We established strong professional and personal relationships with them. In many cases, those relationships continue at the personal level to this very day. When one looks at the mission, the bravery, the commitment, and the professionalism of these soldiers, one realizes what an honor it was to serve with such men. We of the 281st Assault Helicopter Company became the US Army's first Special Operations Helicopter Company to be attached to and serve with this most professional Army organization. We flew above the best.

PROJECT DELTA

Project Delta was a covert Special Forces operation in Vietnam which began May 15, 1964. A single Special Forces detachment, B-52, was tasked with training the Civilian Irregular Defense Group (CIDG) and the South Vietnamese Special Forces, known as the Luc Luong Dac Biet (LLDB), in conducting long-

range reconnaissance patrols in uncontrolled and enemy territory. The operation, code named Leaping Lena in 1964, actually started as an entity of the Central Intelligence Agency. It was composed of selected teams from the 1st Special Forces Group (Airborne) in Okinawa, Japan, and 7th Special Forces Group (Airborne) Fort Bragg, N.C. The RECONDO School was also developed from Detachment B-52 to train personnel in forming long-range recon patrol (LRRP) companies within each division. These teams were designed to strike deep into uncontrolled territory, seeking out Viet Cong and NVA units and their sources of supplies. Normally sent out on five-day operations, the teams performed a wide variety of missions: locating enemy units, intelligence gathering, bomb damage assessment, artillery and air strike coordination, hunter-killer missions, special purpose raids, wiretapping, POW snatches and conducting harassing and deception missions. In addition to the American Special Forces, there were more than 1,200 South Vietnamese and ethnic Chinese soldiers divided into two CIDG companies and the 81st South Vietnamese Airborne Ranger Battalion. One CIDG company was the Nung Strike Force, a platoon-size, rapid reaction force made up of ethnic Chinese soldiers. The other company was known as the Roadrunners.

The Roadrunners were select indigenous members from various groups. These soldiers showed an extra measure of courage when they would go undercover within a North Vietnamese unit to gather intelligence. Once a North Vietnamese unit had been found,

the Roadrunners would be prepped and fitted with the appropriate equipment before being inserted to link up with the enemy and collect information. Their missions were top secret and when transporting to and from the aircraft, they wore ponchos to cover their uniforms and protect the objective of their missions.

Although a variety of assets were represented in Project Delta, the core mission surrounded the six-man recon teams. Originally the teams were made up of six Americans, but they eventually evolved into teams of two Americans and four indigenous personnel, typically Vietnamese Special Forces. These Recon Teams were the mainstay of Project Delta. As the effectiveness of the small recon teams evolved, other units were formed, such as Projects Gamma, Omega and Sigma. With the formation of Military Assistance Command Vietnam Studies and Observations Group (MACV-SOG), the other Special Projects or "Greek Letter Units" within the 5th Special Forces Group (ABN) were absorbed by this group to provide the necessary trained personnel to perform their mission. Project Delta remained an element of the 5th SFG (A) for the duration of the war. According to Jim Morris, a noted author and military historian as well as a former Special Forces Major who served three tours in Vietnam, Project Delta is credited with providing 40% of the creditable and actionable intelligence gathered within the borders of Vietnam.

A special bond developed between our men and Delta Recon that has continued to current times. Delta Recon knew the 281st would be there when they needed them, and nothing would stand in the way of their being extracted, whether in the rain, at night or under heavy fire from the NVA. There were more 281st aircraft hit by enemy fire or completely shot out of the sky and air crewmen wounded or killed during emergency extractions than from any other phase of the operations.

Suggested reading:

Carpenter, Steven A. Project Delta Recon (2010) Boots on the Ground., Charleston, SC

Morris, R. C. U.S. Army Special Forces Detachment B-52, Project Delta. (2009) The Ether Zone. Hell Gate Press. Hellgatepress.com.

MACV RECONDO SCHOOL

After General Westmoreland became commander of the American forces in Vietnam, in 1966, he ordered the building of the Military Army Command of Vietnam (MACV) Recondo School at Nha Trang to replace the training functions of Project LEAPING LENA, later Project DELTA. This was a relief for Project DELTA as they were spending their down time between operations training other soldiers. The major commands were augmented with elements of the 75th Rangers to be utilized as Long Range Reconnaissance Patrols (LRRP), but until Westmoreland's MACV took over Recondo, short for reconnaissance commando, there was no training available for these commands. The 5th Special Forces Group personnel were assigned to train American soldiers, as well as members of other allied forces, in the art of long-range reconnaissance patrolling techniques. Besides a high level of physical fitness, the course required knowledge of patrolling techniques, land navigation, weapons and air-mobility techniques, including insertions, extractions, the use of rope ladders, hoist operations, and the McGuire rig. The course concluded with the insertion of an actual combat patrol, which gave the students the chance to demonstrate their new skills.

The MACV Recondo School was established and operated by the 5th Special Forces Group and was located next to the group compound in Nha Trang. The Recondo compound was a showplace with a large, wooden archway at the entrance. In the center of the archway was the Recondo badge next to the Special Forces patch. On the left side were the words Recondo School, and on the right side were the same words written in Vietnamese. Most of the structures inside the compound were old Quonset huts which contained a first aid station, an operations center, a supply building, one main classroom, the Recondo Headquarters office, and a row of student barracks. The coveted Recondo badge was visible on most of the structures and was painted in two color variations, either white and black or olive drab and black. The badge was shaped like an arrowhead pointing down. In the center was a black "V" and above it the word "Recondo." The arrowhead symbolized wood lore, while the "V" stood for the wearer's ability to move against the enemy by air-drop transport, day or night. That is where the 281st became involved.

The Redondo School was a grueling course that lasted three weeks. It had an attrition rate of about fifty percent. It was a non-stop professional school taught by experienced and well-tested Special Forces instructors.

Rappelling…Rope ladders…McGuire rigs were all part of the training
McGuire rig photo Courtesy Chester Howard Project Delta

Because most of the new "in country" 281st helicopter crews had little or no experience with the techniques required for Special Operations, the Recondo School offered the unit an opportunity to provide aviation support to the school while giving its young, inexperienced crews realistic training which would put them in good standing when they became involved in supporting Project Delta. Training with insertions by rope ladders and rappelling and extractions by hoist, the McGuire Rig and later the STABO Rig would often be put to good use throughout their tour with the unit. This was the real thing. During the last week of the course, the 281st crews would insert teams into a known enemy territory and would support them throughout the mission, who often required aerial gun support from the Wolf Pack and/or immediate extractions when the students were engaged by the enemy and could not break contact to continue the mission. The Recondo School was often referred to as the deadliest school on earth because the NVA provided the live fire for the final exam. The Recondo School and the 281st AHC worked together, trained together and fought together. The 281st Assault Helicopter Company flew above the best.

DEADLY RESUPPLY MISSION

We were two miles from the landing zone at fifteen hundred feet above the ground, on final approach to a nightmare. I lowered the collective, which controlled the altitude on my Huey, and eased out of the safe zone. We Army aviators in Vietnam had learned from experience that flying at tree top level or at least fifteen hundred feet above the terrain put us in safe areas. Fifteen hundred feet or more above ground level kept us above the small arms fire from the enemy. Go below, and we were in the "dead man zone," within range of the enemy's deadly AK-47 until we returned to tree top level.

I made the necessary corrections with the anti-torque pedals to maintain our flight path to the point of touchdown. It was when leaving the safe area that the butterflies in my stomach started flapping faster than the rotor blades overhead were turning. My crew and I were tense. We didn't like the way the day was shaping up at all! My co-pilot had earlier called over the radio for helicopter gunship support to assist us on this emergency mission. "Sorry" and "Unable to help," were the replies we heard from scattered gunship teams throughout the area of operations. It sounded like they already had their hands full. It was shortly after sunrise in the Republic of South Vietnam, and, like it or not, my crew and I were committed to a single-ship ammunition resupply mission without gunship support.

A rude awakening

It had been much earlier that morning at 0330 hours, when someone had grabbed my shoulders and shook me hard. "Major! Major! Wake up," a voice in the dark had yelled. "Our Mike Force is in big trouble." At first I did not comprehend what the shouting was all about. My crew and I had been flying missions eight to ten hours a day for the past four days. We had piled into our bunks not more than four hours before this rude awakening. It was a minute before my weary eyes recognized the duty officer of the Special Forces camp in Pleiku, in the highlands of South Vietnam. The Mike Force was a unit of Montagnard tribesmen who were led and trained by American Special Forces, both officers and noncommissioned officers. The tribesmen were known to be fierce fighters. Their leaders, from the U.S. Army's elite SF group, were tough and fearless.

Although my senses were not fully awake, the duty officer wasted no time in briefing me on the dangerous predicament the Mike Force was in. The previous day the Mike Force had been deployed west of Pleiku near a dry lakebed, very close to Cambodia and Laos. Intelligence reports said that North Vietnamese Army elements were in the area. The Mike Force's mission was to move about the area and try to stir up a fight with the enemy. The purpose was to find the enemy, fix their location, and determine their number. The 4th Infantry Division, which had been in Vietnam for a short time, would then engage them in their first combat operation in country. This would be their "baptism of fire."

The Mike Force had found a fight all right, with a North Vietnamese (NVA) regiment. The encounter started out as a small skirmish, but became a major firefight very quickly as the NVA committed their full force. The Mike Force would throw out a hail of fire, then withdraw quickly, stop and fire again. This had gone on from late afternoon throughout the night. The duty officer continued, "Our troops are running out of ammunition and water. They need to hold out just a little bit longer until the 4th Infantry can get there. Major Cartwright, we need you and your crew to fly your chopper out there at first light and resupply them with ammo and water. They need our help desperately." He gasped for breath, and as he ran out the door, he added, "I have every available man in the camp loading up carbine ammo clips and putting them and two canteens of water into burlap sandbags for you to carry out to them."

By this time I had thrown on my jungle fatigues, laced my boots, grabbed my "brain bucket" (flight helmet) and had run out the door to waken my crew. My copilot was a young 23 year-old first lieutenant who acted like an old man. He had been in Vietnam too long and seen too much. The Huey crew chief was even younger, barely 19 years old, and his pride and joy was the helicopter (tail number 711) that we were about to fly. The gunner was an older sergeant, all of 23, who had only been with us for the past few days. The Sergeant was filling in for our regular gunner, who was on rest and recreation leave (R&R) for seven days. The Sergeant only had eighteen days left in Vietnam. He should have been back at the base camp waiting to climb on the jet home.

I arrived at the aircraft and began a quick pre-flight inspection. It was a good thing that the whole crew had pitched in the night before to make sure the helicopter was refueled and inspected and that the door guns were clean and loaded. She was ready to go. The rest of the crew was there within minutes and went about their tasks to make ready for the flight.

The camp was like a hornet's nest that had just been drop kicked. Men were all over the place loading the sandbags with ammo and canteens of water and tossing them into the Huey. The troop seats had been removed and numerous burlap bags were piled in the middle of the cabin floor. A Special Forces first lieutenant came up to me and requested to go on the flight. He was the assistant supply officer who had supervised the putting together of this emergency resupply. "I can help unload the bags when we get there," he pleaded. For the life of me, I could not figure out why he wanted to tag along. I guess he wanted to get out to where the action was.

The Huey was fully loaded and ready to go. It was getting close to first light. I rolled the throttle over to the indent position and backed it off slightly. This was the time in the starting procedure when you "light the fire." The turbine engine ignites and starts turning slowly. When it whines, you know it's a good start. The rotor blades grudgingly started turning, and the throttle was carefully rolled on to full power. I pulled up the collective, made the helicopter light on the skids, and made ready to hover out to the helipad for takeoff.

Captain Clyde Sincere, a Special Forces officer, ran up to the aircraft, poked his head into my open window and yelled loud enough to be heard over the noise of the rotor blades, "I want to go out with you." He was the commander of the Mike Force that was in trouble. He had flown back to the base camp the day before with some NVA prisoners that had been captured in order to coordinate the battle plan with officers of the new infantry division in the area. He added, "I've got to get back to my men. Where do you want me to sit?" I nodded, tilted my head towards the left rear of the cabin and yelled, "Sit next to the crew chief." I made one last glance around the cabin. The supply lieutenant was buckled up next to the gunner on the right side of the aircraft. In front of the gunner was an M-60 machine gun mounted on a pedestal. The crew chief and the captain were ready to go on the left side. The crew chief also had a machine gun in front of him.

On the way, hurry!

There was a reassuring jump up as the helicopter transitioned from the hover to a climb out. She felt a little heavy with the load but was flying well. Initially we flew at treetop level, and then Huey 711 headed for fifteen hundred feet like a homesick angel. We were finally on our way. Captain Sincere was anxious to get back to his men with this load of ammo and water. "Hurry, please," his plea echoed over the intercom.

The Vietnam countryside was beautiful as the rising sun cast early morning shadows over the lush green terrain. There was certain serenity to flying along at a safe altitude, hearing the steady popping of the rotor blades as they grabbed air. This is when most pilots say to God. "Oh, Lord, I'm asking you to get us through this day. Protect my crew and let us be there in time to help, and please let us see the sunset." My reverence was shattered when the gunner and crew chief fired off a couple of rounds from their machine guns. This was standard procedure to make sure the guns were in operating condition, ready for any situation. I noticed that down below; some soldiers were pitching a large tent with a red cross on a large white square emblazoned on the top of the canvas. It was a battalion aid station getting ready for casualties. Along our route the tattoos of war were already evident. Tops of hills were being cleared of trees and firebases established. The trees had been blasted away and bunkers built as the new division prepared for its first combat operation. Concertina wire was installed around the camps in wiggly paths with claymore mines interlaced with the barbwire every few feet. Trees and bushes were cut to the ground for several hundred yards out from the perimeters of the camps to allow fields of fire. The United States Army certainly knew how to change the landscape. I began the approach. Our thirty-minute flight of sightseeing had just ended.

The smell and sound of battle

The altimeter needles moved in a counter-clockwise direction and began unwinding as we left fifteen hundred feet. At that moment the smell of the battlefield invaded my nostrils. It was the first time this had ever happened to me. A dense, acrid odor of gunpowder was everywhere. I was amazed that the smell had reached our altitude. I envisioned the battle that would produce such a phenomenon. I looked out the windshield at a good-sized dry lakebed (if you can imagine anything dry in Vietnam) and the wooded area next to it. Smoke was everywhere. A layer hung above the ground and trees like a giant comforter. It reminded me of the smog in L.A. but nastier.

As the Huey sliced through one thousand feet, the sounds of the battlefield reached our ears. There was so much gunfire it sounded like popcorn being popped at the neighborhood movie theater. "Listen up!" I told the crew on the intercom, "I have contact with the Mike Force on the ground." An anxious Clyde wanted to know what the situation was. "Boss," the voice on the radio replied over the radio, "We've been fighting all night, and we're down to the last of our ammo. We can hold them a little bit longer, but we are counting on you to bring the ammo in." I told them to throw a smoke grenade, so we could pinpoint the unit's position. Yellow smoke appeared on the East Side of the lakebed, about fifty yards into the wood line. I acknowledged the yellow smoke. Our aircraft was heading north, so the smoke was at our right front. "O.K., Sarge, you and the lieutenant be on the alert," I ordered them on the intercom, "Get your weapons at the ready. It's hot down there. Watch out for our guys." On the other side of the aircraft, Captain Sincere was making ready to join his troops. As aircraft commander, I was getting so busy that a prayer was stuck in my throat.

Five hundred feet, four hundred feet, lower and lower we went as I focused on where we were going to land. I wanted to get as close to the wood line as possible, so that the troops unloading the aircraft wouldn't be way out in the open and exposed to fire. I could hear the gunner's and Special Forces lieutenant's initial bursts of rounds from their weapons. "I see 'em; I see 'em," yelled the sergeant over the intercom. The bursts of machine gun and M-16 fire were amplified over the intercom as he talked and fired at the same time. The sound of the rapid fire from the gunner's machine gun abruptly stopped. Then I heard no more.

Thirty feet above the ground, twenty, fifteen, I was just about to set the bird down. There was no time to stop at a hover. "Fly her right to the ground," I instructed myself. The crackling of bullets was all around us. Thump, thump, thump. I heard a bunch of rounds hit the chopper.

On the other side of the Huey, the Mike Force commander leaped from the helicopter as we passed through about ten feet of altitude. He really wanted to get to his troops! Everything was going crazy. Sincere ran under the skids (landing gear) of the aircraft just before it touched down. Just as he cleared the right skid, the supply lieutenant's M-16 rifle fell from above, hit Captain Sincere on the shoulder, and then toppled to the ground. He glanced up to see both the sergeant and lieutenant slumped in their seats. The skids of the chopper touched the ground and we slid a few feet forward and came to a full stop.

All hell broke loose

I turned my head quickly to the right to look for our troops running out of the wood line to unload the aircraft of its precious cargo. Instead, I saw NVA soldiers walking out of the woods firing their weapons at us. They were no more than forty yards away. These were regulars, not the black pajama clad Viet Cong we were used to seeing. I yelled over the intercom, "NVA! NVA!" I guess they had broken through the Mike Force's flank at the very last moment. "Fire! Fire!" I ordered, not knowing if anyone was listening. I did not hear our weapons fire. "Get 'em," I yelled, as I glanced back to see both men with their heads slumped, as if they were asleep.

My head jerked forward as I looked for a way to get out of this mess. If we stayed there, we would be destroyed. At that moment the Special Forces captain picked up the M-16 that had fallen from his comrade's hand and ran directly at the North Vietnamese. He was blazing away at them with an M-16 in each hand. I was witnessing an incredible act of bravery by a combat leader determined to get back to his men. It was like a scene from a John Wayne or a Rambo movie. Nothing was going to get in his way, not even a dozen well-armed enemy soldiers.

Thunk, thunk, thunk. More rounds were hitting my side of the aircraft. "We've got to get out of here." An adrenaline rush seemed to take over my mouth. "We're taking too many hits." I took one last glance. The Captain had created enough havoc running and firing at the NVA that they split. I saw them fall back to the wood line. I remember saying out loud, "Good luck, buddy. God help you."

There was just enough time for me to pull power and take off right from the ground without hovering. Fifty-foot trees loomed in front of me, not more than a hundred yards ahead. I wanted to get the chopper up over the trees and at least have some protection from all the rounds being fired at us. It became apparent in the next few moments that I might not be able to coax the chopper over the trees with the yet unloaded ammo and water in the cabin. I could not turn right, so I cranked the aircraft into a left turn out over the dry lakebed, figuring I would go back over the treetops as soon as we had sufficient airspeed and altitude. In the left turn, the top of the helicopter was exposed to the NVA small arms fire still coming from the wood line. Sure enough there was the "thump, thump, thump," sounds of rounds hitting the rotor blades and the roof of the cabin. "Lord, help us!" Was I yelling, or were those my thoughts screaming?

Bright warning lights

Trying to keep calm and collected without caving in to the terror around us was becoming increasingly more difficult. Between the pilot and copilot seats was an instrument control panel lined with about twenty warning lights. When the light indicators are not on, everything is okay. If they are lit, watch out; there is trouble. There is nothing brighter than warning lights. Lights were coming on showing problems in the transmission oil temperature and pressure and engine oil pressure. We had really been hit hard. Why were we still flying?

Normal procedure when warning lights come on is to set the aircraft down and fix it, or call for help if you can't fix it. There was no way we could set the Huey down in the middle of this open area and survive. By this time we had sufficient altitude and airspeed to turn east and get over the trees. At least we would have some protection from ground fire.

Wrestling up all the courage I could, I told the copilot, "I don't know how much longer this bird will fly, but we have got to get this ammo to our guys somehow. They'll get slaughtered if we don't." I couldn't help wondering what had happened to Captain Sincere who had run right into all that mess. What had happened to the radio operator whose radio transmission was abruptly cut off? Had the North Vietnamese taken the Mike Force's position?

A final attempt

At that moment I saw the lingering yellow smoke from the smoke grenade that had been thrown earlier by the Mike Force to mark their position. It seemed like an eternity ago, but it had only been a couple of minutes earlier. "I'm going to fly a steep right turn around that smoke," I briefed the crew chief, who had been on the opposite side of the aircraft during all the chaos. "I want you to get out of your seat and kick as many of those bags as you can out the door." As an afterthought I added, "I don't know how much longer we can fly, so do it as fast as you can; now!" I yelled.

Bloody Cockpit

Tears in his eyes, he moved around the machine gun pedestal and positioned himself in front of the load. I banked the aircraft and kept it as close to the smoke as I could. It worked! He began pushing, shoving, and kicking with a vengeance, as if he were mad at the world. The bags of ammunition and water fell quickly through the trees to the ground. I prayed that our people would be able to get to the bags and use the ammo. I circled the area three times as the crew chief worked furiously to keep a flow of bags falling like manna from heaven. Another warning light came on. "This is it," I acknowledged with a heavy heart. "We have to go." I eased the chopper into a climb and turned to the east. I just wanted to get away from all the terrible things that had been happening to us. How could Huey 711 possibly fly any further? The crew chief, exhausted, crawled over the remaining bags on the floor to check on the gunner and the Special Forces supply officer. What he cried out, I did not want to hear. "They're dead! They're dead! Oh, God, they're dead!" He was bawling like the young boy that he was. "Buckle up" I said. Trying to encourage him and myself, I added, "We'll be home soon."

What happened next was worse than anything that had already happened to us. The mission had been flown with the large sliding doors of the cabin open so that the crew could man their machine guns. In flight the wind enters the rear of the cabin and then swirls and burbles toward the front windshield. The very blood that had sustained life just a few minutes before was now being sprayed around the cabin and against the windshield as the wind rushed past our two fallen comrades. Where to now? All I could think of was to gain as much altitude as I could before she quit. At least I might be able to auto-rotate the helicopter into a safe area. But the reality was that there was nowhere to go except into the treetops. The events that had just taken place were overwhelming. I just wanted to get us out of there. Not one of us wanted to stay there, crash and be right in the middle of all that war.

The clear plastic visor on the flight helmet that covered my face and eyes was turning crimson with blood. Not thinking, I reached up with my left hand to wipe it away. Instead, my flight gloves smeared the blood across my visor. Attempts to wipe away the blood on the windshield resulted in the same smeared mess. It was becoming harder and harder to see outside the aircraft. A red haze was everywhere. When I opened my mouth to talk on the intercom, I tasted it. I rolled my visor up, hoping to see a little better, and the blood covered my face.

I was scared. I didn't know how we were going to make it back. All those warning lights were flashing at me. I couldn't see zilch. There was nowhere to land. There were two courageous men dead on my aircraft. I was getting nauseous. I felt helpless. I was the old man of the crew at 32, and wanted to cry with my crew chief. I looked upward, not realizing that I was yelling, and pleaded, "God, can't you stop all this? Please take us away from all this blood and death." The situation looked hopeless.

I glanced at my copilot. His lips were moving. I knew he was praying too because nothing was coming over the intercom. I looked around the cockpit in utter disbelief.

There was the crew chief, the lone survivor in the back, with tears still running down his cheeks. He was hunched over and sagging in his seat, looking not at me but through me. The remnants of a precious cargo were at his feet. The copilot's eyes were focused straight ahead as if he were trying to pierce the red veil before him. I sensed that they were waiting for the inevitable to happen. There was an eerie silence that seemed louder than the rushing wind and the screaming engine. They were waiting for the final, ear-shattering silence of an engine that would quit at any moment. My eyes scanned the instrument panel, cross-checking flight and engine instruments that were sprinkled with blood. I was startled again as I looked down at the warning lights that were on. The windshield was difficult to look through. I shook my head thinking, "Ol' 711 is going to die an ugly death today." My eyes trailed off to the right. All of a sudden, I saw a spot on the windshield that was not covered with blood. It was at the furthermost point of the windshield on the very bottom. It was only about a three-inch diameter circle. Then I saw it! I could not believe it. There, through that small circle, I spotted a large red cross on a white background. It was the same battalion aid station tent that we had seen being erected on our flight out! I abandoned my coaxing, tender touch on the controls and quickly dropped the collective so that the chopper would start an immediate descent. Throughout the 270 degree turn, I was asking, "Are we going to make it, Lord? Are we going to make it, Lord?" A helipad had been built near the tent. My heart was pounding in cadence with the rotor blades. This had to be the most precise and quickest approach that I had ever made. I slowed, flared the helicopter, and made small adjustments so that the chopper would touchdown in the middle of the circle with an "H" painted on it.

There was no stopping to establish a hover. I took her right down to the perforated steel planking (PSP) that formed the helipad. The rear of the landing skids touched the landing pad, and I carefully eased the nose down so that the front of the skids fully rested on the pad. At that very moment the engine quit! I had not rolled the power off; I had not turned any switches off. Huey 711 had just died, and the silence was deafening. A team of medics ran out to the aircraft, immediately unbuckled the two that had given their lives and carried them inside the tent. The rotor blades stopped, and I noticed my trembling hands turning off the switches. My hands seemed like they belonged to someone else. I collapsed in my seat as the last ounce of adrenaline left me. In retrospect, I wish I had said, "Thank you, Lord, for bringing us to our place of refuge." Instead I just said, "Thank you, Lord."

Major Alvin Cartwright,
Aircraft Commander
November 11, 1966

As described in the above incident we lost **Sergeant Henry T. Leonard** *when he was flying as a door gunner on that desperate attempt to resupply a Special Forces team that was about to be overrun. He had volunteered to fly even though he only had a few days left before he went home.*

On 2 December 1966, while flying on a rescue mission, we lost four brave men to enemy fire: Specialist Four William Joseph Bodzick, a crew chief; Specialist Four Lee Joseph Boudreaux, Jr., a door gunner; and Warrant Officer Donald Harrison, a co-pilot. Warrant Officer Arthur Sulander, the aircraft commander is still missing. Their helicopter was shot down in Laos while trying to rescue a recon team that was about to be overrun by a large North Vietnamese enemy force.

In flight school pilots have to memorize the entire cockpit panel; the location of each instrument, circuit breaker, radios and controls. The pilot flies with his head "on a swivel", constantly scanning the instruments. As with any school there are some contingencies the student is never prepared for. Blood spattered instruments; windshield and helmet visor definitely falls into the category of an unplanned contingency. In combat, the rules and regulations of flying are discarded and flying is done by "the seat of the pants." If any pilot utilized any of the combat skills in flight school he would have been washed out and never graduated. Combat develops a set of skills that can never be taught in school. The machine and man became one. The pilot wasn't climbing into the helicopter; he was strapping it to his back.

The following illustration shows exactly what every pilot sees and dreams about:

A PRECISE SEQUENCE

1. Overhead Console
2. Flight Instruments
3. Engine and System Instruments
4. Center Console and Radios
5. Tail Rotor Control Pedals
6. Collective Control
7. Cyclic Control

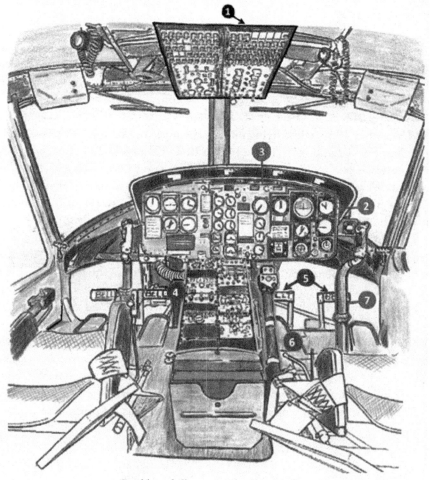

Dashboard illustration by Lou Lerda

THE CREW CHIEF

Although the crew chief was never on the controls of the aircraft, he, along with the door gunner, was the success of every mission. Not only did he man the M-60, he was the pilot's eyes on the left side and left rear of the helicopter. The pilot had to do exactly what the crew chief told him and the crew chief trusted the pilot to follow his instructions. A helicopter could never make it into or out of a hover hole without this teamwork.

It was always "my helicopter." Never did a crew chief speak of the helicopter that he was the crew chief on without using this possessive term. It was as if he had brought the machine into the world and had bought and paid for it with his own money. Consequently, it was his helicopter. The pride that each crew chief showed with the care given day in and day out, month after month to the care and maintenance of his Huey was obvious with every crew chief of the 281st. It was his pride and joy. If every soldier in the Army from the top to the bottom had the can-do attitude and commitment and performed his duties as did the helicopter crew chiefs, we would have one heck of a well-maintained Army. The crew chief's concern for his helicopter was natural since his very life, as well as those of the crew and passengers, depended on the excellent care of his helicopter.

The army helicopters required a lot of maintenance. With this flying machine you had to think ahead and anticipate all the "what ifs" that could go wrong. Helicopters are made of thousands of moving parts all going in opposite directions to keep it flying. The crew chief could detect the slightest unusual noise or vibration, and when he informed the pilots that something was wrong, there was no doubt that they would immediately be looking for a place to land.

The Army helicopter crew chief was highly respected because he performed so many duties and answered to so many different people. First, he was under the direct supervision of his platoon sergeant and his platoon leader. Following them, he answered to the maintenance officer, the first sergeant, the company commander and to each pilot who flew his helicopter.

While in flight, he was the gunner on the left side. He needed to know everything that the gunner knew; how to fire, how to lead when firing, how to load and reload and how to correct malfunctions in flight. He had to know the weight and balance chart and be able to determine how much load the helicopter could carry to balance the load against the fuel required for the mission. All of this information was critical for a safe and successful mission. He also made sure that each passenger was secured and safe inside the cabin. It was not uncommon for a loaded aircraft to actually carry animals like pigs and chickens, which the Vietnamese soldiers would not leave behind. Making sure they were secure was a problem, for they could shift the balance of the aircraft. At times, he had to train a new door gunner. He knew how to start the helicopter and how to shut it down safely. Moreover, most of the crew chiefs could take off and land the helicopter in case of an emergency.

Each person in the 281st performed his duties in an excellent manner, but the helicopter crew chief was a standout and made all of us look good. All Intruder pilots will tell you that they frequently owed their life to the crew who sat in the back, out in the open, protecting them on every mission. Most of our pilots wanted the whole crew to receive the same medals they did, and they should have.

THE DOOR GUNNER

Aaah; our door gunners… They were the counterpart of the crew chief. He was the eyes and gun security on the right. Without the team work of the crew chief and door gunner, there would be many more dead pilots. A daughter of a door gunner thanked a pilot for bringing her daddy home safely. The pilot responded, "your dad brought me home safely!" We were so fortunate and so blessed to have such brave men! Almost to the man, each one was a professional and loved being a part of the crew. Over the years their typical remark has been "If I had to do it all over again, I wouldn't change a thing. I would do it again with the 281st as a door gunner." What made them brave? Moreover, can bravery be acquired, or is it a quality you have at birth? The answer is nuanced and complex. Bravery taps the mind, brain and heart. It issues from instinct, training, and empathy. Today, neurologists, psychologists, and other medical researchers are studying bravery to unravel the mystery. I think the researchers would do well to look at our helicopter door gunners. First of all, most had already served on the ground as infantrymen. They knew what the men on the ground were going through because they had experienced it themselves. Most had already been awarded the Combat Infantryman Badge and numerous other medals. They came to us as brave men who volunteered to stay in Vietnam for an extra period of time to serve as helicopter door gunners. Generally speaking, Intruder pilots will tell you they would not be alive today if it had not been for the door gunners and crew chiefs. But as skilled as they were on the ground, maintaining that skill in a moving helicopter required practice. Once in the helicopter, the door gunner was on a moving platform and had to compensate for wind, ground speed and turbulence. When these factors were mastered, these modern day "gun slingers" were God's gift to the entire flight crew.

Their assigned weapon was the M-60 7.62mm machine gun, the standard utility helicopter door armament system. Initially, the door guns were mounted on solid swiveling mounts bolted to the aircraft in order to retain and steady the guns. As the war progressed, crew chiefs and door gunners resorted to bungee cords in order to suspend and retain the machine guns. This became a common practice, for the newfound maneuverability of these "bungeed" weapons allowed for increased firing angles. This practice was commonly referred to as using a Free 60. However, some door gunners simply continued to hand-wield the weapon for a maximum level of maneuverability of fire. Door gunners were normally restrained for safety within the aircraft, often by using a standard lap belt. If the gunner wanted more freedom of movement within the aircraft without being restrained, he used a monkey harness, which was a GI safety harness worn on the torso and anchored to the aircraft floor or to the cabin wall. The monkey harness allowed a door gunner and crew chief greater mobility, including leaning outward on the helicopter skids to get a better firing angle. The door gunner's position on the Huey was on the right side, exposed to the elements and an easy target for the enemy due to the position of manning a machine gun in the open door of a helicopter. According to popular legend, the door gunner on a Vietnam era combat assault mission had a lifespan of five minutes. This might be exaggeration, but it accurately describes the hazards of this particular military job at the time.

A door gunner had to thoroughly know aviation lingo because he was the pilot's eyes on his side of the helicopter, particularly when descending into a small area. He made sure both machine guns were in excellent condition and had plenty of ammunition. He assisted the combat team exiting and entering the aircraft while still firing his machine gun to keep the enemy at bay; being careful not to hit any of his own men. In addition, he often served as a medic, rendering lifesaving first aid to those who came aboard wounded.

He also helped the crew chief with maintaining the aircraft, and, as time went on, he became quite proficient with all aspects of caring for the helicopter. Eventually, several of these brave young men became skilled crew chiefs. The bonds that developed between the crew chief and door gunner were strong and in many cases still exist. The door gunner was not only a gun slinger; he was a key contributing member of our combat aviation team and helped make this unit so special. It was also good to hear the door gunner's words, "Clear on the right."

Door Gunner Den

THE PLATOON SERGEANT

Moving to and operating from an FOB in the field was never an easy task. Moving a small town of people; living quarters, food, showers, toilets and more was a daunting affair. The flight elements were broken down into their individual platoons and the platoon sergeant became the lubricant that kept that unit operating smoothly.

The platoon sergeant had a very demanding job. In most cases, he had already been a crew chief or a maintenance man. He knew the helicopter inside and out and served as a role model for his men. The platoon sergeant assigned the crew for each mission and made sure that each time the helicopter flew, it was in the best of shape with highly skilled crew members on board. When needed, he was there to help with maintenance. He was the overall watchdog, looking out for the welfare of his men. The platoon sergeant answered to the platoon leader, to the maintenance officer, to the company commander and to the first sergeant. He also was the barrack's sergeant, making sure that everything was ready for an unannounced inspection by the first sergeant or company commander. In addition, he also flew as a crew chief or door gunner when needed. In some cases, the crew chief was the platoon sergeant. The system worked; each man stepped up to make sure every mission was successful. The platoon sergeant had the sad job of inventorying the personal belongings of men who were missing or killed in action. Our platoon sergeants, no matter what their occupation was, met the challenge every day. We had some of the very best non-commissioned officers. They were the backbone of our company, and they deserve considerable credit for our overall success.

Two of our platoon sergeants were killed in action while flying as crew members: Sergeant Henry T. Leonard and Staff Sergeant Bobbie H. Brewer.

WARRANT OFFICERS

During the Vietnam War, most Army helicopter pilots were warrant officers. Warrant officers were in a command layer between non-commissioned and commissioned officers. They had a narrow area of expertise and authority called a Warrant rather than a Commission. In the US Army, warrant officers were addressed as "Mister." With the improvements in helicopter design, the war in Vietnam became more of a helicopter war. By regulations, a pilot had to be either a commissioned officer or a warrant officer, and the demand could not be met using only commissioned officers. As fighting increased, the Army was forced to train an ever-increasing number of warrant officer pilots for the ever-increasing demand.

This demand led to the expansion of the Warrant Officer Flight Training program. Many of the warrant officers had initially joined the Army to go to helicopter flight school, while others were enlisted men who had requested transfers. Warrant Officer candidates had to be at least eighteen and have at least a high school education, and qualify for a "secret clearance." Warrant Officer Candidate School combined warrant officer training with flight training.

In 1957, the first published definition for Army Warrant Officers was established in Army Regulation 611-112 and defined the Warrant Officer: "The Warrant Officer is a highly skilled technician who is provided to fill those positions above the enlisted level which are too specialized in scope to permit effective development and continued utilization of broadly trained, branch qualified commissioned officers."

In short, a Warrant Officer was highly trained in a particular field, such as aviation or maintenance. The main difference between a warrant officer and a commissioned officer was a Warrant Officer could not have any command responsibility, such as a platoon leader or company commander. They had all the rights and privileges of a commissioned officer but none of the responsibilities. Their job was simply to fly helicopters.

Jim Baker,
Chief Warrant Officer

THE CHEMIST

Most of our door gunners came to us well qualified in the use of an M-60 machine gun. Most had been trained as infantrymen, and most had already earned their Combat Infantryman Badge, which verified their combat experience. Their MOS in most cases was 11B20. In addition, these men had volunteered to extend their tour to serve as door gunners. But what training does a chemist have? How does a chemist with MOS 92C meet the qualifications of a door gunner?

My story with the 281st begins when I was sent to the 10th Combat Aviation Battalion for my assignment. I had bunked with door gunners the night before, and they told me that they really needed gunners. I was assigned to be a chemist, but I was not committed to that job. The next morning, when I told the soldier assigning me my MOS 92C20 I was a chemist, he told me that he didn't know what that was. All I could think was I would be filling sandbags for the foreseeable future. Rather than insist I was supposed to be a chemist; I told him I wanted to be a door gunner. He said I couldn't, but I started arguing with him, telling him what the gunners had told me the night before. It got heated, and a colonel working in the back came up to find out what was going on. I told him the same story. He grabbed my arm to see how strong I was and then told the specialist to give me the job. I wondered what my strength had to do with it. They told me I would be going to the Special Forces Compound in Nha Trang with one other fellow. By now there were five other men who were also changing their MOS to become gunners. Because only one more gunner was needed, the five were told to pick a number between one and ten. This is how I met my new friend Richard Cooper. He won the assignment by letting the other men pick a number first before he chose the closest number. Turns out he was a gambler.

We were flown to the compound, assigned bunks, and the next day assigned a ship, a gunship in my case. I was told to outfit it and started doing that. The company was in the field when I got there, and the next thing I knew a ship was returning with Sergeant Goff, who had lost his ship and needed a new one. Sergeant Goff told me that he would take my ship because he had seniority, and I told him fine because I was totally new at this. I helped him to get everything ready, trying to learn from him. When the ship was ready, they took off for a test flight and were immediately shot down. With luck, they managed to crash land, and no one was hurt. At that point, I knew I was going to make it home. On one of Cooper's first flights, the Viet Cong shot 57 holes in his ship. He was rethinking his luck at gambling.

I should tell you about my first mission, a camping trip with the company. We flew along the coast to Da Nang, then inland to the Special Forces Camp at Khe Sanh. It started out sunny, and we camped in big wall tents along the air strip. We were inserting teams to recon near the DMZ and Laotian border. It wasn't too long before it started to rain and got windy enough to tear a large hole in the top of our tent. That's when I started sleeping in our ship; at least it was dry. It rained so much that the C-130s resupplying us couldn't land on the air strip.

It wasn't long before we were running out of food. I remember getting lettuce and peas for breakfast, and while leaving the mess tent with my tray, the wind blew the food off my plate; I picked it up off the ground and ate it anyway. The Special Forces Colonel in charge was very upset and said the lack of preparedness wouldn't happen again. We got a break for Christmas, and when we returned the Green Berets had relieved the Navy of two large refrigerators and a few jeeps.

It was during this mission that we lost contact with a recon team. We searched for them for a long time. I remember finding two of the Chinese mercenaries alive but so tired they couldn't climb the rope ladder we dropped to them. The Special Forces sergeant with us jumped out of the ship and helped them up, so we could pull them in. We never got the Americans back.

My last ship was the first gunship in Vietnam to get the new flex mini guns. That happened after the gunship I was crewing was raked from front to rear by a 28mm anti-aircraft gun. I still have a piece of the half-inch plate of steel that was suspended under my seat as a memento. It stopped an armor piercing round that ended up blowing a six-inch hole in our fuel cell, which fortunately was almost empty. We made it back, but the ship never flew again. The new flex mini guns gave us a lot more gun power.

Russell Erbe
Door Gunner 1966-1967

GETTING READY FOR THE MISSION

The process required to get a helicopter ready for takeoff is extremely complicated because of the many details and the importance of doing everything in a precise sequence. The day was already off to a bad start: the weather was lousy and the mission area had been changed at the last minute. Thankfully, the "old man" had the new area reconned before last light the day before, and all the available info was passed on to us during the brief. As soon as the mission briefing is over, it's time to preflight and get ready to launch. You look for your crew and hit the flight line to make sure everything is in order.

Arriving at the aircraft, you stow your gear and make sure that the helmets and "chicken plates" (ceramic armor chest protector) are located on the seat, so you can easily retrieve them when your preflight is completed. You need to check the log book one more time to see if there are any new maintenance write-ups. Everything appears to be in order. It's time for the preflight walk around. Start from the right front and end at the same point. Check the condition of the sheet metal, Plexiglas and flight controls. Look for leaks or visible signs of any previous damage and open up the cowlings. Check the engine, transmission, rotor blades, drive shafts, synch elevator and tail rotor. You've done this hundreds of times, but the seriousness of these checks never diminishes. You can't spend less time on this inspection and still be true to yourself and the people you're carrying.

Remove all covers and tie downs as you go. Everything looks good, so you button it all back up and double-check your locking fasteners; you don't need any loose panels flapping around in flight. Check weapons, look for any loose equipment in the main cargo area and secure or dispose of it; you don't want anything flying out of the aircraft and getting tangled in the rotors or flight controls once we get the bird started. While you are back here, be sure to check the level of the transmission oil.

Returning to the pilot's seat, you put on your helmet, gloves and chicken plate and begin your preliminary check of the electronics, radios, navigation equipment and all circuit breakers before pulling the start trigger.

You brief your crew and passengers as required and make sure all maps and radio frequencies required for the mission are either set in the avionics or readily available. You enter your flight crew data to the flight log and stow the log book in the map case.

Start your checks with your left hand over your head and aft, at the rear of the overhead console. Make a semicircular sweep of the overhead console, the flight instruments and the center console to make sure that the appropriate switches and circuit breakers are in the correct on/off or select position. Adjust the pilot's seat and tail rotor pedals to suit your comfort level. Make a static check of the cyclic control, the collective and tail rotor pedals to ensure correct movement, and verify that there is no binding of the controls. All engine gauges and applicable switches are OK. The prestart check is complete. You ensure that the engine instrument indicators will be in the horizontal position once everything is operating normally, which makes your cross checks easier. (It assures you can spot a malfunctioning system faster.)

Post the crew chief and door gunner as fire guards. Check that the rotor blades are untied and all tie downs are stowed securely. Your copilot is following you with the check list in hand, serving as your second set of eyes. Flip the ignition switch to ON. Now turn on the battery switch, open the fuel valve, check fuel switches and set the governor switch on automatic. Depress the engine/rotor rpm switch on the throttle control for ten seconds to set it at the low rpm setting, then reach down with your left hand to grasp the collective pitch lever and set the throttle to the start position on the bottom side of the detent, so you can roll the throttle to off if there is an incorrect start condition. Now set the altimeters and the clock.

The next forty-five seconds require the total concentration of both pilots as you pull the starter trigger. The familiar turbine whine of the Lycoming turbine softly screams in your ears as it starts to spin. Now turn on the main inverter and monitor the engine instruments to ensure that you have correct engine and transmission pressures and temperatures. Also make sure that there are no indications of an incorrect start. At fifteen seconds, the rotors should be turning and the turbine should be on its way to 40 percent of engine operating rpm. Roll the throttle clockwise to the low rpm setting of 6000 rpm, and make sure that the engine start temperature does not exceed a maximum of 760 degrees centigrade, Set the starter generator switch to standby and check all systems for correct operating limits and temperatures. Now advance throttle and insure that the rpm is at 6600. Set all radios and avionics. Check all flight instruments; set and readjust as necessary. Next you perform the engine Health Indicator Check. As you bring the bird to a hover, you run a quick power check against the engine decal on the instrument panel.

Combat flying, once again, changes all basic procedures. All the aircraft are checked upon arrival from a mission. All pre-flight procedures are completed to ensure the aircraft is ready to fly. When a tactical emergency occurs, the co-pilot jumps in... flips on the battery switch...pulls the start trigger and the engine starts its beautiful sound. While the co-pilot is "cranking" the engine, the A/C is putting on his helmet and strapping in. He takes the controls from the co-pilot and brings the engine up to full throttle (6600 rpm) while the co-pilot puts his helmet on and straps in. If all goes well, the aircraft can be in the air in one minute!

Hovering is the most difficult operating mode of this bird. You recall that when you were in flight school, you were given 22 acres of open space and one distinctive tree. You were to keep the helicopter centered on the tree and within the confines of the field. It was very difficult, but you have become very proficient at this, and you swear you can hover the Huey over a postage stamp in your sleep.

You are making constant corrections as you operate the collective to maintain your altitude, the rotor pedals to compensate for power changes and the cyclic control for finite control movements. As you do this you check your torque gauge to compare the torque required to hover against the manufacturer's test results on that particular engine as to what it is capable of producing, but you also have to remember that the drivetrain will limit you to 50 psi torque because of the drivetrain component design and materials' limits.

The entire flight is now at a hover, and the lead ship gives the command to depart. You are careful to not have your hover cushion blown away as the other birds in the formation take off around you. The bird drops momentarily as you move forward and suddenly go into your liftoff mode, gaining forward airspeed. Moving into your flight formation position, the last ship to take off announces that all ships for this mission are airborne. Gently easing the cyclic forward, you main-tain the speed of the others in the formation and adjust all controls accordingly. There is a constant cross checking of flight and engine instruments to ensure that all is going well, and you are staying in formation as you head for the release point. Airspeed is running between 90 and 100 knots, and the altitude is being dictated by the terrain, weather and the mission.

LZ with elephant grass

For today's mission the RP is code named Baltimore, and only one slick has a team on board. However, three slicks are going to descend to designated landing zones to try to confuse the enemy as to where we are really dropping the team. Our coded LZ is Richmond; the others are Wilmington and Frederick. As we call the RP, we are each cleared to our des-ignated LZ. These are single-ship missions, and often the LZ isn't large enough to accommodate more than one Huey. Your adrenaline starts to increase as you begin your descent to your area. Checking your rpm to insure that you are at 6600 and per-forming a quick systems check, you lower the collective pitch to begin your descent. You are aware that recovery is questionable if something goes wrong, and this only adds to the tension. The LZ looks OK; there appears to be room for a recovery bird if necessary, but there is elephant grass in the area, and you can't really determine how tall it is. You double-check all wind indicators, slow your forward speed to 80 knots and do a banking turn into the wind while monitoring your rate of descent. The area appears to be surrounded by trees 120 to 150 foot high, and you plan your approach to land in the middle of the clearing at about a 10-foot hover. Around 500 feet, you begin a reduction of forward airspeed and slow the descent rate for better control. The LZ appears level, but the grass is still a problem as you can't estimate its height or determine if the landing area is level or sloped. Crossing over the trees, you quickly decrease your airspeed to 20 knots and literally drop to the height of the elephant grass, decreasing forward speed as you descend.

You come to a hover with the grass just over your skids and slowly lower the bird until the grass is up to your windows; time for your team to exit.

They disappear into the elephant grass, and you waste no time applying power for an immediate departure. Total time since beginning your descent is about three minutes. You clear the trees and with a sweeping right-hand turn, climb back to altitude to rejoin the other birds and return to the Forward Operating Base. Another successful day in Vietnam. Mission complete.

Colonel Lou Lerda,
U.S. Army Retired
Reconstructed from memory after 48 years

Delta recon team ready for insertion
photo courtesy of Chester Howard
team leader on the right with the headband

1967

STAFF SERGEANT WILLIS

SSG Willis

I had just arrived in Vietnam and was assigned as a helicopter mechanic with the 281st Assault Helicopter Company. Most of the time, we worked on the helicopters right out on the flight line. It was always noisy. On one particular day I was sent out to work on one of the rotor heads of a Huey. I had my tools and was hard at it. All types of aircraft were taking off and landing. Just down the flight line, a Huey was getting ready to depart. I was concentrating on what I was doing when I happened to look down. A sergeant was asking me something, but it was so noisy that I couldn't make out what he was saying. I just shook my head and said, "I don't know." I watched as he went over to the next crew that was working on another helicopter, and I guess he asked the same question. They pointed back at me.

He made a quick turn, came back and ordered me to get my *@# down. I climbed down, and then he asked, "How come you don't know your *@# name?" Most army staff sergeants are good at getting their point across with colorful expressions, and this sergeant was no exception. After giving me hell he ordered me to follow him. We walked over to helicopter tail number 725, and he said, "This is your aircraft. You are going to Bien Hoa early tomorrow morning, so make sure you have 1,000 pounds of fuel in the tank." He handed me the red log book and continued, "Your gunner will be mounting both M-60 machine guns shortly." With a smirk he added, "I know you can't remember your name, but can you remember that mine is Sergeant Willis and that this is your helicopter?" He walked away with a swagger as if he were a Mafia boss man and said over his shoulder, "Good luck." After Sergeant Willis walked away, I remember just standing there. I kept looking at the tail section, the rotor head, and the nose, and then looking again several more times. I was thinking, "What the hell do I do now?" I was just nineteen years old. I could feel the weight of my responsibility on my shoulders.

As Sergeant Willis left, my gunner Ron Renfrow showed up. Renfrow and I made a good team. We had a good Huey. Number 725 was my baby, and the pilots always complimented me on how well I took care of it. One morning I woke up very sick and had to go to the Special Forces Dispensary to see what was wrong with me. Sergeant Willis found another crew chief to take my place, and while on a recovery mission 725 was shot down. All the crew was badly burned. Renfrow still suffers to this day. Sergeant Wills was a great guy, and I often wonder what happened to him.

Frank Little
Crew Chief
Jan '67 - Jan '68

On 11 February 1967, Major Allen "Al" Junko assumed command of the company.

GRUMPY

In every war, a combat unit inevitably adopts a stray dog for its mascot, Grumpy was ours. He wandered into our area. He looked bad, was hungry and needed a home. We fed him lots of good army chow: c-rations and whatever we could beg, borrow or steal from the mess hall. We cleaned him up. We adopted him into our platoon. He was just a pup, only months old, yet he acted like an old man. Because he was not particularly friendly, we named him Grumpy. Of course, he lived in the barracks with us, and when we went on extended missions, we took him along. Grumpy loved to fly and would hang his head out the door to look around, especially during takeoffs and landings. We made sure there was a bulletproof flak vest on the floor for him to lie on, but more so to protect him in case we received ground fire from below.

Grumpy was an extraordinary combat dog. It is estimated that he had well over 100 hours of combat time, which would have earned a human soldier three air medals. All his flight time was in the UH-1C gunship, which carried 36 rockets, 250 40mm grenades with two M-60 machine guns, one on each side. PFC Grumpy was not just a dog; he was a member of our platoon. HE WAS FAMILY.

William Perren
Door Gunner 1966 - 1967

On 21 May 1967, we lost Walter Francis Wrobleski and Michael Patrick Gallagher from enemy fire, Chief Warrant Officer Wrobleski is still missing.

NEVER AGAIN

On 6 August 1967, we were working with Delta and a team called for an extraction. The guys were on the top of a ridge which was fairly clear and made for a relatively easy landing. On short final, the bad guys opened up and the aircraft was shot down. The pilot was able to hit the ridge line but he had too much air speed and he bounced off the ridge and over the air. The aircraft exploded on impact. Everyone on the operation was stunned. We just lost an aircraft and entire crew. Horrified, C&C had to maintain composure. There was still a team on the ground that had to be extracted. Suddenly, an excited team leader reported the downed aircraft crew was alive and scrambling up the hill to his location. They had survived the crash and were alive and well. Now not only was there a team to recover but also an entire flight crew. As plans were being formulated, the backup recovery aircrafts reported low on fuel and had to return to base for refueling.

Nearby, listening to the action, was an Air Force "Jolly Green" ready to assist. The LZ was too small for the ship so the decision was made to use a hoist. There was only enough room for three people on the hoist so "Delta" loaded three of the crew onto it and cleared the Jolly Green to go.

As big as these aircraft were, they were not designed for this kind of load on the hoist. Usually their missions were for one person at a time. As the pilot started to take off, an engine fire warning alarm went off. Thinking there was a fire and he was in an overload condition, he flared the aircraft to get control. This action caused the three crew members to sling out over the steep ridge and jungle below. The hoist operator panicked and cut the hoist cable sending the three crew members to their death. Never again would we use anyone other than our people to work our mission.

On 6 August 1967, we lost Private First Class John Camden Soper, Door Gunner; Private First Class Michael Anthony Goffredo, Crew Chief; and Warrant Officer Daryl Leroy Miller. They were all killed when the Jolly Green Giant helicopter, which was recovering them with a hoist, "developed engine problems" because the helicopter was overloaded. They were cut free and fell to their deaths.

Jolly green giant helicopter

MO VS. JOE

Joe, a nineteen year old tough infantryman, was a door gunner from the Bronx, a well-known borough of New York City, where he had earned a reputation as a tough Irish kid. Joe wanted to be transferred from the lift platoon to the gunship platoon. When he heard the request, Captain Mo replied, "No, you're a good man, and I want to keep you here." A few days later Joe made his request again to Captain Mo. With a tough look on his face, he said, "I know I am a good man, and I am a sure shot with an M-60, but I really want to switch platoons so I can fly with my friend Frankie, who is also from the Bronx." The captain was getting annoyed with Joe. Captain Moberg looked straight in the eyes of this tough kid and said, "If you can kick my @*#, I will let you transfer." Joe was about 5'10" and weighed close to 190 pounds; he was all muscle. Captain Mo was about 6'2" and weighed about the same as Joe, maybe a few pounds more. He had less muscle but was lean.

Joe wore a crooked smile and a warm feeling as he and the captain stood toe to toe and eye to eye. He now had a chance to kick this captain's rear end. He was thinking he could make a name for himself. After he took care of the captain, he would be held in high esteem by all his friends in the 281st, and he would also have a good story to tell his kids and grandkids as he grew old. In his eyes, the captain was an old man, almost 36 years old. Joe was sure this was going to be an easy fight; one, two, three and it would be over.

Each man took off his shirt. Joe turned sideways and then slowly turned again, coming face to face with the captain. As he was eyeballing the adversary, he thought how easy this fight would be; way too easy. He gave the captain his crooked grin and then made a fast move to the left trying to fake the captain off side. Mo just stood his ground and did not blink an eye. Then Joe stepped back and made his next move. As he came forward, Mo stepped forward too and grabbed Joe's arm and, using his momen-

tum, took him down to the ground, putting his knee in the middle of his back. It was so smooth, just one continuous movement. Joe was begging for mercy. In just a few seconds, the fight was over. Captain Mo released his grip, grabbed Joe by the neck, picked him up and said, "Now get your butt out of here; you're going to the gun platoon."

Joseph (Joe) Corney, Sr. and Francisco (Frankie) Esquilin Wolf Pack friends for life

Joe dusted himself off with a what-the-heck-happened look on his face, shook hands with the captain and moved on down the flight line toward his new home. The captain watched him go and was heard saying, "There goes a damn good man."

For the next few weeks, Joe was admired for taking on the captain, but he also took a lot of ribbing for letting an old man get the best of him. Joe became a top notch gunner for the Wolf Pack Gunship Platoon and is a valuable member of the 281st Assault Helicopter Company. To this day, Joe Carney and Frankie Esquilin still live in the Bronx and are still the best of friends. They see each other almost every day.

FLIGHT OPERATIONS

The 281st Assault Helicopter Company Flight Operations was comprised of a major as the operations officer, a captain as his assistant, a sergeant first class and four flight specialists.

Flight operations was the hub of just about everything that went on in the company and for most soldiers this was an exciting place to work. It usually took a while to get settled in and become familiar with how the system worked; to get to know the pilots, crews, maintenance teams, and what was expected of you. The flight operations sergeant, of course, answered to the flight operations officer and he was usually the headquarters platoon sergeant. With that position he answered to the first sergeant.

The flight operations specialists were well trained. They knew they had a good job, even though they might work sixteen hours or more, seven days a week. The 5th Special Forces was always engaged, always busy, so we were on continuous standby just in case they needed us. Their lives depended on all of us and even more on our pilots and crew to come rescue them if they got into trouble. It was a well-known fact that we would all risk our lives to always bring them to safety; ALWAYS.

The flight operations building at Nha Trang was not much more than a shack, with one level and two rooms. One room was for the operations personnel; the other room was a pilot briefing room. The two rooms were connected by a wide hallway. The entire building might have been or could have been made out of wooden ammo boxes. The sides were open with screens attached to keep the flies out. There were large flaps that we could close when it rained. It was a very simple building that served its purpose quite well in spite of being cramped.

Most of the time the flight operations sergeant manned and monitored the radios, answered all the telephones, called in all the reports (there were always reports to be called in) and made sure the flight specialists had all the information needed to keep the flight records up to date. Keeping the flight crews' records (DD form 759-1) up to date was a constant chore each day; there was no getting behind on this. He kept track of all the missions and shuttle runs and kept a list of passengers who needed a ride to wherever. He was always in contact with maintenance as to the status of all the aircraft, the crew chiefs and the platoon leaders of the three platoons. But most important of all, operations had to anticipate all the "what ifs". They always made sure that there was an aircraft and crew ready to go on a minute's notice. The gunship platoon was always available if needed. Maybe it should be said we all were ready if needed.

Albert Alvardo and Jack Interstein

PILOT CLASSIFICATIONS

SIP- Standardization Instructor Pilot
IP -Instructor Pilot
AC- Aircraft Commander
P –Pilot
PIC -Pilot In-Command
CP- Copilot, sometimes called Peter Pilot
C&C - Command and Control

In the 281st, the Company SIP's were charged with the responsibility of ensuring all IPs and ACs were trained to perform in accordance with the mission requirements of the unit. These requirements varied with the mission of each platoon, and therefore there were separate IPs for the lift platoons and the weapons platoons. Normally, they were individuals who had extensive experience in the aircraft and the mission.

Instructor pilots were individuals who were certified to qualify or transition a pilot into a new type of aircraft and/or re-qualify a new pilot joining the unit. Thus, they gave initial and ongoing check rides to ensure standardization within the unit. Instructor pilots were generally designated as such on unit special orders. Again, they usually were individuals with extensive experience in an aircraft type.

Aircraft commanders were individuals who had accumulated experience and skill, related to the mission of the unit and thus were in charge of the aircraft crew and held responsibility for mission performance. In the 281st each platoon had different standards for designating an individual as an AC.

The new pilots were individuals who were being trained to perform duties such as preflight inspections, inflight map following and flying the aircraft when the AC felt it was safe. Most individuals were assigned to a specific AC who was responsible for teaching them how to fly and perform the maneuvers required by the mission. Most pilots arrived in the company with 200 hours of flight time, all of which were accumulated in the flight school environment, resulting in the term Peter Pilot. Copilot was the designation for the second pilot when he was flying with an individual who was not yet designated as an AC.

C&C was the designation of the aircraft being flown by an individual in charge of a mission requiring two or more aircraft. Normally the Commander of the ground troops would fly in this aircraft, as well.

When a new pilot had been on a number of missions as a copilot and had accumulated a required number of flight hours, he would be recommended to become an aircraft commander. Once he passed his AC check ride, he was given a call sign and assigned an aircraft and a crew for which he would be responsible.

The use of company call signs was designed for simplicity and ease of control. When in a training environment, such as flight school, the pilots would use the last three aircraft tail numbers. If the aircraft tail number were 00-34567, then the aircraft call sign would be Army 567. This was very confusing when there were a number of aircraft operating at the same time. It was almost impossible to keep track of who was in what aircraft by just the tail number.

The unit call sign was used for quick identification. An example would be the call sign "Intruder 6." The word "Intruder" identified the 281st Assault Helicopter Company, and the number "6" identified the company commander. Now, let's break it down further.

Within the 281st Assault Helicopter Company, there were three flight platoons. The first platoon was the Rat Pack. Rat Pack 16 would be the platoon leader's call sign. The number "1" represented the 1st platoon, and the "6" identified the platoon leader. The second platoon was the Bandits. Bandit 26 would be the platoon leader. The number "2" represented the 2nd platoon, and the number "6" identified the platoon leader. The third platoon was the Wolf Pack. Wolf Pack 36 would be the platoon leader. The number "3" represented the 3rd platoon, and the number "6" identified the platoon leader.

How we did it

Pilots never seemed to really leave the training environment, even in combat. A newly assigned pilot would be given an "In Country" check ride. During the course of this evaluation, which was done by the unit instructor pilot (IP) or platoon instructor pilot, the newly assigned pilot would be evaluated on his flying skills and knowledge of the aircraft and its systems. After the initial check ride, the IP would meet with the commander or platoon leader and let him know what he needed to know about his newly assigned pilot. The IP would determine what areas of improvement, if any, the new pilot needed. This additional training typically would be done with an aircraft commander. Normally, a pilot would need 300 hours of flight time before he would be considered for AC. The IP would take input from the ACs who had been flying with him and platoon leader whose responsibility it was to recommend a pilot for an AC check ride. Assuming the pilot did well on his AC ride, he would be placed on orders as an aircraft commander and would log that type of time in the aircraft log book.

Individual call signs were supposed to be used in a tactical environment only. Flight following with air traffic control was always done with the last three numbers of the tail number preceded by the company's call sign, as in Intruder 567. This made it easier for air traffic control (ATC) to know who you were and whom to contact if contact with the aircraft was lost. When I was there, we always used our tactical call signs when on mission except when the flight was being followed by ATC because we did not want to be confused with some rear echelon company. We wanted the supported unit to know that Bandit 24 was the guy who pulled his butt out of the jam, not some rear echelon company that only flew milk runs.

If we were doing a combat assault led by a company commander and using aircraft and pilots from both lift platoons, we would use the Intruder call signs. Wolf Pack was always Wolf Pack. An operation like that was very rare, and I don't recall being on more than one or two of these during my tour. Most of the time the combat assaults were platoon size and led by the platoon leader. The majority of the time when we were not on Delta Operation, we operated as single aircraft supporting small units such as Special Forces A Teams and such. We always used platoon call signs on Delta Operations.

Chief Warrant Officer Robert (Bob) Mitchell
Bandit Platoon

RESCUING ROBBIE

The rescue crew included Warrant Officer Kenneth M. Johnson, who was the copilot, Crew Chief Michael J. Smith, Door Gunner Joseph Corney, Special Forces SFC Walter (Doc) Simpson operating the hoist, and me, Bob Moberg, in the left seat as the AC. The Recon Team had been pursued on the ground for two days by the North Vietnamese. Earlier, one of our helicopters had succeeded in rescuing three of the team members. Major Eldon Smith had been flying the command and control helicopter (C&C) with Major Charles (Bruiser) Allen, the Delta Commander. The forward air controller had spotted the team through a small opening in the canopy. The jungle penetrator hoist was being lowered under heavy fire and taking numerous hits. Major Allen and Major Smith called off the aircraft and ordered SFC Orville G. (Robbie) Robinette, the team leader on the ground, to "Get your stuff in order and find a safe LZ!" Robbie replied, "I got my stuff in order. I'm just looking for that slick you promised would get us out of here!" Knowing the Recon Team could not defend itself for long with only three remaining men; I requested that C&C give me directions to locate them, as I hovered down the ridge with skids in the trees using the triple canopy for concealment. The C&C gave us directions: right 3 degrees, left 5 degrees, hold heading, etc. It worked. I looked down, and there they were. Doc ran the hoist down its full length, over 200 feet. They couldn't quite reach it. I settled lower, and the blades were just starting to clip the top of the trees as the gunner and crew chief reported receiving heavy fire. Doc reported that Staff Sergeant Jay Graves was on the hoist. We couldn't move for fear of dragging Graves into the trees.

We are hit

About that time I felt the aircraft rise as the bottom windscreens disappeared and the cockpit filled with blue smoke. My right leg was knocked left off the pedal by the buckled radio console. I was sure we had been hit by a B40 rocket but could not confirm. The aircraft, still at a hover, started to drift left. As I tried to correct, I glanced at Johnson's death grip on the cyclic, the control for horizontal movement. I screamed, "I got it." The aircraft continued drifting, and I realized I had no cyclic or pedals. I made the decision to crash in the trees rather than 500 feet over the valley. I bottomed the collective, the control for vertical movement, and saw the brush spinning around us as the aircraft went nose down and then rolled upside down, stopping about six feet from the ground. I couldn't get the door open and screamed, "Where the hell is my gun?" Doc poked me with his M16 from below and said, "Here, take mine and get the hell out of there!" I crawled out through the nose. Doc and Smith had been thrown out and had broken ribs. Johnson and I climbed out with only broken pride! Doc and I climbed back up into the aircraft to shut off the inverters that were still whining, and Doc removed the M-60 machine guns and survival kit. I also found my M-15 carbine. Graves came over, kissed me on the head and said, "I knew you'd come get me!" Robbie came over and asked me if I wanted to take command, even though the policy was the Recon team leader was supposed to remain in command. I gladly told him he was doing a fine job, to keep trucking, and asked him what he wanted us to do. Robbie assigned us positions and fields of fire in the ambush above a trail running well below the downed aircraft. Bruiser advised us by PRC 25 to stay put until he could find an LZ to send in a platoon from the 93rd Ranger Battalion assigned to Delta for backup. I portioned out the water and ammo from the survival kit as Doc set up an M-60 above and behind me. It became really quiet, and as I lay there looking at my field of fire, I heard Vietnamese jabbering. I saw a man stop running about 20 yards from me, looking away and down the hill. As he stopped, the rest of his squad ran into him, bunching up. I was expecting the rescue Rangers but realized the pith helmet and crossed harness looked strange. I glanced over at Robbie, who was licking his lips and slowly taking careful aim with his M-15 Carbine. As I looked back at the bunched up men in front of me, the leader spun around. The red star on his helmet stood out like a rotating beacon. Seeing the Huey hanging above us, he pointed and started to scream as my first burst hit him. As I was trying to change magazines, I was aware of the constant M-60 fire over my head and numerous hand grenades being tossed into the now totally decimated squad of NVA in front of me. Robbie gave a pullback signal, and I helped Doc carry the M-60 and extra ammo back up the ridge north of the aircraft, where we set up a small perimeter defense in a clump of tall elephant grass.

No better way to die

As we lay there, unable to even see three feet in front of us, we could hear enemy troops coming up the other side of the ridge and firing into the trees above our heads. One of our crew started shaking violently. Afraid he might start firing and give our position away, I quickly crawled down to him, grabbed him hard by the shoulder and whispered, "Just remember, this is a great day to die for your country." He nodded in agreement and immediately settled down. I have pondered that moment in similar circumstances many times since and wondered what the Hell prompted me to make such a statement! There is no good way to die! And if you're fighting for your life, that is exactly what you're fighting for; your life, not your country. A few minutes later Robbie crawled over and told me the Rangers were in-bound follow him north. As we were pulling out, we heard Vietnamese screaming back and forth at each other and then heavy firing to our front. Graves told me later they were telling us that they were not armed, just as he and the Viet lieutenant opened fire on them. The Viet lieutenant later told me they were saying, "Don't shoot! We are out of ammo!" I have often wondered if we could have taken them prisoner. We kept moving and started sliding down the hill to the east, away from the NVA. I could see Smithy having a problem carrying the other M-60, so I took it and gave him my carbine. We fought our way through the undergrowth for what seemed like three or four hours until Graves made contact with the Viet Rangers. The Rangers set up a blocking force, and we passed through to a small LZ in a stream at the bottom of the mountain. A Marine CH-46 came in, and I started helping everyone aboard. I stood there in a daze from exhaustion and an adrenaline let down. I watched the ramp of the CH-46 close, and it started to take off with some small saplings caught in the ramp. I realized I was NOT aboard when the aircraft settled back, the ramp opened, and Robbie reached out, grabbing me by the back of the harness and dragging me into the aircraft like a sack of potatoes. We took off, receiving a couple of hits as the gunners on the Marine CH-46 were firing in all directions. One of them even pulled out his .45 caliber pistol and fired out the window. I often wondered if he knew the Rangers were right below us. As we landed at Dong Ha for refueling and inspection of the hits, I saw that I was almost naked from the waist down. Those cheap tiger fatigues had been completely torn off in the brush. I have worn skivvies and two pair of "issue" pants on every operation ever since! Slicks from the 281st picked us up and took us back to Phu Bai. Major Smith met me as we landed, put his arm around me, welcomed me home, and escorted us to the TOC, Tactical Operation Center, for debriefing. After a short debrief, Bruiser ordered us all to Marble Mountain for more debriefing and rest. The medics dug the thorns out of our rear ends and taped up Doc's and Smithy's ribs. I guess if we had brought back documents, Robbie would have been awarded the Silver Star instead of the Bronze Star with Valor. I received an Army Commendation Medal with Valor. I think the crew members each received an Air Medal with Valor, but I am not sure. I am sure that they all deserved a medal.

CH-46 Marine helicopter

Captain Robert J. "Mo" Moberg,
Aircraft Commander
Bandit Platoon Leader 1967

On 9 September 1967, Major John W. "Jack" Mayhew assumed command of the company.

Major Mayhew and Captain Moberg

FLYING WITH THE BEAR

I was a Senior Aviator with a lot of experience flying fixed-wing and rotary-wing single and multi-engine aircraft, I had spent three years in South East Asia flying a Caribou into landing strips that were too small for a Caribou and taking off overloaded while receiving enemy fire. I had a considerable number of hours in an UH-1D and was a seasoned army aviator. At least I thought I was until I met the Intruders of the 281st. I had only been in the unit for a few weeks when we headed to An Hoa and Happy Valley for my first Delta operation. My old friend Captain Bob Moberg had warned me that this would be different, but I had to see it for myself. I watched the operation for a few days from the command and control helicopter and decided that it was time to join the troops in an insertion. Captain Moberg had told me that Warrant Officer Petrevich was a seasoned Bandit and was calm under pressure. His friends called him "Bear." I decided that if anyone could put up with me, it would be him. Consequently, I joined his crew as his Peter Pilot (Copilot) and went on the ride of my life with the "Bear" and his crew. It was almost dark as we made the approach into what looked like the smallest landing hole that I had ever seen in the jungle. I did not think an OH-13 would fit in that opening. Maybe a jeep could if dropped straight down. I followed the Bear's instructions: hands lightly on the controls and feet on the pedals, just in case something happened, while keeping my eyes on the instruments and calling out the torque readings. He quickly maneuvered the aircraft into the small opening and gently hovered it down through the dense jungle. The main rotor blades were clipping leaves from the trees on both sides. With the help of an excellent crew chief and door gunner, he made a perfect landing, placing the tail rotor between two trees with only inches to spare on each side. I sat there in awe watching the coordinated moves between him and his crew. Working together they had backed the helicopter into the hole, and I was a bit concerned that this was going to be my home for a while.

Once we were close to the ground, the Recon team quickly exited the aircraft, and we were on our way out. It was then that the Bear let me perform my only function when he told me to call "Bingo" to signal that the insertion was a success and that we were climbing out. The insertion had only taken minutes, but it had seemed like hours to me.

On the way back, I kept looking at the Bear and his crew with admiration; this team was as professional as they came. I asked over the intercom so both the crew chief and door gunner could hear me, "Do you guys do this for a living?"

Throughout the rest of the flight, everyone was silent. Suddenly I heard over the company net a voice that became a trademark to signal the end of a successful mission. It was the voice of an Intruder who has only recently been identified. He keyed the mike and broke the silence with the Road Runner's trade mark sound: "Beep Beep." I knew then that I was among young men who were true professionals before their time, and I knew that I was in for the time of my life with them. And I was!

1962 Captain Jack Mayhew transporting South Vietnam President Diem and his aids in Caribou, tail number 080, VNAF A1-E's escorted the flight

Major John (Jack) Mayhew,
Company Commander
Intruder 06

SIE

On one of Delta's missions was to evacuate villages which were occupied by the jungle natives living close to the Ho Chi Minh Trail, used by the NVA to transport equipment and supplies to South Vietnam. This required us to transport teams of American SF and South Vietnam Rangers into the village at daybreak. They surrounded the village, rounded up everyone and disarmed anyone who might have a weapon. The occupants were then loaded on our helicopters and flown to a staging point where they were transferred to air force C-130s for transport to a location in the southern part of South Vietnam. On one of these operations, as we were leaving the pickup point after the 130s had left, we noticed that there was a small boy still there. Bob Moberg picked him up and brought him with us to Nha Trang, which was our home base. When we were in Nha Trang several of us lived in a large villa, and Bob as our company executive officer, was our villa manager. Bob took Sie under his wing, and he lived with us. We all taught him English, which was not necessarily a good thing. He was a bright young man and we asked the good sisters at the local orphanage school to let him go to their school, which was close by. Because we supported them, they agreed. One afternoon the head sister of the school came by to tell us Sie was very bright and doing well. However, she suggested that we refrain from teaching him additional English as his vocabulary was already a bit too colorful for the school.

A few years ago, a chap who returned to Vietnam tried to find the school and could not do so. The school was part of a Catholic orphanage that we supported. (We have additional stories about that.) The Nuns were both French and Vietnamese. Bob left Vietnam in 1968 and asked a friend to watch over Sie until he could get back to get him. Bob went back several times but was never able to locate him, and his friend had died. About five years ago we launched a drive to find Sie, and the most we could find was that he had returned to his village near Bong Son. We had a person visit the village, but, unfortunately, no one would come forth with any information.

FOB KONTUM

Beginning 14 December 1967 and continuing through 16 December, we were focused on the forward operating base of Kontum in the Polei Kleng operation. From the Project Delta Advance Base located at the small Polei Kleng air strip, west of Kontum, the 281st Assault Helicopter Company inserted an Army of the Republic of Vietnam (ARVN) Special Forces Ranger company and a recon team with the mission of conducting a recon of a B-52 bomb strike that had taken place the night before. The target of the bomb strike was North Vietnam troops, who were reported to be moving through and/ or operating in the area. The ARVN Special Forces Company was under the command of an ARVN Ranger Captain with First Lieutenant Charlie Ford, United States Army Special Forces, serving as the senior officer and advisor to the ARVN Rangers. As we were preparing to depart the base camp, Lieutenant Ford came to me and reminded me that his date of return from overseas assignment (DEROS) was only a few days off, and he would appreciate our bringing him back. We shook hands, and I promised him that we would bring him back in time for him to catch the "bird" to Cam Ranh Bay. The insertion and first day's activities went as planned without incident. At first light on the second day of the operation, the Wolf Pack, the Bandit rescue helicopters and the Command and Control (C&C) helicopter flew directly to the area of operation (AO) from Kontum. The remainder of the flight went to the forward base at Polei Kleng. Major Charles "Chuck" Allen, AKA "Bruiser," the Project Delta Commander, and a communications sergeant were on board the C&C helicopter. The Delta forward air controller (FAC), an Air Force captain, was flying an L-19 single-engine airplane called the Bird Dog over the ranger unit on the ground. The Wolf Pack gun platoon was under the command of Captain Fred Mentzer. The Bandit Platoon slicks were under the command of Captain John Wehr. Arriving in the area we quickly saw that during the night North Vietnamese soldiers had moved into the area by way of a small river that ran adjacent to the area of operations where we had inserted the rangers. The NVA were either brazen or very confident of success, for they had left their fleet of small rafts beached on the bank of the river. The Wolf Pack set up a flight pattern around the site, and contact was made with Lieutenant Ford on the ground. At this point the ground forces were in light contact with the North Vietnamese Army troops. However, within a short time the situation escalated to the point that there was heavy, close contact, and several individuals were either killed or wounded in action. An attempt was made to extract the wounded, but ground contact was so close that each recovery ship sent in took heavy fire and was unable to stay over the site long enough to allow the ground troops to load the individuals onto the jungle penetrators that were lowered from the aircraft.

The forward air controller immediately requested air support. We set up holding patterns, while Captain Wehr set up a resupply schedule and initiated a refueling rotation plan for his flight platoon. At the time it appeared that the troops on the ground would require resupply and we would be needed for a long time. I considered that we should have brought our lunch.

The heavy ground contact continued as the forward air controller brought in flight after flight of fighter aircraft, and the Wolf Pack magnificently carried the fight to the North Vietnamese Army. At one point the Wolf Pack gunships were working one side of a line of contact, while the fighters were bombing and strafing in the other direction, all within extremely close proximity to each other. Early in the morning the forward air controller left as a result of engine trouble, and tactical close air coordination was transferred to us in the C&C helicopter. We stacked as many fighters and bombers as we could beg, borrow or steal over the area, and continued the pressure from the air while the Rangers pressed the North Vietnamese on the ground.

In midmorning, we responded to an urgent request for ammunition and called for the first resupply ship, which was loaded and waiting at the base camp. The resupply ship, flown by First Lieutenant David Alan Villaume and his crew, quickly arrived on site and were vectored over the resupply point. There was no hesitation on the part of the resupply crew even though they knew, and we knew there was little chance of their getting in and out of the site. As we expected, the resupply helicopter hovered over the site for only a few minutes before all hell broke loose, and the aircraft started to take heavy fire. However, Lieutenant Villaume physically held the ship in position to give the Special Forces crew time to off load the ammunition. As the ammunition hit the ground, Lieutenant Villaume was rapidly losing control of the helicopter and had to be vectored to a small open spot where he set it down. The helicopter was all shot up. Within seconds the rescue ship, flown by Warrant Officer Don Torrini, moved over the downed ship and started taking the crew on board. Like the resupply ship, the rescue ship was under intense heavy fire coming from the North Vietnamese Army, who had a clear view of both aircraft. During the rescue operation all the individuals operating the aircraft showed their true mettle by insuring everyone got on board. In one case, a severely wounded crew chief was literately pushing individuals up the rope ladder into the rescue ship. Within thirty minutes Don Torrini and his crew had transported the wounded and injured crew members to the evacuation hospital.

Within a short time after the resupply mission, we attempted to recover some of the seriously wounded rangers from the Army of the Republic of Vietnam from a small opening near the line of contact. The helicopter flying the rescue came under heavy fire, and while maneuvering to the pickup site, it was shot down. There were no injuries.

Shortly after noon Bruiser elected to commit the rest of the ranger battalion, and

Captain John Wehr's Bandits went about inserting them into the area of operation. The lift went without incident, and we spent the rest of the afternoon controlling the tactical air, which ranged from United States Air Forces jets to Marine prop aircraft. They provided close support to Wolf Pack. The operation continued throughout the day and into the night. At the end of the day, we had lost three UH-1Ds, which were destroyed with dispatch by the mighty Wolf Pack.

By early the next day, the North Vietnamese had broken off contact and fled the area. We then evacuated the wounded and killed in action, followed by an evacuation of the ARVN Rangers. The last individual recovered was Lieutenant Ford, who was transported to Nha Trang before he left for the United States. His tour of duty had ended while he was on the ground. I had kept my promise.

****

This mission took place while the remainder of the Bandit Platoon stood watch over the Delta Recon teams that were operating in other areas of the sector. The 281st crew members assigned to support a recon team took great pride in their jobs and maintained a constant watch over the progress of their teams when they were on the ground. The crews maintained a constant state of readiness and were prepared to instantly respond to the needs of their assigned recon team.

This operation clearly highlighted the strong points of the 281st. First and foremost was the unselfish sacrifices made by the young crew members of the 281st, who on a daily basis, and without a second thought, provided a level of support to the US and ARVN SF ground troops that is unmatched in history. Of equal importance is the fact that on a daily basis these young men laid their lives on the line for their fellow crew members. Lieutenant Villaume and his crew had only one thought when they headed for the resupply site: The troops on the ground needed ammo, and he and his crew were going to deliver it. There was only one thought in Warrant Officer Don Torrini's mind when he and his crew rescued the downed crew: A 281st crew was on the ground, and it was their job to get them out. Truly, the 281st lived by the creed of leaving no man behind.

The 281st was a totally self-supporting unit. It trained its own inexperienced pilots to provide complex aviation support that included insertions and extractions from craters created by bomb drops in dense jungle environments and small openings in the jungle that always appeared to be smaller than the helicopter. The type of combat aviation support provided by the 281st normally would have only been provided by highly-trained pilots in special aviation units. In Vietnam the average age of the Intruder pilots was 20, and the crew members averaged 19. The experience level of these crews consisted of flight school and on-the-job training. These crews, in addition to the complex and dangerous recon missions of the 281st, provided resupply to the ground troops on a daily basis, evacuated the wounded and killed in action and recovered its own downed crew members. (I personally never saw a medical evacuation chopper in the 281st area of operation.) The 281st provided and directed its own fire support and often served as the forward air controller, directing the activities of the fighter/bomber aircraft that were called in to support Delta Operations. However, most of Delta's fire support came from Captain Fred Mentzer's Wolf Pack and his gunship pilots like Warrant Officers Lance Ham and Joe Anderson, Wolf Pack 33, who on the day of the mission were flying the Hog Frog "Snoopy," tail number 449, along with Crew Chief Dan DiGenova and Gunner Don Creed. Joe, Dan and Don were shot down in the A Shau Valley in the same aircraft in March of 1968 and were recovered by the 281st. Ken Donald, John Stevens, Monty Montgomery, and Joe Bilitzke were counted on to protect the 281st slicks and to provide deadly accurate fire in support of the Special Forces troops on the ground. There were several very real parallels that existed between the Wolf Pack crews and the fighter pilots of other wars. In fact, I often thought that many of them may well have been reincarnated members of Pappy Boyington's Black Sheep Squadron. Sergeant David Bitle, the Wolf Pack platoon sergeant, along with his crew chiefs and support personnel, did a job that was above and beyond call, in keeping the gunships operating and rearmed, patching the holes and painting the daily kill tally on the side of each aircraft. The door gunners that flew the Wolf Pack ships had more exposure to enemy fire than any other individuals in the war. Although these pilots and crew members were constantly in the line of fire, I personally never heard a word of discontent from one of them, and each and every one was held in the highest esteem by all. A large percentage of the door gunners for both the Wolf Pack and the Bandit platoon were individuals who had been wounded in ground combat units and had extended to stay in country as aircraft door gunners. At the end of the war, there were 100 individuals missing in action from the 1st Aviation Brigade, and 10% of them were from the 281st AHC. Of the 60+ aviation companies that were assigned to the Brigade, the average number killed in action during the war was 28. The 281st lost 52 or 65% more than its sister companies. At the end of each day, we could count on replacement aircraft arriving before the day was over, and thanks to the magnificent, round-the-clock work of the members of the unit maintenance section and the attached 483rd Maintenance Detachment, commanded by Major Don Ruskoff and Master Sergeant Robert "Bob" Ohmes, we were never short on aircraft. The 281st had the best land and air communications available, provided by its own signal attachment. To round out the 281st, its spiritual souls were brought up to speed on a regular basis by the rotund traveling priest of the 10th Aviation Brigade.

The 281st performed all of this and was constantly on the move. Most assault helicopter companies provided support from a fixed base and returned to that facility each evening. In contrast, most of the members of the 281st spent the majority of their tours in a "UH-1" or in a tent surrounded by sand bags and trenches.

The memories of the Kontum/ Polei Kleng operation are etched in my mind forever. They not only reflect the greatness of the unit, but they clearly showcase the magnificence of the individuals who served in the unit. I know, without a doubt, that each and every person who served in the 281st AHC is a true American Hero.

Major John (Jack) Mayhew,
Company Commander
Intruder 06

MR. BELL, WE SALUTE YOU!

At this point, it is a good idea to provide the readers not familiar with aviation and the military with a few pages of terms and photos. This will provide a better understanding of the jargon that we used to refer to the events and items in our typical day.

The UH-1C was specifically developed as a gunship. The "C", or Charlie model, was designed with more power to carry the added weapons of a gunship. The core of the main rotor blades was increased from 21 inches to 27 inches. It was configured with the 540 rotor system. The armament, as stated earlier was limited only to the imagination of the crew chiefs and they all had vivid imaginations. At their disposal was 2.75 inch folding fin rockets often fitted with 17 pound warheads, flex-mini guns, M-60 7.62 mm machine guns operated by the crew chief and door gunner, the nose mounted 79mm grenade launcher and whatever they could conjure in their minds.

The test for the correct amount of ammo was simple. The pilot would try to bring the aircraft up to a hover and if he succeeded, more was added until the only way the pilot could take off was with a running takeoff.

Wolf Pack UH-1C Hog Frog with rocket pods waiting for Grumpy to board

LOBO

By late 1968, the Wolf Pack had grown into a force to be reckoned with. Not satisfied with the "status quo" they constantly added airborne weapons to their already lethal arsenal. Later that year they reached the top of the pinnacle with the creation of Lobo, "The Wolf." An unknown unit had left a D model Huey in the company area and failed to return for it. The Wolf Pack, living up to their motto, took it into their den and proceeded to convert it to the most heavily armed helicopter in Vietnam. Based on its special operations mission, the 281st had the authority to improve their weapons system as needed to accomplish their mission. To obtain the needed weapons for Lobo, Paul Maledy collected trading materials consisting of weapons, knives, flags, and other items obtained from the Special Forces units and headed south. When Paul returned with his stash of weapons, Dave Bitle and his Wolf Pack buddies went about installing hand cranked 40 mm grenade launchers in the door gunner den and the crew chief station, as well as a 50 caliber machine gun in the cargo compartment. External weapons were flexible mini guns.

Lobo was deployed in support of Delta and other combat support missions and operated successfully for several months until it was discovered that there were large cracks in the airframe caused by vibrations from the new weapons. It was supposed to go to the salvage yard, but Wolf Pack made the decision to honor Lobo's service by giving it a burial at sea. Under Gary Stagman's directions, it was rigged appropriately for sling transport. With the help of a Chinook it went for its last ride. Before reaching the salvage yard, the rigging failed, as planned, and it dropped into the South China Sea. RIP, Lobo.

Thus ends the life of Lobo whose story reflects the motivation, creativity, drive, and skill of the Intruders of the 281st.

Warrant Officer Stephens and Specialist Stanley, LOBO Crew.

Specialist Goldrich and Sergeant Bitle, LOBO Crew.

"LOBO"

*...twin 60's on each side...50 Cal
and hand crank 40 mm on each side...the
recoil of the 50 cracked the fuselage of the aircraft*

A belt of 40 mm ammo and the hand crank gun

Rocket pod with the flex-mini gun

96

The US Army wanted another version of the Huey that could carry a crew of four, two pilots a crew chief and a door gunner, and also deliver an infantry section of eight to ten soldiers. Bell's solution was to stretch the UH-1B fuselage by 41 inches and use the extra space to fit two sideways-facing seats on either side of the transmission. This brought the total seating capacity to fifteen, including crew seats.

This next model was designated UH-1D by the US Army. The enlarged cabin could also accommodate six stretchers, twice that of the earlier models, making the UH-1D easier to use as a Medevac aircraft, which in combat was referred to as "Dust Off". With further refinement, The UH-1D H was born with a more powerful engine. The "D" had the L-11's while the "H" had the L-13's. The difference was phenomenal and totally changed the capabilities of the slick platoons. The average cost of a new Huey in the 1960's was about $275,000. About 7,000 were deployed to Vietnam and about 3,300 were lost or destroyed. In total, 1,074 Huey pilots were killed, along with 1,103 other crew members. One of every eighteen crew members who served in Vietnam was killed in action.

A UH-1H on Delta stand by at LZ Whip on the Laotian border

WHERE ARE WE GOING, AND WHERE HAVE WE BEEN?

Even though there were no safe places in Vietnam, some flights could have been considered routine. However, most of our missions with the 5th Special Forces Delta teams were highly classified; even the crew knew nothing about the missions. It was frustrating for the men to not know where they were going and where they had been. This flight related by our crew chief Ken Hamilton gives you an idea of what was going on in the late 1960s.

In December of 1967, I was a new crew chief in the Rat Pack. I had just arrived with a bunch of guys from the 61st Assault Helicopter Company. I was assigned crew chief of helicopter tail number 723, one of the original D models that came over with the 281st Assault Helicopter Company from Fort Benning. It was long past its prime. I never knew there were so many shades of OD (olive drab). The tail boom was a different color than the fuselage, and not one of the six doors matched. My gunner was Dennis Mannone, an experienced door gunner who was good at his job and knew a lot more about the 281st and how it worked than I did.

On one of my first missions, Rat Pack was flying Delta teams out of Plei Djerang, where an old A team camp was just south of the tri-borders of Vietnam, Cambodia and Laos. From the runway you could almost throw a rock into Cambodia. Sergeant Beasley showed up late one afternoon and told me and Dennis to remove our dog tags and IDs. We were in the field wearing camouflage clothing called tiger stripes. A little while later three men in civilian clothes showed up with their gear in suit cases.

We took off heading northwest. As we flew over the Perfume River, I thought, "I'm an American soldier wearing a South Vietnamese uniform flying into Cambodia on a helicopter that's on its last legs." The Cambodia thing wasn't a problem for long because we kept heading northwest into the setting sun, and soon we were in Laos.

We flew for quite a while and finally landed on a mountain top with a helicopter landing pad that wasn't much wider than the skids. The place was covered with little hootches that had radio antennas sticking out of them. Our passengers waved goodbye, and we headed back to Plei Djerang. Arriving home well after dark, the fuel level was down to the twenty-minute warning area. The whole flight was really quite uneventful. I asked the pilots where we had been. They said, "Leghorn." For once I knew where we had been, but not exactly where it was. It took forty years and a lot of maps, but I finally figured out where we had gone. I found Leghorn, a SOG (Special Operation Group) radio relay/NSA radio-listening site in southern Laos. It was about half way between Vietnam and Thailand, just off route 96, a major artery of the Ho Chi Minh Trail. Now I can honestly say that I have been to Leghorn.

Ken Hamilton
Crew Chief
December 67 to October 68

On 21 December 1967, Specialist Four Les Howard Paschall died in a helicopter accident.

COST OF LIVING AND BASE PAY 1967–1968

In 1967 in America the average income was $7,850, the minimum wage per hour was $1.40. A new house cost $14,250. The average monthly rent was $125.00 if you could find a place to rent close to an army base. A new car cost about $2,750, and gasoline was 33 cents per gallon.

We were among the highest paid military at that time. Yet, it was hard for the common soldier to make ends meet. There were some soldiers who only lived from payday to payday; others found a way to save something from each pay check. The Army encouraged everyone to take part in the U.S. Saving Bond program. Most of us thought we were doing okay.

The monthly base pay of a private first class was $128.70, and if he were married, it was sixty dollars more with the added dependent; increases depended on the number of dependents. A South Vietnamese soldier with the same rank made $40.00 per month. By the end of 1971, the South Vietnamese soldier's pay had dropped to $19.00 per month. Compared to the costs of living 45 years later, these pays offered in mid '60's were meager. We had "room and board" but the most important benefit for the men of the 281st was the friends and brother they served with.

****

On rare occasions, when not flying "Delta" the slicks were used to fly ash and trash missions for other units. On one trip a small fishing village was visited to check on the advancement of the VC. Just how far was the war spreading, and were there indigenous people needing assistance? It was a quaint village, far removed from the war…simple people living a peaceful life. The images of these people brought home the reason why we were fighting in a foreign country.

1968

CHINESE NUNGS

Special Forces needed their own dedicated reaction forces, but where would they get them? There weren't enough Green Berets available to fully staff the fighting camps, much less provide the manpower necessary for an effective reaction force. Indigenous troops led by a Special Forces cadre were an obvious answer, but where would they get reliable, hardy troops who would actually fight? No one was impressed with the soldierly qualities of the South Vietnamese. The big question was how the Viet Cong could fight so well and their adversaries so poorly.

By 1965 Special Forces troops had been in Vietnam for nearly five years and had formed some pretty good ideas about who was dependable. One group that often came to mind was the Nungs. The Nungs were ethnic Chinese who had, at various times, fled that country and settled in and around Cholon, a suburb of Saigon. Recruited by Special Forces advisors, paid far more than their ARVN counterparts, and properly led, they had established a reputation as dependable, fierce fighters who could more than hold their own against the Viet Cong.

Many of them were already in service as camp guard forces, forming some of the Civilian Irregular Defense Group (CIDG) companies in various "A" camps, or acting as bodyguards for important people. More could be recruited and trained. The nucleus was a company of Nung CIDG troops who had survived a fierce battle at Special Forces Camp Ben Cat, located adjacent to War Zones C and D, at the edge of the infamous "Iron Triangle." Led by Captain (later Brigadier General) Joseph Stringham, the Nungs were given less than two weeks to recruit new troops, issue equipment, train, and be ready to fight. Fight they did, in places like Bu Gia Map, Bu Dop, and Loc Ninh. Their reputation served as a deterrent, and just the presence of a camp was often enough to convince the VC to shift their attention elsewhere. When it didn't, the fighting spirit and leadership of the Mike Forces were enough to bloody the noses of units far larger than they were, even though they were not only outnumbered but outgunned as well. The Mike Force was armed with American weapons left over from past wars. In the early days of Special Forces involvement, when the CIDG program was still under the authority of the CIA's Combined Study Division, a bewildering plethora of German, Danish, Swedish, French, English, and even obsolete Soviet weapons had been purchased from arms dealers all over the world. However, in spite of the advantage of having all these weapons, the VC was usually defeated by the Nungs. We were glad to have them on our side.

A captured document by the 101st Airborne Division stated that the NVA were planning a nationwide attack to be launched 31 January 68 during Tet. No one took the document seriously.

TET 1968

Guard bunker at 281st Villa

North Vietnam had asked for a truce, and the U.S. Commanders, along with the South Vietnamese Army and government agreed with the proposition. That was a good thing for us. Our men needed a rest, and our equipment needed attention. Buddha's birthday was coming up, and the tradition was a country-wide celebration with good food, family and fun. The event was to start at the end of January. The truce was in place and agreed upon by both sides, but the communist government and their generals had a few tricks up their sleeves. The communist north had secretly been planning the TET offensive for the better part of a year. At the end of January 1968 every soldier in South Vietnam was awakened by fierce gunfire, and the battle of Tet was on. Our cooks, company clerks, supply personnel and many others immediately became infantrymen, each one manning a rifle or a machine gun. All of us sensed we were in mortal danger.

Tet arrived at midnight. The villa that several of the unit's officers and warrant officers were living in was surrounded by several ARVN compounds, and at midnight the soldiers celebrated for an hour or so by firing their weapons in the air, while our civilian neighbors celebrated with fire crackers and rockets. At about 1 a.m. the celebrations stopped, and it became quiet. Around 2 a.m. Sie, a young boy we had unofficially "adopted," kicked open the bedroom doors shouting, "Get up, get up, the **+=#@*VC are coming!" Needless to say, that got everyone's attention.

A battalion-sized North Vietnamese Army unit (approximately 300 soldiers) had entered the south side of Nha Trang and marched north in formation on the beach road which led into the city of Nha Trang. In preparation for their entry, they had placed operatives in the city that had built tunnels and occupied other points of interest. The U. S. and Korean field forces were located along the beach road, as were the villas occupied by the 17th Aviation Group and the 281st AHC. As the NVA unit headed toward the city, they passed the first of these buildings and were not challenged by the guards. By the time they reached the 281st area, they had started to branch out into the side streets, where they were challenged by the local ARVN units. The Nung guards assigned to the villa by Project Delta were firing down the side street and, with the help of the Intruders living there, were able to keep them out of the area.

The battle went on most of the night and into the next day, with the Wolf Pack playing a major role. Wolf Pack provided support fire for the Ranger Battalion and took on missions to remove NVA individuals from key facilities, like the city water tower. Recent information suggests Captain Fred Mentzer, Wolf Pack 36, was responsible for the rounds that hit the city ESSO service station and blew it up in a ball of fire. Major Tu and his 91st Ranger Battalion met The NVA unit head on, and when the main battle ended the next day, each member of the NVA unit was dead and accounted for. The Ranger Battalion suffered three killed in action and, sadly, our friend Major Tu was one of them.

Nha Trang Esso Service Station (POL) before the Wolf Pack blew it up during the Tet uprising

On 31 January 1968, there were more American deaths than on any other single day of the war: 245.

"In aviation there are old pilots and bold pilots, but very few old, bold pilots."

On 8 February 1968, Donald "Don" Ruskauff assumed command of the company.

5 + 40 = 39

As a 23 year-old I was considered an older pilot, not old but older than a number of the other warrant officer pilots. We were at Camp Enari, a small operation base not far from Pleiku. I was an aircraft commander assigned to the third platoon. My radio call sign was "Wolf Pack 39" (pronounced three nine). There is never a good day to die, especially in Vietnam, especially on your birthday. February the 19th was my birthday, so I requested that day off. I did not want to chance it. We were helping the 4th Infantry Division, and they kept us very busy. My platoon leader granted my request, so to celebrate the day I turned 24, I slept in. My crew had the day off also.

The Tet Offensive of 68 was supposedly over, but we were still going through some tough times. We had been flying every day. On our first day off in a long time, my crew and I got some much needed rest. I spent some time enjoying a few cups of morning coffee and later had a birthday drink of warm beer. Around noon I was informed that I was to report to flight operations immediately. As I got up I asked, "On my day off?" There was no response.

A five-man recon team was in trouble and needed immediate extraction; they were about to be surrounded by a large enemy force. My crew was already on its way. While I was being briefed, my crew was loading rockets and ammunition and pre-flighting the aircraft. We had as much fire power as could be loaded on the UH-1C gunship. I made a run to the flight line, climbed in and buckled up as my copilot Ken Donald started the engine. We were so loaded that the Huey could just barely hover.

We were ready to go; all the gauges were in the green. We hovered out to the runway. I turned into the wind and nosed her over as Ken called out the power settings. We bounced once, twice, and we were flying. Other helicopters that had been on site were returning for more fuel and ammunition. We were needed at the area of operation as soon as we could get there.

The location and map coordinates had been given to me at the briefing. I was flying, and Ken was watching the instruments while following our flight path on the map. I had a good crew. We all had been on similar missions and had been battle tested. I established radio contact with the team on the ground and asked for a situation report. The reply was there were four wounded, and they were about out of ammo. As I got closer, they popped smoke.

This was really Indian country; the jungle was triple canopied, so obviously there was no place to land a helicopter. It was going to be a ladder or McGuire rig extraction. We went to work at keeping the enemy at bay. The recon team on the ground was moving to a place where they could be extracted. We were bringing hell from above on the NVA as the slicks returned after refueling. Everything was in place for the extraction. The first ship got two men out with the McGuire rig, but there were still three to go. It seemed like forever before the other three were in the lift ships, but finally all five were on their way back to safety. We had remained on location even after our mini guns jammed; our door gunners were doing a great job with their M-60 machine guns. We did our job; it was just another day in the war. The best thing for me was the bullet with my name on it did not come my way. The five-man team was recovered, and that was a great birthday present for me.

****

A few years ago at the 281st reunion held in St. Louis, Missouri, I was approached by a gentleman who introduced himself as Bob Stein. He informed me he was writing a book about a recon team. He planned to call it "Ghost Warriors." This fellow had been a school mate of Ed Haas, a fellow pilot with the 281st. As we got into the conversation, he looked at his notes and mentioned the date of February 19, 1968. Well, now he had my undivided attention. How could I ever forget that date and that mission?

I was then introduced to some of the members of the recon team that were rescued that day. We had a great time talking, and I will never forget how they looked me in the eye, shook my hand and thanked me. All five of the men had been single when they were rescued. During the passing 40 years, these five soldiers had married, had children, and now there were grandchildren. All together there were 39 family members. Each former soldier said that, without a doubt, if we had not shown up just when we did, they would have all been killed. There would have been no wife, no kids, no grand kids; only five gravestones.

The five men were Oscar Carsoway, Delbert Ayers, Lou Hansen, John Wishart and Robert P. Johnson.

So, 5 men plus 40 years equals 39 people.

Colonel Jim Fisher
U.S. Army, Retired

A SHAU VALLEY

The A Shau Valley and Khe Sanh were like magnets for Delta. Khe Sanh is best known for the NVA siege during the Tet offensive. With all the places to go in Vietnam, why here? This was Indian country, where the Ho Chi Minh trail crossed the border from Laos into South Vietnam. It was about as far northwest as you could get in the country and still be in it. Most of the guys in the 281st did not comprehend the seriousness of these missions. All they knew was Delta was going there and we had to go with them. It was beyond comprehension how these guys had the courage to go into the jungle there. Probably the best comparison would be stirring up a large bed of fire ants! Imagine the bravery of these men going into that environment to gather intelligence and get out of the area without being detected. Frequently, they were not successful and called for the "Cavalry."

A day in the A Shau

In early March 1968 Project Delta was running operation Samurai in the A Shau Valley. I inserted a team to recon a certain area. It didn't take them long to find out there was a bee hive of activity there; thousands of NVA…trucks, tanks, roads, bunkers, supplies, commo wires, antenna and more. The team was extracted and a plan was conceived to run an operation with rangers to clear the area of the enemy. A couple of weeks later the assault began with the insertion of rangers. They barely got off the aircraft when they were in contact with the enemy. The battle ensued with the wounded piling up. The 281st worked to extract the KIA and wounded for the next two days. March 16th was to be my day off because my aircraft was badly damaged. I was nine days short for my R&R to Australia. Because of the shortage of aircraft, maintenance patched up my ship and I flew the mission that day. Three aircraft went into an LZ barely made for two, and things got very crowded. I lifted out of the LZ to make room for the other aircraft and climbed above the trees. I was in a steep left bank when the ship took fire from a .50 cal. gun emplacement that was supposed to have been taken out the day before. Two armored piercing rounds hit the aircraft; one breaking the ammo link on the door gunner's gun on the right side of the aircraft, and the other through two armored plates on my seat hitting me in the left leg just above the knee shattering the bone in my leg and severing the sciatic nerve. The round continued on to the right leg causing a lateral break in that leg and lodging against the bone. The impact of the round caused me to lurch out of my seat hitting my head against the greenhouse and letting go of the cyclic. The cyclic went full forward and the aircraft went into a dive. I was able to grab the cyclic and pull it back leveling the aircraft. However, without the use of my legs, I had no control of the pedals and told the co-pilot I had been hit and to take over. As I reached for the first aid kit above my head I passed out and the remaining story was related to me by the crew.

The co-pilot, Lieutenant Lyle Beltch, got the aircraft down into a small area with trees, losing part of the blades as it went down. Jim Rogers, the crew chief, jumped to my aid trying to open the door to pull me out. Realizing it was impossible to extract me through the door he jumped into the cargo area and pulled the release pins on the back of my seat allowing the seat to fall back. He pulled me out and immediately went to work on my legs. Using my belt for a tourniquet, he tied off my left leg and with his own belt tied off the right leg, splinting it to keep it from flopping around.

While all this action was going on, Warrant Officer Don Torrini, flying the recovery ship, landed as close as he could at the bottom of a hill near my downed aircraft. The crew dragged me down the hill as I fell in and out of consciousness. A group of Vietnamese rangers was right behind us. When they got close to the aircraft, they scrambled on board leaving no room for me. With not so gentle persuasion from the Delta guys, some of the rangers got off making room for me. With the aircraft fully loaded, there was no room left for the crew. Left behind, they had to E&E (escape and evade) the enemy for about 45 minutes until Don could return. On the aircraft, I was thought to be near death and Doc Simpson from Delta pumped two cans of albumin into me because of the loss of blood. Don radioed ahead to the marine hospital letting them know he was inbound with a badly wounded pilot. At the helipad, they unloaded me on to a stretcher and Don took off to refuel and go back for the rest of the crew.

The marines had a standing order only marines would be treated at the marine hospital and I was left on the helipad while the Army hospital was called to send an ambulance. After what seemed an eternity, the ambulance arrived and got me to the hospital for treatment and eventual medevac to Japan and home. The story of my being abandoned on the helipad at the marine hospital made its way to the commanding general of I Corp who took action to assure nothing like this would ever happen again.

Back at the crash site, FAC remained on station to keep track of the crew and guide Don in to them. The aircraft was being stripped by the bad guys; weapons, radios and whatever they could get their hands on. Whenever an aircraft went down, protocol called for the crew to follow the Delta guys and do whatever they were told. The area was swarming with bad guys and a lopsided gun fight was not in the plan. Once again, the Delta guys were in a run for their lives but this time they had an aviation crew to look after. Lt. Beltch started telling the Delta guys exactly where the enemy was and where they were headed! He spoke and understood Vietnamese and understood everything the bad guys were doing! He was a spy on the ground and kept the good guys a step ahead of the bad guys. His knowledge and leadership enabled a successful extraction of all the guys.

Aaron Rich,
Rat Pack Aircraft Commander

First Lieutenant Lyle Beltch was awarded the Silver Star for valor, the Nation's third highest award, for his actions on the ground.

KHE SANH

Khe Sanh is best known for the NVA siege during the Tet offensive. The battle raged, lives were lost, later in 1968 the Marines began their withdrawal taking all salvageable supplies and destroying the rest. The only thing left was the barren airstrip. Now the Viet Cong flag is flying about Khe Sanh airstrip.

Op orders came down and more information was needed. Even further Northwest from Khe Sanh was the little hamlet of Mai Loc. We would be boxed into a corner. All the missions required McGuire rig (strings) extraction. No LZ's, just tiny holes in the jungle canopy to pull the guys up through. Sitting in strings at a high altitude and flying at 50-60 knots was very cold after sweating on the ground. The weight of their bodies would cause the narrow straps to dig into their legs and cut off circulation. They had to be transferred inside the aircraft as soon as possible.

Remember that abandoned airstrip with the VC flag on it? Yup, that became our transfer point. We would have to lower the guys down slowly. Remember, they are on the end of a 120 foot rope

Emergency Team Extraction
Jets Bomb First Smoke

As soon as their feet hit the ground, we dropped as fast as we could. The guys jumped in with the gathered strings and we were off in a matter of seconds. We dodged a lot of Indians during these missions. Damn, I hate fire ants!

Warrant Officer Brian Paine,
Aircraft Commander
Bandit 24

The abandoned airstrip at Khe Sanh

CHALLENGING AND REWARDING

My number came up and I reported to the draft board; not ready or willing, but report I did. Then off I went to basic training at Fort Dix, New Jersey. The army needed men as ground soldiers, combat arms, infantrymen, tankers and artillery. I was a draftee and suspected I would be assigned to the infantry after my basic training. I made up my mind to make the most out of this once-in-a-life time experience. I accepted the army's challenge, did my best and hoped for the best. The last week of training I was told to report to the orderly room, where I was told I had achieved high scores in every battery of tests that I had taken. As a result, the army was going to make me a 71P. "What is a 71P?" I asked. The company clerk looked it up and said, "Flight Operations Specialist". I wondered, "What is a Flight Operations Specialist?"

After basic I was sent to Fort Rucker, Alabama for a very extensive twelve-week course, which covered weather reporting, radio control procedures, air traffic control, weights and balances, air field operations, maintenance of flight records and much more. There was so much to learn, but it was all interesting. The whole class of about thirty trainees was told that most of the class would be sent to Vietnam after graduation, so I was mentally prepared when I got my orders to report to Travis Air Force Base in California.

It was a long flight to the war-torn country of Vietnam. Upon arrival, I was assigned to the 281st Assault Helicopter Company, stationed in Nha Trang, South Vietnam. This turned out to be the right place, the right assignment and the right job for me. From the very first day, I was busy, and as time went on, even more so. Flight operations was a very busy place, with people in and out all day long. There were pilot briefings, constant radio traffic, and incessant ringing phones. Most importantly, I shared the responsibility for maintaining as many as 275 flight records on a daily basis. I can honestly say I enjoyed my job, and later I was promoted ahead of my peers to specialist fourth class.

When I was sent to the forward operation base, my duties doubled. I had received on-the-job training as a door gunner, and a number of times I was called upon to fill in when needed. I was contributing to a team effort by helping to reload our gunships, refueling helicopters, performing guard duty at night, and at times guarding prisoners. My efforts were appreciated; we all worked together to accomplish the mission. What an honor it was to be serving my country as an Intruder and working with the Fifth Special Forces soldiers, the Green Berets! My tour of duty with the 281st Assault Helicopter Company was challenging and rewarding. If I had to do it all over again, I would not change a thing.

Specialist Four Alexander H. Trotter,
Flight Operations,
January 67 – July 69

BAMBOO THICKET

Bamboo Thicket along the Ho Chi Minh Trail

Mid-morning the 13th of March 68 our ship inserted a Delta recon team out in our area of operations. The ship was piloted by aircraft commander Don Torrini and Joe Bilitzke. Both were warrant officers. I was the crew chief, and Bill Henderson was my gunner. "Salem" was the team's call sign. We four Americans and two Vietnamese made up our team. The five-day mission was to watch some trails that crossed through the area.

By mid-afternoon all of that changed when we got a call from the forward air controller (FAC) working out in the AO that the recon team had made contact with a large force of the North Vietnamese Army (NVA) and needed immediate extraction. The crews scrambled to their ships. The extraction flight was made up of our ship, another hole ship, our two recovery ships and the command and control ship (C&C). A heavy fire team from Wolf Pack had left just before we did.

Upon reaching the area of operation, we were told by the FAC the team was in a bamboo thicket and surrounded by the enemy. There was some confusion about the point man not being with the team and maybe cut off from them. We could not confirm this with the team because the enemy was so close, talking would reveal the location. The decision was made to go in cold because we did not want to risk hitting the point man. The bamboo was so thick no signaling device would work to locate the exact position except a pen flare, but, again, using it would reveal the location. As soon as C&C released us, we dropped down and came to a hover over the bamboo thicket to look for the team. Spotting it through a small opening, Henderson dropped the ladder on his side down to the men. It was the old style rope ladder, light but hard to climb on. The ladder was just long enough to reach the men, and they would have to climb the entire length of it. The first man up was having a hard time climbing the ladder. What was keeping us from going any lower was a small tree at our 11 o'clock position. At this rate we knew we would be hovering for a while before the team got on board. Mr. Torrini asked me if the rotor blades could take chewing into the tree limbs, which would make a shorter climb for the rest of the team. I told him they would, and he brought it down slowly until we had taken about six feet or so out of the climb. We could go no lower because the tail rotor was almost in the bamboo. We were sitting in the bamboo like a bird in a nest. Hovering there, not being able to see through the foliage and not being able to lay down covering fire, made for some very tense moments. We knew the enemy was nearby, so we could be fired upon at any moment. But where would it come from? When the first team member got on board, we could see why he was having trouble. He had a bad wound across the palm of his hand. The second man up was one of the Vietnamese. He did not have too much trouble. The next man was the other Vietnamese. He was having trouble climbing the ladder. A team member on the ground grabbed the ladder and pulled it tight to make it easier to climb, but in doing so he put too much weight on the right side of the ship. Mr. Torrini said he was running out of left cyclic. Bill could not get the man on the ground to let go. Mr. Torrini said he had to pull up or risk hitting the tail rotor. We pulled up to a higher hover. The sergeant with the wounded hand tried to pull up the ladder but could not. He and Bill traded places. Bill tried pulling the ladder up with the Vietnamese on it, but the rungs slid on the ropes. Bill was lying on his stomach, with the Vietnamese on board holding his legs, so he could reach farther down, but the next rung was just out of reach. Mr. Torrini said he was still short on left cyclic. So I grabbed the Vietnamese and made him sit next to me to improve the center of gravity. Then all hell broke loose. Several things happened in just a second or two. We heard the sound of AK weapons right underneath us. I saw Mr. Bilitzke jolt in his seat and then slump over. Next I saw the muzzle

flash of a machine gun from the slope of the hill. The Vietnamese next to me was hit and knocked backwards. The Vietnamese on the ladder hung on for a moment or two before falling off. I could feel the ship shudder from all the hits we were taking. I began to lay down suppressive fire, first on that muzzle flash up the hill, then firing back through the foliage at the NVA underneath us. I still could not see them, but I could see the leaves being shredded by their fire. Mr. Torrini said we had several warning lights on, but the ship was still flying, and the controls felt good. Bill and the sergeant traded places again, and he began laying down suppressive fire.

With us down to one pilot and with two wounded team members on board, it was time to get out. As we were climbing out, Mr. Torrini informed me we had a fuel boost pump warning light on, even though the fuel pressure gauge was still in the green. We talked briefly about how high we could fly if we lost both pumps. After gaining enough altitude to get above small arms fire, I helped the Delta sergeant put bandages on the Vietnamese, who had taken several rounds in the stomach area and was in bad shape. Mr. Torrini had been trying to get some response from Mr. Bilitzke, who was finally starting to come around. We asked him where he was hit, and he said he was shot in the foot. We were escorted out of the valley by one of the recovery ships crewed by Ken Hamilton. They were taking bets on whether we would make it out of the valley because they could see we were losing fuel. On our approach to Phu Bai airport, we were told to give way to an air force C-130, also on final to the airport. Mr. Torrini informed the tower we were coming in with wounded. Before tower could say anything, the C-130 pilot said they would give way to the Huey and make a go-around. We landed at the base of the tower. Medical people came out and removed the two wounded team members. Bill and I helped Mr. Bilitzke out of the ship to have his foot looked at. As all this was going on, we were gathering several spectators. I guess we made quite a sight. Both ladders had bamboo still stuck in them, and the rotor blades at ground idle were making all kinds of whistling noises. After getting all the wounded out, we intended to hover over to where our maintenance team was. That is when Ken Hamilton ran over and told us we had a large fuel leak. I looked underneath the ship, and we had a puddle of JP-4 almost as big as the fuselage and growing. I put my ladder back in the ship, closed the cargo door and looked through the fire extinguisher door on the cowling. Fuel was spraying everywhere on the engine. Why it never caught fire is still a mystery. Mr. Torrini shut it down right on that spot. We had them bring out a fire truck in case it caught fire. Later on I looked at the engine and saw that one of the fuel lines at the fuel control had been shot into. We got our equipment out and caught a flight to our FOB. Our day was finished. While we were flying out of the AO, we heard two more attempts had been made to get the rest of the team out of that thicket. The other recovery ship went in and got hit bad also. They only made it a few kilometers from there and had to set the ship down. The other hole ship went in, had a tail rotor strike and had to depart. Hamilton's recovery ship had refueled and was returning to the AO. First, it escorted the tail rotor strike ship for few minutes to make sure it would make it out okay and then returned to pick up the crew of the ship that had gone down. After extracting the crew and their equipment, the flight returned to the FOB.

The next day the FAC made contact with the rest of the Delta team. Hamilton's recovery ship went in and used the hoist to pull them out. Ken told me on the way back the team leader had removed his web gear and pack and while looking at them, saw several bullet holes in the canteens, the stock of his M16 and his shirt. But he was without a scratch.

Three days later I was crewing the C&C ship being flown by Major Ruskauff and Mr. Albright. Also on board was Major Allen, the Delta commander. We led the flight back out into the AO. We were going to look for the back seater of an Air Force F-4 that had gone down two days before. Hamilton's ship had recovered the pilot that day but not the back seater. Flying over the area we thought he might be in, I spotted what looked like a signal panel through a hole in the jungle. I told Major Allen, and we circled back around. We both saw it! He sent one of the gunships over the opening to have a better look. They saw it and also spotted someone lying close to it. Having drawn no fire, the recovery ship was sent down for the rescue. The Delta medic on board rode the hoist down and got the man lying there. After they had him on board, we were told it was the Vietnamese that had fallen off the ladder on my ship three days before. He had removed his clothes and was just in his underwear. He was in bad shape but still alive. It took four days to get the whole team extracted from the AO. The team had two men KIA, both were Vietnamese: the Vietnamese that was shot on our ship and died on the flight back in, and the one who fell off the ladder. He died on the operating table in Da Nang. I know that one sergeant who was on board our ship was wounded, but I don't know if any of the others were or not. We had two pilots that had foot wounds.

We also lost one recovery ship. A big loss was the loss of the hoist that was on board. A hoist was harder to come by than a new ship. Two gunships were hit also. My ship was down for a month getting repaired. The rotor blades were destroyed, not only by the tree we chewed up, but also by the bamboo we had hit and by all the small arms fire.

The 281st would be involved in many more insertions and extractions in the months to come. A lot of them would be hot. We had a great working relationship with Project Delta. There was a kind of mutual feeling that each thought the other was crazy to do the job that they did. Maybe that is why we would risk all for one another. We flew above the best.

Paul Maledy,
Crew Chief

Air Force C-130

HAPPY VALLEY

Happy Valley...Death and destruction in a little valley on a map

Happy Valley was a major Viet Cong and North Vietnamese Army base camp, storage area and supply infiltration route. Men and materials would move from the base areas near Ai Yen 20 km east of the Laotian border and down Route 614 to units operating near Song Tuy Loan or other positions overlooking or surrounding the Da Nang vital area. This area comprised Da Nang City, Da Nang Air Base, Red Beach Base area, port facilities, and Marble Mountain Air Facility. The NVA would fire 122mm rockets, which had a range of 12 km, from the hills overlooking Da Nang at the city and U.S. military facilities. There were so many rockets fired it was called the "rocket belt". The Happy Valley area was covered by dense undergrowth and with elephant grass seven to ten feet tall. It was a very difficult area to land in and lift out of, which made it extremely dangerous. The following account exemplifies the difficulty and danger:

Happy Valley was never a happy place for the 281st Assault Helicopter Company. I had been assigned to the 281st Assault Helicopter Company and had only been in country a couple of months when we were sent to Hue Phu Bai to replace the first platoon "Rat Pack" in support of Project Delta. The day of the incident was hot and sunny. After the officers got a briefing, we left the forward operating base around midday. We were assigned as medical recovery and would fly behind the command and control ship. Our job was to pick up wounded or downed members when directed to by C&C.

The mission for the platoon that day was to insert a company of Army of the Republic of Vietnam Rangers and some Nungs, along with their American advisors, in a combat assault in reaction to intelligence gathered earlier by Delta. This was not a typical Delta mission, and this was my first hot combat assault.

Warrant Officer Robin Hicks was the aircraft commander; a maintenance warrant officer, Warrant Officer Wendell Allen, was the copilot; and Lionel Wesley was the gunner. We also had a Special Forces medic with us. In addition to our normal equipment, we had a McGuire Rig and a power winch with litter basket.

The combat assault got underway with three slicks from the 281st on the initial insertion. Helicopter 135 was shot down in the landing zone amidst heavy enemy fire. The other two helicopters went in and then flew out. A marine helicopter, a CH-46, came in and received some direct hits. It was smoking around the pylon as it came out, but it was able to make it out safely. The next marine CH-46 came in and made a crash landing. We were at a higher altitude, fairly far away, and sometimes I was on the wrong side of the ship to be able to describe everything that went on in the landing zone up to that time. However, I know two ships were shot down in the landing zone: helicopter 135 and the CH-46. There was a lot of discussion over the radios, and I think another one of our helicopters went down and picked up the crew from 135. Any way, we were all about out of fuel and flew back to the forward operating base.

Warrant Officer McCoig and Warrant Officer Norm Kaufman were the pilots on helicopter 135. After their rescue, they were taken back to the forward operating base. Mr. Kaufman had been wounded in the foot and was airlifted to the hospital. There was some discussion whether or not to attempt flying the 135 out, so Mr. McCoig volunteered to take the maintenance officer's place on my helicopter and for some reason flew left seat while Warrant Officer Robin Hicks moved over to the right seat. After refueling we hurried back to the landing zone.

When we got back to the area of operations, the Wolf Pack gunships had already set up a pattern, and we went in with C&C and marked the area with smoke. By that time the remainder of the flight had caught up with us. We went into the LZ to drop

114

off the recovery and maintenance people for both 135 and the Marine 46 and to pick up our wounded. All aircraft including the gunships were reporting heavy ground fire. About that time C&C decided that the LZ wasn't secure enough to conduct recovery to the downed aircraft crew. The recovery ships were ordered to go in and pick up the men on the ground. Aircraft 127 made it in and out, but aircraft 228 went in, was shot up and had to return to the LZ. Helicopters 113 and 129 recovered the crew of the downed helicopters, maintenance personnel and some wounded. Then another Marine 46 crashed hard in the LZ. As I looked down, it looked like a junk yard for helicopters. We were ordered to go down and rescue the crew of the marine CH-46. I was on the left side and Mr. McCoig had me go hot with my M-60 real early because my side was where all the ground fire was coming from. Wesley, on the other side of the ship, couldn't fire because the friendlies were there. Mr. McCoig flew into the LZ, and we quickly loaded the downed crew members from the marine CH-46. With the medic, who was already on board, and eight passengers, it was a full load. Upon departure from the LZ, we received ground fire. **The very first bullet hit Mr. McCoig directly in the forehead, killing him instantly.**

Then all hell broke loose. I was out of M-60 ammo by this time and grabbed my M-14, trying to get a clip into it. Fuel was flying all over my face. In the meanwhile, Hicks jumped on the controls as the aircraft went into a nose high position with a tremendous yaw to the right. Hicks kept screaming for me to come up and get McCoig off the controls, but centrifugal force was trying to throw me out, and I was holding on to anything I could grab just to stay in the aircraft. I could not make it forward no matter how hard I tried. Finally McCoig's death grip on the controls relaxed enough to allow Hicks to gain control. Hick's masterful flying skills somehow got us back into the LZ.

Once on the ground, we continued receiving constant fire from the tree line, but this time I was on the friendly side. Mr. Hicks couldn't exit out the right door because the enemy had him zeroed in, and every time he moved his armor plate, they would hit it. He eventually crawled out over the console and came out the left cargo door. Wesley had made it out somehow and crawled under the nose cone with both his and my M-60 and all the ammo that he had left. There was a bomb crater about 20 feet from where the aircraft landed, and using our downed ship as cover, we eventually made it to the bomb crater. After the fire died down a little, due in large part to Air Force fighters working the tree line, we recovered McCoig's body and moved him inside the perimeter of a defensive position that a small ranger team had established next to the LZ. By this time darkness and bad weather forced us to remain on the ground that night. We received steady mortar, B-40 rockets, and small arms fire. It was a long and scary night. Early the next morning we were told that a large North Vietnamese Army force was headed our way and that we needed to find an LZ which could be used to recover our dead and wounded. We would definitely not leave anyone behind. We headed out with first me and Wesley and then Hicks carrying Mr. McCoig's body. It was particularly difficult for Hicks because he weighed less than McCoig. There were several dead and wounded in our group.

One SV soldier had taken a direct hit from a mortar, and it didn't require a very big poncho to carry his remains. The gunner from the CH-46 was really unlucky. He had been hit in the left side when we loaded him, but then took another round in his lower gut when we came back into the LZ. We were carrying his dead body. One Special Forces guy had two bullets in his chest and was white as a sheet from the loss of blood, but somehow, someway, he walked out with us. As we left, I looked back at the five helicopters that had been shot down. We left carrying our wounded and dead; we were determined to make it out. We moved toward the river and with all that water around us, we had nothing to drink. Man, I was thirsty. At the time, I was carrying a wounded Special Forces captain's web gear. It had a canteen with some purifying tablets taped to it, so I filled it with that nasty river water, threw in a handful of tablets, shook it a couple times and drank it down. We walked all morning, then all afternoon. Mr. Hicks heroically continued to carry McCoig's body; it was all he could do to keep moving. It was slow going for all of us. Once we got out of the river, the terrain was nothing but dense bush. I remember seeing aircraft of all makes and services in the air, and the artillery from Firebase Bastogne was pounding the mountains surrounding us. The weather had lifted, and it was hot and muggy in the jungle. My mouth was dry as a bone. The Special Forces guy with the two holes in his chest gave me some hard candy but I couldn't develop enough spit to swallow it. Sometime in the late afternoon of that day, we located a clearing that could be used as a pickup point. We watched the guns work over the sides of the pickup zone, and between the napalm and other work, the pickup zone was secured. Just before dusk, we got out of that place. Marine helicopters picked up the dead and wounded first, and then the 281st helicopters came in to rescue everyone else. I was one of the last out and was taken all the way back to the forward operating base.

I don't remember how many days we stayed at the FOB before we went back to our home base at Nha Trang, but it wasn't long. Once back I was assigned to another ship but got real deep in the bottle, and eventually I asked to be reassigned to the maintenance platoon, where I stayed the remainder of my tour. Most everything after that day is blurred in my memory, due either to the alcohol or my mind giving me some relief from the guilt, fear, and other emotions I felt at the time. The one thing clear in my mind, and I will never forget, is the heroic actions throughout the mission of Chief Warrant Officer Robin Hicks. He was and is my hero.

Private First Class Kenneth R. Ebrey,
Crew Chief

Ken Ebrey died in 2006 after a long struggle with cancer. At Ken's funeral Robin Hicks placed his own Silver Star, the nation's third highest award for valor in combat, which Robin received for his actions during the mission, into Ken's coffin, a gesture which clearly signified the bond that existed between these two Intruder heroes.

Marine CH-46 Sea Knight

VINH SON ORPHANAGE

Sister Le looked at me with the saddest eyes and said in broken English "Baby die soon." Captain Surry Roberts, a Special Forces doctor, and I watched as she cuddled this small, doll-like baby in her arms. We were staring death right in the face, as the nun rocked this almost lifeless, tiny baby back and forth. The baby had been left on the front steps the night before.

Captain Roberts had a look of urgency on his face; we left in a hurry. He needed a helicopter right away and also needed to make an emergency phone call. After so many years I do not remember where we flew, but we found and brought back an incubator. The nuns had never seen such a thing; Doc Roberts gave them instructions on its use.

Specialist Doug Simpson and Sister Imelda with orphan children

The nuns were praying aloud as we left.

The Orphanage was a small building located in downtown Nha Trang. It could house about 30 children comfortably but had 65, sometimes even more. The nuns somehow, someway took care of all the children, who ranged from new-born babies to homeless children more than twelve years old. Every foot of the building was used; children slept in the hallways, offices, closets and the kitchen. They needed all the space they could find and all the help they could get. The building had been an older Catholic Church that the nuns and their staff had converted into an orphan home. It was crowded but they made it work.

On a number of occasions I had flown Captain Roberts and his medical team to Montagnard villages deep into the jungles of the highlands of South Vietnam. He and his medical team attended to the needs of the people living there. Sometimes it would be an all-day thing, as men, woman and children lined up to receive medical aid from this man who came down from the sky to help them.

From the first time I met Surry Roberts, I took a liking to him because he went out of his way to help those who could not help themselves. He was the main doctor, the officer in charge of the 5th Special Forces Medical Group. I was amazed at his talent; he was the right man at the right time for this position.

With the permission of my company commander, I asked the 281st Company to help me with a most worthy cause, and they did, in a grand way. A collection table was set up on paydays for needed cash donations. Most of the time we would get at least $100.00, at times over $300.00, and that was a lot of money back then. Captain Roberts and I did not give the money to the orphanage; we took the money and purchased what they needed.

I asked our men to have their families back home mail care packages of clothing, toys, baby diapers, and blankets. Soon we were receiving a number of items needed by the orphanage. Churches back home also got involved, and what a sight it was to see when we delivered boxes of needed clothing and toys to the kids living at the orphanage. It was Christmas each time. Most active were the NCOs who, in most cases, had children back home. From time to time a number of us would go out and just mingle with the kids. It was pure joy, for the kids wanted so much attention from us. Though we did not speak Vietnamese, both we and they understood the language of love. The smiles on their faces were worth more than we could ever give back. I think most troops are pretty darn good about supporting something like this. I cannot say enough about the help we received from our men.

Captain Surry Roberts not only helped the nuns and the children, he went out of his way to help the village people. He was their life line as he provided much needed medical care. He was usually the first and only doctor they had ever seen. We were most fortunate to have a man of his caliber, kindness and professionalism as our doctor. We became friends over 47 years ago, and we are still the best of friends. He developed a special friendship with the Montagnard tribal people and to this day he is still helping them.

The men of the 281st came through for me, as we all wanted to be a part of helping these war torn children who had been left to fend for themselves.

I was proud to have been a soldier and a pilot with the 281st, but, to this very day, my involvement with the orphanage project is the most important and satisfying thing I have ever done in my whole life. I cannot and will not forget those kids that needed love, a touch and our attention.

Chief Warrant Officer Paul Morsen,
Pilot
August 1968 - July 1969

Special Forces Sergeant First Class Bright, Sister Imelda and Chief Warrant Officer Paul Morsen. Paul is holding the little baby who's life he and Captain Roberts helped saved.

TEAM 10

We had to get the team on the ground out, or they would be killed within minutes. The opening in the jungle was so small; in my opinion it was not large enough to get the helicopter through it. The aircraft commander had only one thought in his mind. We had to get them out now! He turned the helicopter on its side and made a dive for the small opening while I held my breath. I had been in Vietnam for just over a year. I was a seasoned helicopter pilot with more than 1,200 hours and had been an aircraft commander for eight months. I had completed my first tour with the 48th Assault Helicopter Company, whose base was at Ninh Hoa. Over the past year, I had been in some tight spots, been shot at and had flown some hectic missions. I was young and enjoyed flying, so I extended for six more months. I went home on a thirty-day leave, and when I reported back to Vietnam, I was pleasantly surprised to be sent to the 281st Assault Helicopter Company. I was starting over again as a copilot. I was assigned to the 2nd flight platoon known as the Bandits.

Warrant Officer Donald Torrini was the Bandit platoon's instructor pilot. I had the good fortune of being assigned to fly with him as part of my orientation and qualification check flight to become an aircraft commander. Each unit had different standards, even each platoon. Torrini demanded that on each flight he and I work as a team with the Crew Chief Specialist Five Charles Fredricy, and Door Gunner Sergeant Robert Carl.

Our crew had successfully inserted this six-man project Delta long-range reconnaissance team without any contact, and for the past four days, we had followed their mission performance. We were on standby and ready to go at a minute's notice. We were their life line in case they got into trouble, and the team knew that no matter what, we would come and get them. Their team depended on our team.

These recon teams of Delta were the best of the best; they were well trained, had nerves of steel and were the bravest men I had ever known. On the morning of 4 May, the team's location was compromised, and they were engaged with a large hostile North Vietnamese Army force. They were in trouble and needed immediate extraction. Within minutes of hearing their urgent message, we were on the way, accompanied by Major Ruskauff, our commanding officer, and Major Allen, the Delta commander, both of whom were flying in the command and control helicopter. Wolf Pack gunships were on the way, ready to bring "hell from above." There were back-up helicopters because this was a total company mission to save the team on the ground. Even the United States Air Force Forward Air Controller in his observation airplane was there to help guide us to the closest pick-up zone. This was both nerve wrecking and exciting for me and was going to get even more so.

Within minutes we arrived over the area and found the team to be in an escape and evade mode in very rugged mountainous terrain. The team on the ground had been trying to get to a pick-up zone but had been cut off by the North Vietnamese Army. Now they were being chased downhill to a small river. We were on location fiercely searching for a hole in the thick jungle canopy, looking for an opening to get down to them.

The river was 80 feet wide, at most, with trees and a dense jungle canopy covering. This was not a landing zone, nor could it be a pick-up zone. There was no way for a rope or McGuire extraction to be used. The only way was to get down to the river, and we had to do it now. The command and control said there was a small opening in the canopy a short way upstream. Warrant Officer Torrini put the Huey in a very sharp turn and made a dive for the hole. As the copilot and an experienced helicopter pilot, I knew this was not a pick-up zone that I or anyone else would attempt to use under any circumstances. I was holding my breath. Officer Torrini was in a hurry; through the small opening I could see the river. The crew and I were along for the ride of a life time in route to rescue the team. The hole in the jungle did not get any bigger as we got closer. How was he going to get through, how was he going to get this thing down and under that triple canopy forest? More importantly, how would we ever get out? I reminded myself that in the back of the Huey, we had two of the best men manning the M-60 machine guns. They would be our eyes on each side and life savers for all of us.

In the past, it had not been a problem to nip a few leaves or small branches with the main rotor blades, but never with the tail rotor. Officer Torrini's flying skills allowed him to somehow get the helicopter through the holes in the jungle canopy cover without any tail rotor contact. I still don't know how he did it. Once we got down to the river, we had to hover under the tree branches with our skids in the water. There were only inches to spare on each side; this was way too close for comfort.

Now our goal was to find the team, and this is where it takes teamwork to make the team work. The command and control, the forward air controller, and the team number 10 helped us get to the right spot in the river. Wolf Pack was flying above ready to bring hell from above on the enemy. Once we arrived and were hovering downstream, this became a single-crew mission because in that area of the river, the jungle canopy was only large enough for one helicopter. There was no way for us to see the aircraft above us, nor for them to see us. It kind of surprised me to see how swift the current was. Specialist Fredricy and Sergeant Carl were very busy providing covering fire for the team that was being pursued by a clearly visible enemy force. Once the team was in the river, Fredricy and Carl continued to fire the M-60 machine guns with one hand while hauling each soaking wet team member onto the helicopter with the other hand. It was Officer Torrini's job to fly the helicopter while my job was to monitor the instruments, watch everything, and keep him informed. He listened to my every word. I was constantly talking to him saying, "Keep it steady, move a little to the left, or come this way a few inches and so on." I was not so much scared as I was busy. Let's just say that I was very intense. This was a fairly new UH-1H, and the helicopter was torque limited at 50 PSI. I noticed the torque meter climbing as each man came aboard. The skids were in the water, which helped each team member to climb aboard more easily. The crew in the back was very busy, sometimes firing with one hand and helping the team board with the other. Suddenly I noticed that the helicopter was off balance. The alert crew chief noticed it too and started to bring the team members in on his side, which solved the problem. With our six wet team members and one prisoner all on board, the torque meter was bouncing off 50.

121

We were in the hole and still in the water with the team safely on board, and in my estimation the only way out was the same way we came in, which was more than a hundred feet straight up with a heavily loaded helicopter. How could we do it?

Officer Torrini knew that he could not get out the way he came in because the helicopter was loaded to its limit. The command and control aircraft advised us there was a small hole in the forest canopy downstream. We made our way down, made a slight right turn and spotted the very small hole. The UH-1H helicopter rotor blades are forty-eight feet from tip to tip. The hole could not have been more that a total of forty-nine feet. I was watching the instruments as Officer Torrini moved slowly with the torque meter pegged at 50, taking the fully loaded helicopter between solid tree trunks and emerging on the other side with amazingly no rotor blade contact. His feather-light touch on the controls was beyond amazing. I watched in awe as he inched his way around, over and under obstacles to make our way out. I was getting good at holding my breath. The pucker factor was in the red. With a slight right turn, we were suddenly in the clear and were almost immediately flying as we came up and away from the area. The captured NVA prisoner was severely wounded, with most of his intestines exposed. The crew chief was administering emergency first aid trying to ease his pain and keep him alive. What a great bunch of men I was serving with. I looked to the left at Warrant Officer Donald Torrini and felt the greatest admiration that I have ever felt for any person in my entire life. What an honor it was for me to be in the same cockpit with him. My hands were wet with sweat and shaking, but I could finally stop holding my breath and breathe.

The only possible pick-up point for that recon team just happened to be right where they were at in their flight from their pursuers. Had the decision been made that we could not pick them up due to the weather and terrain; the decision would have been justified. However, Warrant Officer Torrini was willing to risk his life to save them. With a great team effort from the whole 281st Assault Helicopter Company, we rescued the team from the jaws of death. We had made the impossible possible.

Now, 49 years later, Colonel Donald Torrini still insists that without the door gunner, the crew chief and his copilot, we would have crashed and died in the swift running waters of that mountain river. It takes teamwork to make the team work.

Chief Warrant Officer George Thomas Dodd,
Bandit and Wolf Pack pilot

For his actions in rescuing Team 10, Warrant Officer Donald Torrini was recommended for the Congressional Medal of Honor, our nation's highest award for bravery in combat. He was awarded the Silver Star, the third highest award for bravery.

On 8 May 1968, Chief Warrant Officer Leslie Dayton, Chief Warrant Officer George Thomas Condrey III, Sergeant Daniel Edward Jurecko, and Specialist Four Robert Earl Jenne were shot down, and all are still missing.

Air Force Bird Dog on target as a Forward Air Controller (FAC)

YOU CAN'T PARK HERE!

My crew and I had been sent out to help the 4th Infantry Division at Pleiku. We made the three-hour trip in our UH-1C gunship. About a mile out, I called Pleiku flight tower and requested landing instructions. They gave me instructions for the approach and told me where to land. We came in low and slow and hovered into one of the L-shaped revetments. After shutting down and securing everything, we hoisted all our stuff on our shoulders, made the long walk to the operations building and reported in. It was getting late, and I asked where we could get something to eat and where they were going to house me and my crew. A real live officer, I think he was a first lieutenant, got up from behind his desk with that "hey, I am in charge" look on his face, and informed me I had to go back out and move the helicopter to another revetment. Naturally, I asked why. His face turned a bright red, and he said, "Go move it now because that space belongs to the operations officer."

I said, "Okay." We walked back out, untied the blade, fired up and hovered over to another spot. We secured everything for the second time. One of the maintenance men came over, drove us to a tent and told us where the mess tent was located. We got settled in for the night. It had been a long day. During the early morning hours, the Viet Cong decided to lob a

123

few rockets on the base. We hunkered down until it was over.

The next morning as we walked back to the pilots' area for briefing, I saw the spot where I had first parked. I could not help but smile at my good fortune. The operations officer's helicopter was a pile of junk. A Viet Cong rocket had found its mark. After the briefing I walked by the lieutenant, reached out to shake his hand, and thanked him. I don't think he knew what I was thanking him for.

Warrant Officer Jim Fisher,
Aircraft Commander
Wolf Pack

A PLETHORA OF MISSIONS

Although there were no Delta missions scheduled in the near future, I was still flying a plethora of missions. Many involved convoy cover with some major in the back who kept yakking on the radio to his lieutenant colonel who was on the ground, in an attempt to impress him, I think, because most of what he said was useless. I would hear, "The convoy has passed checkpoint A. I can confirm. There is no enemy activity, but we will continue to monitor from the air."

As I flew more missions, I noticed that some of the Special Forces officers we flew attached a whole lot of importance to themselves, and not all of them really liked us. Many of them refused to roll down their sleeves before takeoff. Sleeves down was a rule, and we never let them get away with breaking it. They loved to keep us out after dark, something else we had a rule about. The rule stated we only flew at night on combat missions, not on administrative flights.

Martha Raye

I remember one Special Forces captain who was inside Dong Tre fire base camp as it was getting dark. While he was doing whatever he needed to do, Warrant Officer Ken Glaze noticed that this captain's camera had been left in his seat in the back of the aircraft. He picked it up and snapped a whole bunch of inappropriate pictures. Then we cranked up the aircraft, picked it up to a high hover and made a few 360 degree pedal turns. This attracted the attention of the SF captain. We landed. The captain reappeared shortly thereafter, ready for his return flight. The camera was where he had left it. I wonder what he did with those pictures. We also did a few Recondo extractions. I remember one where the pickup zone was at the edge of a stream beside a trail. The hole was barely large enough for us to set down, but set down we did. After about fifteen seconds, out came the team, all in camo, weapons pointing in all directions except at our ship. Then came

Sergeant First Class Hines with his huge handlebar mustache. He was walking backwards and pointing his weapon in front of him. It was surreal and straight out of the movies. He bent down, scooted in, gave us a thumbs up and off we went. His retrieval had been requested because he had the flu; he looked like hell but still kept performing his mission. He defined soldier to me. The next day we flew Colonel Aaron, the 5th Special Forces Commander. As soon as he sat down, he put on his homemade pull-on sleeves. He didn't roll down his sleeves, but he met the requirement of long sleeves. He smiled and joked the entire flight, quite the opposite of most of the other officers we flew. Maybe that's why he went on to get three stars.

We also flew the comedian Martha Raye a lot, which was interesting. She was gracious, friendly, talked all the time, autographed the inside of a few of our helicopters and gave each of us her home address in LA, telling us all to stop by and stay a few days and take advantage of her hospitality. She was my one time close-to-fame moment as we happened to share a C-Ration lunch sitting on the floor in back of our helicopter. How many civilians get to do that?

Jeff Murray
Warrant Officer

WHAT THE HECK!

I reported to the flight line early; the morning light had not yet come alive, yet it was already hot and humid. This was my first flight as door gunner on this helicopter. Jay Hays, the crew chief was already there checking and preflighting the helicopter. I checked the machine guns; they were clean, in good working order and had plenty of ammunition. As the pilots climbed into the cockpit, I pushed their bullet-proof plates up into the forward position and made sure their doors were secure. I then clipped my c-ration can onto the machine gun and loaded the ammo into the gun. With one last look on my side, I climbed up into the gunner's den, reached over and plugged in my flight helmet. I was ready. The engine started its whine as the pilots fired up the turbine. The crew chief said, "Clear on the left," and I looked again and said, "Clear on the right." The pilot said, "Okay, coming out," as he pulled pitch and hovered out of the revetment. We hovered over to the helo pad, picked up our passengers and some cargo, and we were ready to go. I was really excited even though it was just a routine flight.

I then heard the crew chief's voice in my headset say, "Good morning. I would like to welcome you aboard. Our destination today will be Pleiku. We will be flying at 1500 feet at approximately 110 knots. The flight time will be 2 hours and 27 minutes. The weather in route is reported to be clear to partly cloudy. For your additional information, we will be flying over hostile territory, and there is a good chance we will be receiving enemy fire from below. Rest assured, if that happens, we will bring down hell on them from above. Again, welcome aboard. Sit back and enjoy the flight."

I am sitting on the other side listening to this, laughing and shaking my head as I think, "What the heck is going on with this guy?" It sounded like I was on a commercial airliner. That just made my day, and even now when I think about it, I still smile. He was a great guy and one of the best crew chiefs. On that day we became friends, and now 49 years later we are still the best of friends.

Richard Schleher
Door Gunner
August 67 – August 68

LADY BUG

Being on a good team, getting the right training and having common sense and lots of good luck can help when the going gets tough. When your life is on the line, and the bad guys are trying to get you, it does not hurt to have some type of good-luck charm in your pocket or hanging around your neck. A lock of your sweetheart's hair and a hundred other items are traditional charms for good luck. But a lady bug?

My wife was from Seattle, so we left flight school in early December 1967 and did a road trip to Houston via New Orleans. At the time her folks lived in Houston because her father was a Boeing Space Physiologist at the Space Center. I was from East Texas about 200 miles north of Houston. We flew from Houston to Seattle as I was scheduled to depart from McCord in early January. We visited a lot of her friends in Seattle for the remainder of the time.

Seattle is pretty cold that time of year, and one does not expect to see ladybugs, that are outdoor summer insects. However, at a friend's house during cocktails before we sat down for dinner, a ladybug landed on the back of my hand. As I moved to swat it away, our hostess exclaimed: "Don't do that; that is Chinese good luck!" I stopped and admired the little creature crawling on the back of my hand. Well, does it work? From that moment on, and to this day, I wear a ladybug on my body some-where. I had ladybug images on my flight helmet, including a little plastic ladybug figure glued to the tip of my helmet microphone and one on the adjusting nut on my helmet. For me the lady bug was my good luck charm. I am still here, healthy and a bit wiser telling my story. It worked then and is still working to this very day.

Ken Smith,
Warrant Officer
Aircraft Commander

IFR

In the real world, which is what we called life back in the good old USA, IFR is a flight term in the Federal Aviation Administration (FAA) which stands for

Instrument Flight Rules. It requires that in certain flying conditions, a pilot must file a flight plan and fly using instruments, rather than sight. IFR flight plans are filed by pilots who want to either fly in very inclement or severe weather conditions or when the pilots are flying a commercial aircraft above flight level (FL) 18 (18,000 feet), also referred to as Class A airspace in worldwide flight rules. There were some pilots in Vietnam who could fly on instruments, but most were not Army helicopter pilots. In training at Ft. Rucker, Alabama, all of the Vietnam-era helicopter pilots were trained in the basics of instrument flying conditions, but, quite frankly, it is the last IFR flying they ever did. A lot of things we did in Vietnam would never be advised or allowed in the real world. One of them was flying in low visibility or close to zero visibility out the front of the cockpit. It was, however, common and accepted practice to fly at low-level visibility along roads. We navigated by watching the path of the road through the chin bubble, the small Plexiglas viewing window between the pilots' feet and the tail rotor control pedals. Believe it or not, we could see quite a lot through this chin bubble, and we used it constantly when we were making recon team insertion/extractions to avoid hitting trees and other objects. Consequently, for Army helicopter pilots, IFR also meant: I FOLLOW ROADS! There was no written procedure on this since any commander would deny it and say, "Of course, that's illegal and not SOP (Standard Operating Procedure)." So the experienced pilots taught new pilots the unwritten rules. A Huey normally flew at about 90 knots or about 100 MPH. If a pilot was IFR, he decreased the speed to around 60 to 70 knots. The second cardinal rule we pilots followed was to always fly on the right side of the road because we knew that some other bold helicopter pilot might be going through the same mountain pass at the same time. If we were both in the middle of the road, the result would be an ugly mid-air collision! I personally applied the two cardinal rules many times, but the time that stands out in my mind was the day a big monsoon storm swept in from the west when we were on a mission for the Special Forces Team near the Cambodian border. The decision to fly was made by the aircraft commander, and I was a seasoned aircraft commander. I determined whether to fly or not, and the rest of the crew was at my mercy. Pleiku was a place that got nightly attacks from mortars and rockets. I decided we could beat the storm and make a run for Nha Trang and the beautiful 5th Special Forces Group Headquarters Officers Club rather than spend a miserable night in Pleiku watching the North Vietnamese Army fireworks. Flight time from Pleiku to Nha Trang was normally about two hours, about the fuel range of a UH-1H. Normally, we would fly over the mountains that surrounded Nha Trang, but as the weather got worse, and I began to lose visibility to fly at our normal safe altitude of 1,500 feet above ground level (AGL), I spotted the major road to the coast and descended to treetop level. Standard operating procedures for Army helicopters was to either fly above 1,500 AGL, which was the safe height to avoid ground fire from small arms like the 7.62 millimeter AK-47 automatic weapons used by the enemy, or to fly on the tree tops, low-level flying. It was hard for small arms to hit a fast moving helicopter at short range through the trees. Between 1,500 feet and tree tops was known as "dead man's zone." At this point, low level flying became very difficult, as the weather was closing in on us, and my visibility went to about 100 feet in front of me. The two cardinal rules of IFR technique became critical. I had to nose the aircraft back to about 60 knots and rely on what I could see below me, the road. As we slowly flew through the Duc My Pass toward the coast and our base in Nha Trang, we met another Huey doing the same thing, but he was westbound in the opposite direction. We safely passed each other at a very close distance, with both of us making a slight maneuver to the right to ensure we did not collide. I can tell you it was a moment of extreme fear as well as excitement when the unwritten rules of I FOLLOW ROADS were observed by both of us pilots, and we made it home safely to fly another day. That night, after a few hefty drinks of Johnnie Walker on the rocks at the Officers' Club, I convinced myself I was one hell of a pilot and God was my copilot. Of course, I needed God on my side, but it was either the luck of the ladybug painted on my helmet or my skill as a helicopter pilot that kept us safe. I'll never know for sure which it was, but I am here to tell the story, and that is what counts!

Warrant Officer Ken Smith,
Aircraft Commander 1968 - 1969

VALLEY OF THE TIGERS

The location was not on any map; it had no name. It was only a valley in the mountain jungles of South Vietnam. Yet, this little spot made the evening news on 13 August 1968 when Walter Cronkite opened his broadcast on CBS by saying, "Now a special report from the Valley of the Tigers". The story which put the valley in the news involved the 281st Assault Helicopter Company.

****

When anyone needed a ride to another location for supplies, food, ammunition, help and a hundred other things, all it usually took was a call to our flight operations center. Supporting the Green Berets was our primary mission. We flew men into battle, and we brought them back to safety. However, we also flew South Vietnamese troops, sometimes with their chickens and pigs, and the soldiers from the Republic of Korea. We were their lifeline too. A request was never denied; the men in flight operations always found a way to help.

Believe it or not, most of the flight crew was not excited about routine missions; they wanted to be in the middle of the action. Flying VIPs, donut dollies, film crews, politicians and reporters was boring, to say the least. The Fifth Special Forces missions were what we were all about. When they called we were always ready.

First Lieutenant Thomas Ross, a Special Forces officer, made a phone call. From the tone of his voice, the flight operations officer who took the call knew it was urgent. This officer was responding to Ross's request with the words, "That is out of our area of operations. What, no artillery support? Civilians? Montagnards?" Whatever Lieutenant Ross told him about the situation, his next response was immediate, "Tell us where you need us to be and at what time."

The 281st Assault Helicopter Company had just accepted the mission to rescue a village of 165 Montagnards: men, woman and children. For the past eight years, these villagers had been forced to carry ammunition and supplies, as well as to grow food, to be used by various enemy units passing through the area. Their story of captivity included tales of brutal beatings and violent atrocities. They were being used as slaves by the VC and NVA. If the village was to be saved, there were only hours in which to act. To be successful this operation would require an extremely quick response. The 281st felt it would be an honor and a privilege to save this village. Reporters and a film crew would be on hand to record the evacuation.

As Americans, we are quick to respond and among the first to send help; this is one of the qualities that defines us as American. It's in our blood. So Ross requested the mission and got it. As the last part of the rescue was being filmed, the reporter asked Lieutenant Ross, "Where are we?" The quick-witted Ross remembered seeing several tigers on the first day of reconnaissance in the valley, and he replied, "We are in the Valley of the Tigers."

His book "Privileges of War" is a must read.

Ross, Thomas A., Privileges of War
American Heritage Publishing
5710 Mt. Repose Lane NW
Norcross, Georgia

Mission complete. Intruders and individuals rescued from the Valley of the Tigers.
Successful mission reported on CBS Nightly News as one of the good stories of the war.

15 August 1968, Major Andrew J. Miller, Jr. assumed command of the company.

DOOR GUNNER WITH A SCREWDRIVER

We were on a mission delivering all kinds of needed supplies to a couple of SF camps in the central highlands. On leaving the first camp, we started receiving small arms fire on my side. It did not appear any of the bullets hit our aircraft. We gained altitude, and everything seemed okay. We were high enough to be in the safe zone from the ground fire. Everything was cool, Bandit 113 was running smoothly, and it was quiet. I sat there enjoying the view below and realized it was too quiet, way too quiet. The only communication we had was the intercom within our aircraft. All the radios up front in the cockpit had stopped working. As the crew chief, I was the only one who could communicate outside the aircraft. The aircraft commander had to say everything over the intercom, and then I would repeat it to the other aircraft or ground personnel. This took additional time, and it kept me busy while returning fire, clearing the left side, kicking out the resupply items such as ammo, food, water, etc. After about 30 minutes, we went up to about 1500 feet for a short flight to get more supplies. My door gunner asked me if I had a screwdriver. I asked back, "What did you say?" He said again, "Do you have a screwdriver?" I said, "Yes. Why?" He replied, "Just find it. I will unbuckle and fix the problem." I climbed around the seats to my tool box and got a screwdriver for him. Here was my door gunner leaning over the seats to remove an electrical panel while we were bouncing around at 1,500 feet. He found a crimped wire that had been bent as a result of something hitting the plastic electrical panel cover. This had caused both pilots' microphones to be grounded. As soon as the problem was corrected, he gave me thumbs up. I informed the pilots to try their radios, and everything was back to normal. My door gunner on this flight was Frank Becker. He is the only person I know of who performed an inflight repair.

Frank, who was an avionics expert, always enjoyed flying as a door gunner if and when he could get some free time. This gave our regular door gunners a rare opportunity to have a day off. Frank and I flew a number of missions together. He always did a great job and as a result, had enough hours to earn a well-deserved air medal. Frank Becker and I have remained lifelong friends.

True to form, as our men get older, this story got better. After a couple of beers, the story was Frank was out on the skids flying at 90 knots per hour while firing the M-60 machine gun with one hand and with the other hand holding a screwdriver to make the inflight repair. And someone will swear it is the truth because he was flying next to us, and that is the way he saw it. And so it goes.

Sergeant Jay Hays,
Crew Chief and Platoon Sergeant
1967– 1968

Helicopter, tail number 113, in a Recondo School training exercise, survived the Vietnam War and came back to the USA. It was later used by the CIA in South America, returned to the US and is now on display at the HEARTS Museum in Huntsville, Texas.

ALL IN A DAY'S WORK

It has always bothered me that I can't remember the time and place in Vietnam when Jay tells his story about me using a screwdriver to make a repair during a flight. However, after thinking about his story, there are enough fact, mixed with the old war stories that have invaded his story these forty-nine or so years, that it is probably true. I did fly when I could get a day off, and most flights were to resupply the Special Forces' team camps. I saw a lot of country that way, as we were on the go all day around the countryside. We often had boxes and supplies stacked in the middle of the craft from the floor to the ceiling, against the wall of the transmission housing. On the top part of that wall there was a junction box for all the wiring of the crew's radios. This was a box we were in often because all the ships had floor switches that the crew chief and door gunner used. We installed it so they could key their mikes to talk with their foot without using their hands. It was kind of an aftermarket upgrade. As far as firing the M-60 and the other stuff in Jay's story, I don't remember doing that. On all the missions I flew, and there were many, no aircraft ever received any fire on those missions. I never got to fire an M-60 at the enemy in the nineteen plus months in country. I tried not to push my luck too far and picked the missions I went on, but on every mission I was always ready for the worst. One time I remember I was thinking about what I was doing after the fact. We were at a forward operating base on a Project Delta Mission, where exactly I don't remember, and for some reason there was one of those hurry up we have to get the Special Forces team out situations. I guess I was out on the flight line, and when they were getting crews on the aircrafts, I was handy, and somebody thought I was good enough to go. I was on the number two recovery Huey as the door gunner. On the way back I got to thinking my guardian angel had worked over time. There was no one trying to shoot us down. The Special Forces team was on board and in good health, there was no shot up helicopter to go recover, and we all returned safely. That's what it was all about; a nice ride in a Huey flying over the countryside, a good day in Vietnam. What all this means is if you were in the 281st Assault Helicopter Company and could do the job at hand, you did it and went on. You were there to do the job, making sure you and the rest of the men in the 281st and Special Forces you were working with made it home safely and got the ride of a lifetime on that big silver bird from Cam Ranh Bay back to the WORLD. Maybe you or someone else remembers it was all in a day's work.

Specialist Five Frank E. Becker,
June 67 - February 69

A HOT REFUELING

It was the fall of 1968 and we were on an operation out of the marine base at An Hoa. We were in heavy contact which called for us to "hot" refuel and rearm. I sat next in line in my aircraft, observing the preparations for fueling the gunship in front of me. It was piloted by the aircraft commander Chief Warrant Officer, Rick Galer. I noted all the rules were followed: the copilot exited the left seat of the aircraft, raised the window, closed the door, and Mr. Galer kept the RPM at 6600, ready to move if necessary. The crew chief went by the book too: sleeves down, visor down, gloves on. He was backed up by the door gunner dressed the same and holding a fire extinguisher. Everything by the book! When the crew chief squeezed the nozzle, it blew out of the tank spewing fuel onto the hot end. Whoosh! Everything was on fire. The crew chief whirled around, throwing burning fuel all over the door gunner, who started rolling on the ground. The sergeant who was in charge of the refueling station immediately came running with another fire extinguisher to extinguish the fire on the door gunner. Mr. Galer quickly picked the helicopter up, moved it away from the fueling point, shut it down and "bailed out." His actions and those of the two crew members were exemplary!

The door gunner had 2nd degree burns and was evacuated. He was lucky to be alive, and his injuries were minor, considering what might have happened. I had called "Mayday" to the tower, and the fire truck arrived quickly, but sadly the aircraft was burned beyond recovery. We learned how valuable it is to train hard and follow your training by the book. This could have been so much worse! The explanation was the fuel pressure to the nozzle was set high for the air force C-130s, which are not manually operated—they lock into the aircraft when refueling. When the crew chief squeezed the nozzle, it blew out and up. So we learned to always check the nozzle pressure. We also learned the door gunner needed to stand further away from the crew chief during refueling, so if this happened he would not be covered with burning fuel. This gave a new meaning to "hot refueling." Good work, Mr. Rick Galer and team!

Captain Bain Black,
Wolf Pack 36

Crew Chief hot refueling while door gunner holds fire extinguisher

WE MADE THE NEWS!

This came as a surprise to us. We were operating secret and top secret missions and there we were in the Stars and Stripes Paper.

"BERETS Smash NVA Road"

"NHA TRANG – Detachment B-52 (Project Delta), a joint U.S. and Vietnamese Special Forces reconnaissance unit, recently received the Valorous Unit Award for helpings smash an NVA attempt to cut a road into the Hue Phu Bai area.

Lieutenant General William R. Peers, former commanding general I Field Force Vietnam, presented the award to Project Delta, the most decorated long range patrol unit of the Vietnam War, at a ceremony in the quadrangle of the 5th Special Forces Group Headquarters here.

Project Delta received the award for extraordinary heroism during an operation near the A Shau Valley. The unit had to locate and interdict a new road system the NVA had developed which left the Hue Phu Bai area open to an all-out attack supported by enemy armor.

Early in the operation, elements of Project Delta discovered the road extremely well-hidden beneath a stretch of triple canopy jungle leading from the A Shau Valley. They monitored the extensive traffic on this which ranged from motorcycles to Soviet built trucks, tanks, and heavy earth-moving equipment.

Then in a daring daylight raid, elements of Project Delta and the 81st ARVN Airborne Ranger Bn. Thrust deep into enemy territory and ambushed a convoy of eight Russian made cargo trucks.

After the initial blow was dealt, helicopter gunships from Delta's air element, the 281st Assault Helicopter Co., completed the destruction of the vehicles and extracted the raiding force.

Having had their own ambush tactics used against them, the NVA greatly curtailed the use of their new road. Soon after Project Delta's successful operation, an allied operation in the A Shau Valley was launched to complete the denial of this avenue of approach for the enemy."

Bomb damage assessment team inspecting the results

YELLOW BRICK ROAD

By the time we got to Mai Loc, our existence in the area was well known by the NVA. There were radio broadcasts from "Hanoi Hanna" welcoming the 281st to the area. They even had bounties out for our heads!

When working out of An Hoa, we were at the end of a valley. We had to fly down a side valley to get the teams where they belonged. The ridges on each side were lined with fortified enemy bunkers; side by side. The bad guys were there to stay. Occasional green tracers going up through the rotor blades brought you back to reality. In flight school, pilots are trained to have a constant vigil for a landing spot to auto rotate into in case there was an engine failure. The valley floor was an endless sea of dark green trees. The jungle was so thick; the aircraft would never hit the ground if it did go down. This would NOT be a good place for an engine failure. The thoughts of inevitable death from a crash were quickly superseded with the view ahead. There in front of us was the "yellow brick road"...the Ho Chi Minh trail...no man's land and we were going right to it! The Delta guys had no fear. They didn't have to. As a good supporter for them, I had enough fear for them and every member off the mission! Suddenly I heard "24 you're clear to go"... "24 roger," and down we went. The procedure was simple; a high overhead approach. You bottomed the pitch but kept the torque at five pounds to avoid a flame out...kick the aircraft out of trim and in one 270 degree turn drop to the trees falling like a rock. It was a controlled crash. As you approached the trees you would pull in power...flare and terminate right over your spot. The guys could rappel and disappear into the jungle and we would return to the flight above.

Chief Warrant Officer Brian Paine
Bandit 24

The Ho Chi Minh Trail aka the yellow brick road

NEW GUY PILOT

I was a regular, checked out, new guy ready to fly. Two incidents, in particular, have stayed in my memory. On the 17th of November 1968, I reported to the flight line for a flight with Warrant Officer Norm Kaufman. I was expecting the worst. Here was this short, round, little guy who had been here forever, and he was frowning. "I had better be on my best behavior," I said to myself, but it was an uneventful flight up to An Khe and back. I didn't know why we went there, but I remember reading about An Khe back in the States, and at any moment, I was half expecting to get shot at. Norm, "Fat Albert" to his friends, was actually not only fun to fly with, but even a quiet, pleasant guy. It was as plain as the dumb-as-a-rock look on my face that this guy knew everything. However, I could maybe successfully start the aircraft two out of three attempts. He told me stories to put me at ease. He even let me land once or twice. In the following weeks, I would get to fly with Norm only a few more times, as he was short, as in going home in a short time, but I got to fly to that hill across the rice paddies from our hooch and out to Hon Tre Island.

The other incident that I recall vividly occurred with Warrant Officer Paul Morsen, who must have called me a new guy about 249 times. We were detailed to transport a body. It was a Vietnamese body, and he must have been important because there were two Vietnamese field grade officers escorting his body, which was in a simple wooden box. The body was ripe. He must have been dead for a while because he stunk to high heaven. I had put my head out the window to escape the smell when Paul told me to fly. I immediately took the new guy liberty to get the wind going from my window to the left, so I could breathe. Morsen immediately did the same on the opposite pedal, and we played pedal tag for a minute or two until I glanced back and saw that the crew chief was gagging. Apparently one of the officers had barfed out the door, but it never made it out; instead, it splattered the crew chief full frontal. That started a chain reaction, and soon everyone in the back of the aircraft was barfing everywhere. I had my head out the window again, and we two pilots managed to get the mission accomplished without barfing too. I remember when we offloaded the non-speaking passenger and his escorts; it was probably another hour before the ship began to even remotely smell close to normal.

Welcome to Vietnam.

Warrant Officer Jeff Murray,
New Guy Pilot

Jeff Murray sitting on the throne with a smile

BAD VIBRATIONS BUT A GOOD ENGINE

I arrived in Vietnam November 1968. Someone noticed on my records that I had been to maintenance and test pilot school. It was then decided that I would have temporary duty orders assigning me to go visit several units throughout the country to see how they were performing maintenance. Consequently, before going to the 281st Assault Helicopter Company at Nha Trang, I spent a few weeks flying, looking, checking and listening to the maintenance people of other aviation units.

For the most part, I was not impressed with the other units' maintenance programs. When I returned to home base, it did not take me long to realize that the 281st had the best team in country. I thought that it would be in the best interest of the other units for them to come see our maintenance program. Our men were maintaining better than 80 percent availability, which is unheard of in a war zone.

In order to keep all the helicopters checked out and ready for early morning missions, I logged many flight hours at night. The men and I did not quit until everything was ready and in good shape; even if it took all night, we stayed and worked. The crew chief was there also. There was no way he would leave his sick ship; of course, it was "his" helicopter.

One night we were changing blades on one of the gunships, a UH-1C. The helicopter had been out somewhere and received a few bullet holes in its blades. We had a "blade" guy who was the best. I think he was a specialist five. I do not remember his name, but he was from South St. Louis. As we worked throughout the night, we talked about all the great pasta places we knew. He was just a kid and really missed his girlfriend back home. I say kid because he was probably 19, and I was all of 25. We got the shot up blades changed. The run up and preflight test results were all in the green. As always, I asked the kid if he wanted to ride along on the test flight. I called Nha Trang tower and received clearance for the main runway departure, as the Special Forces men were firing mortars. It was about 3:00 AM.

Just after liftoff all hell broke loose. We were almost bounced out of our seats; it was a better ride than one at Six Flags. I declared an emergency and aborted the flight, getting the bird (helicopter) stopped at the end of the runway. The air force was pissed off because the tower woke up the crash trucks, and a couple of their big birds had to hold until we got off the runway. All this time, the kid just sat there in the other seat. He knew what was wrong. After we got the ship back to our maintenance area, we made the necessary repairs, fixed the problem and finished the test flight. The helicopter was good to go.

We also had an outstanding engine guy on our team. His name was Specialist Five Budlong. We had received a radio call of a bird down about five miles from our area of operations. Bobbie Stanfill and I and our recovery team boarded the helicopter with the equipment to rig for a sling load. With the team on board, we flew out and found the ship in this beautiful meadow, with trees all around the edge. It was a perfect place for a forced landing. We had been in the meadow for about fifteen minutes when we noticed the trees were beginning to move, which gave us bad feelings. We wondered if we were about to be surrounded by an enemy force, but to our delight an infantry captain came out of the woods and said, "We are on an operation and will provide security while you rig the downed helicopter." Specialist Budlong started checking for the problem, but after a thorough inspection, he could not find anything wrong. We did a run up and ground tests. Everything was in the green and looked good. Specialist Budlong said he felt so good about it he would ride back with me. So I flew the ship back to Nha Trang with Specialist Budlong in the left seat while Bobbie and the rigging crew followed close behind in the recovery helicopter. They were all set to help us if needed. We made it back to Nha Trang without a problem. This time we pissed off the CH-47 guys because they were in route for a sling load when we canceled their mission. Specialist Don Budlong was the greatest. Over the years I have often wondered about professionals like him and all the other team members who gave their best to keep our ships flying safely. They were the best of the best, and I will drink to that!

Captain Jim "MOM" Torbert

The year of 1968 was the bloodiest year in Vietnam. There were 14,589 American Combat deaths.

1969

On January 20, 1969 Richard Nixon took the oath of office for president.

RECONDO SCHOOL PATROL

We were part of the 5th Special Forces Recondo School in Nha Trang, Vietnam. We had broken from our night logger at daybreak on Tuesday, January 21, 1969. We had a lot of area to recon and wanted to be at the midpoint before 1300 hours. I remember the thickness of the brush and the lack of visibility, always a concern for a five-man recon patrol! I was the student team leader, answering to Staff Sergeant Hines, our Special Forces Recondo instructor. Navigating in triple canopy was always a challenge. It was late morning when Sergeant Hines told me to get an aerial fix. There was a USAF A-1 Sky Raider overhead, and it would provide an excellent chance to pinpoint our location.

As I initiated communication with the pilot, my fellow student Marine Lance Corporal Tommy Teague spotted a North Vietnamese Army soldier and fired off a few rounds in his direction. We immediately deployed after the wounded NVA soldier and found him 20 to 30 meters down a ridge line, so badly wounded he died within minutes. I remember his uniform looked new, he appeared to be young, and we didn't find his weapon. Hines assumed control of the patrol and requested an immediate extraction. We were bringing the NVA soldier's body back for analysis because a combat unit's health and disposition can be understood via an autopsy. Hines secured the azimuth (coordinates) to the landing zone, and we proceeded in that direction. Lance Corporal Teague took the point; I was second; one team member carried the body; another team member covered the trees, and Sergeant Hines brought up the rear. We had only traveled a short distance when we were engaged by machine gun and small arms fire. Teague and I were pinned down, but the other team members were able to get to cover. Teague was seriously wounded in the fire fight. Each time we tried to return fire the NVA scattered our position with machine gun fire. Teague and I could do nothing to improve our situation. Although it seemed like hours, the 281st gunships were on our location within minutes. The suppressing fire they provided was a life saver; it was close-in and constant. Sergeant Hines yelled to us, "Once the fire stops, make a run for cover!" I grabbed Teague's weapon and carried him to the team's location. At this point we didn't think we had a chance of staying alive because the NVA was everywhere. When we arrived at the extraction point, it was evident that a chopper couldn't land at the location. We watched as two Hueys turned back from intense fire from the enemy. The third, a USAF helicopter (Husky) succeeded in lifting Teague out with a winch. The four of us set up perimeter defense, awaiting another extraction attempt by the choppers. The NVA were on three sides of our position and searching for us in the under-brush. Ten to fifteen minutes went by before we heard the sound of chopper blades.

Hines popped smoke, and we could see the McGuire Rig working its way through the canopy.

Three of us strapped in and were lifted out. Hines followed on the next drop. Enemy fire continued as we lifted out.

One of the 281st choppers had Staff Sergeant Gies, a Special Forces medic, on board. He had volunteered to assist in the recovery of our team. He was wounded twice during the extraction attempt and died later that afternoon. He was to have met his wife the next day for an R & R in Hawaii. Above all others, this mission stays with me every day. Men risked their lives and Staff Sergeant Gies sacrificed his life so we could live.

U.S. Air Force Husky

First Lieutenant Bob Krajnak,
Recondo Student number 1821

THE EXTRACTION

On the 21st of January, 1969, we were on standby. We had a few Recondo teams in the woods outside the compound close to a half mile away. We got a call for an extraction involving one wounded soldier. We ran to the aircraft, got a briefing, and Staff Sergeant Marvin Gies, a medic, hopped in back as the recovery sergeant. We had heard he was leaving for Hawaii the next morning, and his wife was there waiting for him. We took off, got to altitude and contacted the team. They popped smoke, gave us a direction from the smoke, and we dropped down to get them. We eventually slowed down and hovered over the dense trees as Sergeant Gies directed our movements. "Stop!" he said. "They're right below us."

Our home in Nha Trang was right beside the 05 runway which we used for landings and takeoffs. Due west of the end of the runway was the mountain range called Grand Summit which included a narrow valley. We named that valley "Death Valley" and always flew around it and never through it. Sergeant Hines picked this valley for one of his Recondo training missions and the story is told above and below. It is this mission where

Murray earned the title of "magnet ass."

We stopped. I was looking back at him as we maintained the hover when all of a sudden, all hell broke loose. At least seven rounds came up through the bottom of the helicopter. From his prone position on the floor, Sergeant Gies tried to sit up. We saw a gaping hole in his neck and blood spurting everywhere. Specialist Four Alan Johnson was the gunner; he was new, but he immediately went to Sergeant Gies's aid by applying pressure to the wound. I told the aircraft commander that we had to go. He asked why. Having been looking forward, he had no idea that we had been hit. I quickly explained, and we zipped out of there in a hurry. We immediately called Nha Trang tower to tell them, not ask, that we were overflying their runway with a casualty, would land at the hospital pad, and needed them to clear the traffic for us. We had Gies on the pad within three or four minutes. Besides the hole in his jugular vein, he also had one in his chest. Even though Johnson had kept the pressure on the entire time, Sergeant Gies did not survive the night. Either wound could have been the fatal one. We took our helicopter back to the 281st area, picked up aircraft 715, and keeping our same crew, returned to the area of operations. In the interim, another aircraft had been shot out of the same hole, and an Air Force Husky with a hoist had extracted the most seriously wounded of the Recondo team. It was our turn to go back down again. I distinctly remember hovering over the pick-up zone because the canopy was too dense to get through. I watched Captain Bain Black of Wolf Pack fly his gunship straight at us, spewing 7.62 rounds by the hundreds, interspersed with an occasional rocket. The fire was so close that a piece of shrapnel came in from somewhere and ripped a hole in my nomex, right at my knee. We hoisted the first bunch out and landed back at our area. The second bird did the same, and that ended the mission. The second group included Sergeant Hines, who came to each crew member and shook our hands. For the most part the mission was considered successful. However, the loss of Sergeant Gies and the fact that his wife would receive notification of his death while awaiting him in a paradise of a vacation spot reminded us that war is hell.

Jeff Murray
Warrant Officer

****

Many years later I had an opportunity to speak with Sergeant Hines' wife. I told her we had done nothing extraordinary and if anyone epitomized Special Forces to me, it was Sergeant Hines. That mission also cemented Alan Johnson in my mind as a real soldier, for even though he was new, he performed coolly and calmly under fire and did not hesitate to return for the second attempt at extraction. I left for Wolf Pack shortly thereafter, but on future Delta missions if the Bandits happened to be there, I made it a point to look him up and say a few words. I also put Alan in a for a V Device on his Air Medal, but I have no way of knowing if he ever got it because Alan was killed in action while still serving in Vietnam. After I got back home, I received the same medal. I miss that guy to this day.

Major Jeff Murray,
U.S. Army Retired

On 17 February 1969, Major Ellie E. "Earl" Lynn assumed command of the company.

Recon team ready for extraction

THE TABLE WAS TURNED

Part One

The Intruders of the 281st Assault Helicopter Company were well known for their rescue skills and were often called on for assistance when a unit or team was in trouble. On 18 February 1969, the tables were turned and the United States Air Force came to our rescue. At midday, a Long Range Recon Patrol team from the 4th Infantry Division reported that they were in contact with a large North Vietnamese Army force and were in serious danger of being killed or captured. The 281st mounted a recovery team consisting of troop and gunships and flew to the vicinity of Tuy Hoa to extract them. The crew of the recovery ship consisted of Chief Warrant Officer Victor (Vic) Rose, Aircraft Commander; Warrant Officer Frank Martin, Pilot; Specialist Four Patrick Ronan, Crew Chief; Specialist Four James Norris, Door Gunner; and a Special Forces Sergeant who was on board to handle the recovery gear.

The team on the ground was being chased and was moving as fast as they could through the jungle, which made them difficult to locate from the air. After several attempts to find them, the recovery ship was forced to leave the area for refueling. Upon returning, it flew into the center of the smoke that the team was using to mark their location and was immediately hit by ground fire, which resulted in the aircraft crashing into the jungle.

Specialist Ronan was killed in the crash. Chief Warrant Officer Rose was thrown clear with broken bones in both legs. Specialist Norris and the Special Forces sergeant escaped with no serious injuries, and Warrant Officer Martin was trapped in the wreckage. An Air Force helicopter flying in the vicinity immediately went to the aid of the downed crew by lowering Sergeant Mike Fish, a para-rescue specialist who administered aid to the wounded crew members. The injured and dead crew members were then recovered. However, Warrant Officer Martin was trapped in the wreckage and would require special equipment to free him. Darkness had arrived, and it was determined that Martin would remain in the chopper until daylight when help would be available to free him. Sergeant Fish elected to remain with him overnight. During the night, the LRRP team provided protection for the crew on the ground and crews from the 281st flew cover over the crash site. At daylight, the USAF crew returned to the site and under heavy fire inserted a recovery team and equipment to free Warrant Officer Martin. By early morning, he and the team were recovered.

Sergeant Fish and the pilot of the USAF helicopter were decorated for their actions. Chief Warrant Officer Rose recovered to return to flight status and complete his career as an army aviator. Specialist Fourth Class Ronan's death is remembered on the Vietnam Veterans Memorial Wall in DC and at the website of the 281st. (281st.com)

On 18 February 1969, Sergeant Patrick Joseph Ronan died in a helicopter crash while on a rescue mission.

Part Two

Leaving the team, the air force para-rescue specialist and Frank unprotected, was not a possibility. Jim Carey, aircraft commander; Dean Roesner, crew chief; our door gunner whose name I have forgotten; and me as co-pilot, remained on location. The weather was turning bad, clouds were rolling in, darkness and almost zero visibility made staying on target almost impossible. The extraction equipment had malfunctioned. The long flight time to and from refueling made it even worse. We had made multiple sorties to Phu Hep for hot refueling and re-arming. I will never forget conversing with the team leader, who spoke in a hushed voice because the enemy was so close. In the background, I could hear Frank repeatedly call out, "Get me the &%#@ of here. I'm soaked in JP4." His demand was followed by other choice expletives.

As darkness came, we could see more clouds coming over the mountains. We stayed in the area to provide radio relay and some extra firepower. An Air Force C-47 gunship arrived on scene and took over with some awesome fire power and eventually dropped some flares. We came very close to adding to the already serious problem. The zero visibility was getting to us.

Carey was flying and developed vertigo. He turned the controls over to me. I reverted to basic instruments and attempted to keep us right side up. I was rapidly developing vertigo also. Our crew chief, Dean Roesner, heard our conversations over his head set and knew we only had seconds to live before we rolled over and crashed. He released his seat belt and with his monkey strap on, stepped out onto the gun mount. Within seconds, he got back on his mike and reported that he saw stars at our 10 o'clock high through a hole in the clouds. Carey composed himself, saw the stars, took over the controls and flew up through the hole. Without our Crew Chief Dean Roesner's quick thinking and his actions, we would not have made it back. We returned to Phu Hep and shut down. We had been so lucky.

The reality is that the sequence of events happened in just seconds. In the final analysis, recovering situation awareness, teamwork and training kept us alive.

First Lieutenant David Dosker,

SWEATING BULLETS

On 14 March 1969, Warrant Officer Jerry Badley and I received a mission to fly from Nha Trang to Gia Nghia. The mission was to deliver a load of M-16 rifles for the ARVN camp at Gia Nghia. Gia Nghia was way out west near the Cambodian Border. The weather was lousy. We had to leave Nha Trang and fly north to Ninh Hoa and through the Duc My Pass to Ban Me Thuot. As I said, the weather was lousy with clouds almost down to the ground. So we elected to fly low level from Ninh Hoa past Duc Lap along highway QL 14, which was roughly parallel to the Cambodian border until it turned inland to Gia Nghia.

As we flew along at low level, dodging the trees and hoping that the VC would not shoot us down, the gunner came on the intercom and said, "You'll never guess what just happened." So, I asked him "What?" Then he said, "The cargo door just fell off." He did not have the door pinned back which was the Standard Operating Procedure.

We continued to discuss this for about a minute before we had to dodge a very tall tree. This maneuver forced me to climb into the fog and turn back to the east away from Cambodia and started a 500 foot-per-minute climb. We ran into the cloud bank at about 2000 feet above sea level. As we were climbing, I tried to tune in the Non-Directional Beacon at Ban Me Thuot but there was no signal. We made a call on 243.0 Megahertz, the Guard Channel but no one responded. We finally broke out of the clouds at about 9000 feet. We were sweating bullets the whole time because the mountainous area of Dalat was roughly east of where we went into the clouds.

After we broke out, we turned to the north and headed back to Ban Me Thuot. The cloud deck was a solid under cast until we found a "sucker hole." We could see green jungle through the hole in the clouds, so I made a rapid spiraling descent through the hole and we found our way back to Ban Me Thuot. We refueled the aircraft and inspected the UH-1H, and thankfully there was no damage to any part of the helicopter except the missing right rear cargo door.

We waited for the clouds to clear and then flew down to Gia Nghia at a safe altitude. We delivered the weapons and eventually made our way back to Nha Trang.

The aircraft tail number was 66-17110. Unfortunately, I did not write the name of the crew chief and gunner in my log book. I would sure like to know who they were.

Warrant Officer Dennis Crowe

AGENT ORANGE

From the beginning of operation "Ranch Hand" in 1962, Agent Orange was, and continues to be, a plague on the lives of the American soldiers that served in the Vietnam War and perhaps a greater plague to the civilian and military populations of both South and North Vietnam. The lasting effects of the chemical and its ability to be passed on to succeeding generations will affect millions for years to come.

The involvement of the 281st with Agent Orange came in the form of helicopter spraying equipment, which was mounted in the cargo compartment of the helicopters. The crews of the 281st mounted the equipment, loaded the chemical and disbursed it from the air onto selected targets. From a military viewpoint, the results were excellent, in that the areas sprayed were completely defoliated, so the ground was visible from the air. Unfortunately, little was known or passed on as to what effect it would have on those who came into contact with it. In the air the helicopter blades would suck up the spray, which resulted in the chemical being sucked into the interior of the aircraft, saturating the crew and the aircraft's exterior. On the ground, information concerning the danger the chemical presented in its handling were simply not provided. Other than a field shower, there was no detoxification equipment available, nor did anyone realize it was necessary. Oddly enough, a crew chief mentioned the crews had discovered Agent Orange was excellent for keeping the Plexiglass on the helicopters "sparkling" clean. Imagine this toxic chemical being sprayed right next to their faces! In September of 1996 President Clinton signed a bill which ordered the Veterans Administration to treat all Vietnam Veterans as though they were exposed to Agent Orange without regard to their duty station. This has been the rule for several years; however, it does little to treat the adverse effects on so many of our veterans and their families.

Allan Johnson, Mike Whisenant and Brian Paine with rigged "H" model

THE JUNK YARD

I completed my flight school and maintenance training and earned my MOS as a maintenance officer. The next stop was in Vietnam to work in some unknown unit as their maintenance officer. The Army had its procedure for assigning personnel so I got in line. I made it to the 10th Combat Aviation Battalion which had several aviation companies under its command. After what seemed an eternity, I was told I was assigned to the 281st Assault Helicopter Company. At last, I had a duty assignment and I could go to work. I was told to gather my gear and report to operations for a flight to Nha Trang. Full of enthusiasm, I gathered up my things and went out to catch my ride. Although you were assigned a flight there was no certainty when it would arrive. I just hung out and waited. While waiting, I walked around a bit and checked out the area. Off in the distance I saw a junk pile of helicopters damaged beyond repair. Being a maintenance officer, my curiosity was aroused and I walked over to look at that pile. When I got close enough to inspect it I noticed all the doors had 281 painted on them! My God, what have I gotten into? What kind of pilots did they have in that company? It didn't take me long to learn exactly what that company was about and the high quality of pilots assigned to it. It was a fast education but I learned about the demand and urgency of the mission of the Company and the bravery of the men in it. I was in for some very long days. The crews would bring back their ships broken or leave them in the field for recovery. I spent my tour doing my best to not increase the size of that junk pile.

Captain Walter Pikul,
Maintenance Officer

NAME CHANGE

It was March 1969, and we were in the field at our forward operating base outside the Gia Le Gate of Camp Eagle in support of Project Delta. The Delta tactical operations center (TOC) was located there. I had a busy morning. After lunch I headed to the flight line to test fly an aircraft that the maintenance crew and I had been working on. I noticed the guys in the Delta TOC were enjoying some cold beers. As a matter of fact, from the sounds I heard, most had had more than one. Out on the flight line, I noticed a helicopter on approach to our landing pad. There were three red stars on a panel attached to its side, the rank of a lieutenant general. I sent one of the maintenance crew to the TOC to warn them that a three-star general had just landed and to get rid of the beer and liquor.

I hurried out to meet the general. It was Lieutenant General Richard Stilwell, the CG of the XIV Corps. In an effort to delay him and give the men time to get rid of the beer and liquor, which I assumed he would not appreciate, I saluted and said, "Sir, I'm Captain Pikul. Can I be of assistance, Sir?" My last name has three pronunciations: Pickle, Piekul and Pikool. Pickle is the pronunciation most commonly used in the New York area where I grew up, and that was the pronunciation I had always used. The general's eyes widened. He loudly asked, "How the hell did you pronounce that name?" I responded by again pronouncing my name as Pickle. This time he yelled. "There are no #@% pickles in the XIV Corps. That name is pronounced Piekul." I had never been yelled at by a three-star general before. Because I had a wife and child and needed my job, I responded, "Yes Sir." The general then asked, "Piekul, do you have a job to do?" I replied that I was getting ready to test fly an aircraft. He forcefully said, "Well, get back to your job, and get the hell out of my way." That is exactly what I did. What the general didn't know was the four minutes he had spent correcting the pronunciation of my last name was just enough time for the personnel at the TOC to stash the beer and liquor.

In late 1975 I crossed paths with General Stilwell again. This time he had four stars on his shoulders. I saluted him and pronounced my name "Piekul" (not Pickle) as he had commanded me that day in Vietnam. Even though my last name is spelled Pikul, I have pronounced it "Piekul" ever since my first encounter with the general in March 1969.

Lieutenant Colonel Walter Pikul,
U.S. Army, Retired

WOLF PACK AND DELTA

March 1969 rolled around, and I was evidently headed for Wolf Pack. I didn't really want to go. It was an unknown. I didn't know the guys. However, that did not matter. I reported for duty as ordered. Little did I know I was trained to be here. I got my check flight done right away, flying with the unit Instructor Pilot First Lieutenant Esser, and promptly began flying a few missions. We covered a convoy, a Medevac, spent the night at Phang Rang and had an actual fire mission where I promptly toggled the wrong switch and jammed the mini guns, but I got better. We got mortared at Phan Rang and scrambled aloft, flying under the searchlight of an Air Force C-130 with some huge mini-guns. When they fired, everything lit up. We covered a sniffer mission and destroyed a tree house, not my last tree house encounter, but we fired it up. We also chased some bad guys under the direction of an infantry unit who reported blood trails in the vicinity of where we fired. Evidently these guns work.

Shot down

On 29 March we deployed to Phu Bai, a trip made a bit exciting when Captain Buck Sorem's Huey lost an engine. He put it down in the only patch of level ground for miles, but it was highly inaccessible.

That was my first Delta mission, and I soon discovered it was perhaps the most extreme flying in the country. We made a high level visual recon; the ground was all trees and underbrush with this really nice road going right through the middle of everything. The Yellow Brick Road we named it. We spotted what appeared to be a big, bush-covered garage-sized door, reported it, and behold a few days later a team opened it and discovered a road grader inside.

The weather was always dicey. We lost an entire team when we could not get to their location because of severe fog and rain. Listening to the team asking for help and not being able to respond has bothered me to this day. Perhaps the most eerie thing was when we flew down the road and happened upon a Huey sitting in the trees, identified by its tail number and a 1st Cavalry patch on the tail. The windows were broken out. We reported it back, and a team was sent to investigate. I recall it being a bird that was lost almost a year before with no clue as to the crew's whereabouts. I took a picture, but a month later all my pictures were lost, with just about everything else I owned, when my footlocker fell off the truck on the convoy from one Delta to another.

I usually flew with Rick Galer. He was a strong individual with his own opinions, and most other opinions didn't count. We got off to a bad start, but I guess I grew on him because I kept flying with him, and he actually got friendly after a few missions. It was really hairy in the A Shau Valley. The worst day was when we had three extractions, all of them hot, and for the last one we were almost completely out of ammo.

We identified one team by flying over the one guy who was able to help, a Road Runner lying on his back with the proper panel displayed across his chest. The Delta teams carried a few panels, each side having a different color, and they had to display the proper color to get picked up if we had recognition problems. Recognition was a big problem with Road Runners because they were indigenous and wore enemy uniforms. After we marked this guy, another Wolf Pack ship decided it had found another team, and was going to mark the spot. Galer told the crew not to, and being the Fire Team Lead he had the authority. However, rank prevailed, and down to make the mark went a gunship. It hit a tree bank at about 100 knots and came out the other side at about 10 knots. We spent a good bit of precious time extracting them. Thankfully, no one was killed, but we lost a Charlie Model gunship.

On one of the extractions, we were receiving fairly heavy fire and Galer flew right over the source while I was piling mini-gun rounds into that position as fast as my fingers would let me fire. We got the team out, scooted maybe a half mile away and helped two more Bandits extract a team under fire. We placed our aircraft up the slope from the LZ (landing zone) and fired nothing because we were completely out of ammo. That made us a very noisy blocking dummy. As we climbed out of the valley to head home, the crew chief, who must have been Daryl Evangelho, because I was flying 004 that day, leaned up and said, "Hey, Mr. Murray, look at your seat." I had taken a few rounds under my seat. A few had hit the seat belt retractor and climbed up the belt, notching the belt guide on the top of my seat and exiting out the greenhouse. And I knew nothing. I sure hope I got that sorry shooter. If he had been smart enough to lead us a bit, I would not be here to tell the story.

On April 16, 1969, we tried a Vietnamese Ranger infiltration and had to get some help from the 101st Airborne. They didn't take too kindly to our direction. The lead ship was piloted by their platoon leader and a brand new warrant officer. When they approached the LZ Rick Galer had picked for them, the lead ship came to a hover and the pilot made a radio call that the LZ was completely unsatisfactory and he was going to find a better one. He went down the hill to what he thought was a good place, made an approach and started hovering around. Galer was literally apoplectic, yelling over the FM radio, "Set that aircraft down!" We heard the reply "in a minute" followed immediately by the sounds of enemy fire. The blasts went right into the front of the Huey. The warrant officer was killed immediately; the platoon leader was shot in the leg and had no pedal control. The bird made a few circles and crashed on its side, prompting the Rangers inside to exit stage left. That took us a while to clean up, and it took a lot of "Jim Beam" to calm Mr. Galer down as well. All in all, a sad day made all the sadder by the complete incompetence of the borrowed platoon leader.

We had a few more missions, including the one where Warrant Officer Capo took a round right through his jaw. The flying in the A Shau Valley, as I said, was extremely intense. The Delta folks I met were way more professional than I ever imagined soldiers could be. Our aircrews were equally dedicated to flying successful Delta missions. I saw another side of the guys I knew back in Nha Trang, a good side, a side that knew what to do, how to do it, and refused to give anything less than their absolute best. Wolf Pack was one good group, and I was glad to be a part of it.

Warrant Officer Jeff Murray,
(No longer a new guy)

In April 1969, U.S. Military strength peaked in Vietnam at 543,400.

MY FIRST IN COUNTRY CHECK RIDE

I reported to the Replacement Battalion at Cam Ranh Bay on 5 May 69 along with Warrant Officer Ron Lesonik. Ron and I had been in flight school together, class number 69-5 and were already good buddies. When we arrived in country, we were taken to the center where our arrival was processed. We were assigned to the 17th Aviation Group and told that our orders would be in later. We sat around all day and finally were told that we would be assigned to the 10th Combat Aviation Brigade. We hitched a ride over there and signed in. We sat around for a while, were eventually informed that they did not know which company we would be assigned to and were told to wait for orders. We finally found the Officers Club and proceeded to indulge a little. We wound up spending the night at Dong Ba Thin, where we experienced our first mortar attack.

We went back to the club the next day and sat around with some guys who were going back home. We listened to their war stories. We still had no orders. The guys were from the 281st Helicopter Company. We liked what we heard about the Special Forces Teams and Delta Project. We went down to battalion headquarters and told the personnel clerk that we wanted to go to the 281st. He kind of laughed a little and went over and talked to a major. I think he was the officer in charge. He came over and asked if we were sure about our requests. He tried to discourage us, but we had our minds made up. Finally, the major told us we had been assigned to the 281st, and they would pick us up at the battalion helipad.

Now we were fired up. Thinking that we would be picked up by a Huey, we moved all of our stuff down to the helipad and waited for the helicopter. Several Hueys came in and out during the time we waited. A couple of hours later a first sergeant drove up in a 3/4 ton truck and asked if we were going to the 281st. He told us to throw our stuff in the truck and get in. Talk about culture shock! We were aviators; we were supposed to ride in aircraft, not trucks. The trip from Dong Ba Thin to Nha Trang was actually uneventful, but we were scared to death. I thought, "Here I am, without doubt the best helicopter pilot in the army, and I am riding in a darn 3/4 ton army truck with no weapons." We drove through what I figured was Indian Country. When we arrived in Nha Trang, we found that most of the unit was at An Hoa with Project Delta. It took a couple of more days to get signed in, settled in and draw our basic issue. They gave us a .38 caliber pistol. I said, "What about a .45 caliber?" The weapons guy said they were not issuing .45s to the new pilots. He also gave each of us five bullets. I could not believe it.

We were treated like long-lost cousins by the other aviators. They said they had not had any new replacements for a long time and were short of pilots. Because of the shortage of pilots and the fact that half the Company was on Delta, it took us a while to get our in-country check rides. My buddy, Ron Lesonik, got checked out by someone from the 17th Group and did fine. The 281st instructor pilot (IP) was at An Hoa, so they got a guy from the 201st to check me out. I had a problem. The 201st Aviation Company guy was a jerk.

We went down to Buffalo Flats close to Ninh Hoa to finish the check ride. He insisted on zero-ground run autorotation. I told him that they were not teaching zero-ground run anymore due to all the helicopters that got rolled into balls. That made him mad. He said that I would do them his way or bust the ride. Because I was a recent graduate of flight school, I was still a brand-new warrant officer and still had the warrant officer candidate mentality. I was easily intimidated.

We did one more auto, and I slid about a skid length. This really made the guy mad! He said he wanted zero-ground run. I said, "Yes, sir!" He was a chief warrant officer, expecting an immediate response. We came back around. I sat up and entered, started my deceleration and he went wild. He said, "I want a flare!" He reached over and slapped the cyclic back into my crotch. We were in a D model, and you can guess what happened. With the high-density altitude, we started to fall. I tried to level off, but by then my rate of descent was really building. The tail stinger hit the ground and collapsed, causing the tail rotor blade to contact the ground. It came off. I saw it fly through the air and land in front of us. The aircraft bounced, hit hard again on the tail and then started spinning. I followed the spin with the cyclic. I knew if I powered up, it would only make things worse, so I rode it down. We hit on the right side and slid to a stop with the nose pointing about 45 degrees to the right. The main rotor almost touched the ground at one point. Finally it was over. We came to rest skids down. The IP never touched the controls after the initial slap. I figured that I was in deep do-do. Someone from the 48th helicopter company came out and got us. We were later picked up by a 281st ship and taken to Nha Trang. The aircraft had some major damage.

Here I am; a brand new guy who crashed on his first in-country check ride. I got some looks that afternoon. I told my story to Major Lynn, the company commander. He was pissed, not at me, but at the 201st guy. I never heard anything else about the incident. I took another ride the next week and did well. I was with a 281st guy this time. I can't remember his last name, but I think his first name was Fred. He was a former SF type. He had been around for a while and was really great to me. It could have been either Fred Sherrill or Fred Funk. As you can imagine, my self-esteem was kind of low. After that first flight, I never looked back, and no one ever mentioned the incident again. It was not charged to me and is not on my record.

I started flying as a copilot with different aircraft commanders and got some good training flying with the Recondo School. When the Rat Pack got back from Delta, the Bandits replaced them. I was in the 2nd Platoon then, a Bandit pilot. We arrived at An Hoa in the afternoon. We were given a small informal type brief at the B-52 (Delta) operations tent. We were told they were expecting a ground attack that night, and we were put on red alert. Remembering our five bullets, Warrant Officer Lesonik and I started looking for someone with a .38 to get more bullets. Everyone else had a .45. We finally convinced one of the SF guys that we needed more ammo, and he came up with a case for us. We did get a perimeter probe, but nothing like the yellow horde that they told us to expect.

I flew my first "real" mission the next day. Warrant Officer Brian Paine was the AC. The recon team made their way to the aircraft, checked their equipment, walked away from the aircraft and sat down as if waiting for the ride. The crew chief and door gunner were busying themselves with their duties. I must say I was impressed with the crew chief and the door gunner; they were the best and our life savers. By this time I was finished and standing by, waiting for the AC and the team leader. They finally came walking up, and all the team members loaded on the aircraft. I sat down in the right seat and buckled in. I was not really told a lot about what we were going to do or where we were going. It seemed as if I was just along for the ride.

Mr. Paine handed me a map with a course line drawn on it and told me to keep my eyes on the gauges and my finger on the map. Being a new guy and not wanting to make any waves, I kept my mouth shut and sat there watching the instrument panel with the map in my lap. We got the aircraft started and hovered out for takeoff. We did a hover check, checked the go-no-go placard and lifted off. We left An Hoa and climbed to altitude, heading in a westerly direction. Being a dutiful young Peter Pilot, I immediately found us on the map and began to track our ground path. Mr. Paine said very little. There was a slight tenseness in the air. After several minutes of flight on the westerly heading, I noticed that we were heading toward the Laotian Border. I started to recall my flight school training in calculating times and distances and suddenly realized that we would be in Laos in about five minutes if we continued on that heading. I finally said, "Sir, we will be in Laos in three to four minutes if we stay on this heading." Mr. Paine stared at me for what seemed like an eternity and said, "No kidding, new guy; just keep your finger on the map and watch the gauges."

Still having the sting of the tactical officer's wrath from flight school in my mind, I did as I was told. We went into an LZ, if you can call it that. It was not like the ones we trained in back at Fort Rucker in flight school. It was a hole in the jungle about 200 feet deep. I was amazed. As we let down into the landing zone I remember how the crew worked together. Again, it was the crew chief and door gunner that we counted on to make the aircraft fit into the hole. I called out the torque, N2 and N1, as we hovered. The team rappelled out of the aircraft as we hovered ten to fifteen feet from the jungle floor. I watched as the team disappeared into the jungle.

As we were pulling up, leaving the LZ, I remember Mr. Paine making a radio call, "Coming out with a bingo," he announced. I had no idea what that meant. All I knew was that I was happy to get the heck out of there and be on the way back to the forward operations base. On the way back, we were flying over a small village or hamlet when some guy stepped out of a hut and started shooting at us. I could see the guy firing, and I could see the green tracers coming right at me. The Wolf Pack gunships rolled in on the village, and it was a smoking hole in about ten minutes. We circled around at fairly low altitude after the Wolf Pack did their work and let the door gunners work out.

We stayed at An Hoa for a while longer and eventually rotated back to Nha Trang. By this time I was happy to say that I was not a new guy anymore.

Warrant Officer Bob Mitchell,
Peter Pilot

A TELEPHONE POLE!

Our mission as pilot and crew was to insert recon teams and extract them after they completed their mission, which usually took six days. When we got a call for an early extraction, we knew the team had had an altercation with some bad guys who, as a result, were pissed off. An early call was a guarantee of an exciting flight. I got the early call. A recon team we had inserted was in trouble and needed out. By the time we got on station, the forward air controller had their location pin pointed and had passed it on to the command and control helicopter (C&C.) As I looked down at the jungle, all I saw was a sea of green. There wasn't even the proverbial "big green tree" to use as a landmark. We finally agreed on a point I would aim for, and C&C would guide me in from there. I started my high approach at 1,500 feet, and rolling back on power. The theory was simple. As I fell out of the sky, the rest of the flight would continue on and draw the attention of any bad guys in the area. I terminated at a hover about 100 feet over the tree canopy. It was taking

me seven corrections a second to keep the helicopter hovering. At the same time, I was trying to figure out where and when I would find the recon team and how I was going to get them out. I knew the foliage was so dense that the ropes would never hit the ground. I inched forward, and all of a sudden I heard C&C yell, "Stop! You're right above them"! But I saw only green trees below me. They couldn't be messing with me! The next transmission confirmed my fears. Ladder extractions are never easy. C&C called me and said, "Bandit Two Four, this is going to be a ladder extraction. Drop your ladders and lower slowly". I was trying to figure out how a fifteen-foot ladder would work when a 120-foot rope wouldn't. I descended slowly, and as I got closer to the top of the trees, the leaves parted and right below me under my skid was one of the recon guys looking at me, grinning ear to ear. He and the rest of the team were sitting on top of the tallest concrete telephone pole I had ever seen in my life! That sucker was 100 feet tall! We had similar poles along the perimeter at Nha Trang, but they were only about 60 feet tall. I have often wondered how those poles got there. As I looked down out of my window, these guys looked like cats that had been treed by dogs. They had accomplished their mission and were waiting to be picked up. A couple of explosions on the jungle floor brought me back to the task at hand. Wolf Pack gunships were laying down suppressive fire to keep any bad guys from getting nasty thoughts.

As the guys climbed the ladder hanging over the skid, their weight caused a torque effect which made the helicopter list to the side and drift in that direction. Additionally, as they climbed up the ladder, their extra weight actually pulled the aircraft down and resulted in the need for more power. So what we had was a helicopter that didn't want to stay level while a bunch of guys were pulling it down to the ground. The first concern was to make sure they didn't accomplish this unrecoverable situation and pull us down too much. We could easily be impaled on the telephone pole, like an olive on a toothpick, making for a very bad day. I worked to keep the aircraft level and above the trees while my copilot called out my power. Too much torque could destroy the engine, and we could have a bleed off of rotor speed.

There we sat, hovering out of ground effect using full power. With everyone on board, the only way to get the aircraft flying was a very slow forward motion. I remembered my IP (instructor pilot) and mentor Warrant Officer Norm Kaufman telling me, "Smooth on the controls. You can keep it at a hover if you just don't move the cyclic." Without pulling any more power, I had to get a forward motion of 25 knots and hit translational lift. I moved slowly forward and then began to climb. Fortunately, there was a valley to fly down to gain more and more airspeed, allowing us to climb. Wolf Pack gunships were right behind me with rockets and mini-guns firing to keep the valley clear of bad guys. It was the slowest climb out I had ever made. I finally got to 90 knots and had enough power to join C&C and the flight to head home. I could relax; I had the best crew chief and door gunners ever. I let my copilot take us home. It had been an interesting day with a successful result. |

Warrant Officer Brian Paine,
Aircraft Commander
Bandit 24

THE FOB
(Forward Operating Base)

The entire concept of Delta was to go to the enemy and not wait for them to come to us. Going to them meant remote areas specifically along the Ho Chi Minh Trail along the borders of Vietnam. The enemy used these trails to transport supplies with the efficiency of a colony of ants. The range of the recon teams often exceeded the range of artillery support. Consequently, the support for the teams had to be close enough for quick reaction when the time came. The FOB's were determined by the mission assignments. Phu Bai, An Hoa and Mai Loc were just a few of the locations.

Advance teams were supported by C-130's, truck convoys, and helicopters to

FOB Phu Bai

153

get everything to the location. This seemingly impossible job was completed in a matter of a few days.

One of the most important tasks was to sandbag the tent living quarters, bunkers and all priority locations. Officers and enlisted both worked together to get the job done. The bags were made out of canvas or a woven plastic material. Dust flew everywhere and in the heat and sweat everyone was caked in mud. To insure the task was completed expeditiously, the last thing to be set up was the showers!

Showers, earlier models used an immersion heater for hot water the later models used a 500 gal., black fuel bladder which was solar powered…you had better be at the head of the line!

Home sweet home…note the TV antennae at the Wolf Pack tent

Wolf Pack crew

FOB kitchen

Naturally, with all the hard work, a bunch of young guys can work up a healthy appetite and the Army took good care of the men.

Main Street at FOB Mai Loc before and after monsoon season

Often is the case; location, location, location…Mai Loc created a whole new set of problems for the FOB.

Duty calls even when you are having fun in the field. Delta was running a mission and the team leader had prepped himself and his flight crew for insertion into his AO (area of operation). The LZ seemed to be relatively harmless at the bottom of a steep valley. As the AC brought the aircraft to a hover, all hell broke loose. They were taking fire but this time it was from above. One little bullet hit the left side of the roof and it was in direct line with the co-pilot's left cheek. The round took out his left cheek and teeth and exited the windshield along with his mic. It was not "Lil Al" Capo's lucky day. The AC, Buck Sorem, who was also the platoon leader, "red lined" the aircraft (speed) and flew "Al" to the closest field hospital. Needless to say, the insertion was a failure but things like this went with working for Delta. The first aid administered by the back seaters, the flying by Buck and the doctors at the field hospital all contributed to "Al's" survival. He is alive and well, living in Florida.

The entry hole on the left and the exit holes on the right

LADDER EXTRACTION

The demands of the Delta team leaders were enormous. The LZ's were nearly impossible but if that's where they wanted to go, they got there. Their extraction points were worse. Usually they had made some bad guys mad and were in a run for their lives. A delta team leader later admitted how he picked his extraction points. He ran through the jungle and when he could look up and see blue sky, he was there! It seemed these guys had an affinity for riding McGuire rigs. The flying was so intense, no one in the aircraft had time to look around and take pictures. Additionally these missions were secret and top secret and cameras were not allowed. However, on one mission a gunny crew chief was able to snap one off.

Ladder extraction and Delta team unloading from McGuire rigs (strings) which dangled 120 feet below the helicopter.

VIETNAMESE RANGERS

Procedures often called for the insertion of a company of rangers or more when the recon team found some bad guys who had to be dealt with. As always, the enemy never picked any easy places to hide and inserting the rangers often was as difficult as inserting a recon team. There was never a dull moment with Delta. No multi ship LZ's ever existed and most of the time there was barely enough room for one aircraft. The rangers were put in to do their job and were ready for a ride home. The airlift had to be precisely timed and coordinated. As one ship was loading the next one was on short final for its load.

Extracting a Vietnamese Ranger Company

If the hole ship didn't get out of the way fast enough, the incoming ship was left dangling at a high hover and the probable case of settling with power. Even a good pucker factor would not get the crew out of this dilemma.

The precision needed for this type of flying took continuous practice. Timing, communications, and coordination didn't come easy. Flying to and from locations, returning home from a mission, any time we weren't flying in the trees offered the perfect times to practice. We found ourselves trying to emulate the Blue Angels. Fat chance we could ever compete with them but we gave it one heck of a shot.

TENT MAIDS AND A BUDDHIST CROSS

I remember the hooch maids we had in Nha Trang. For $10.00 a month they washed clothes, shined shoes, cleaned the bathrooms, swept up inside and kept our area clean. In all the time I spent out in the field, though, I can only remember hooch maids on one field operation. It was at An Hoa in May-June 1969. I guess a more accurate term would be "tent maids." I think they were young kids from the local village who did less work for less money.

We had been having a problem with rockets and mortars being sporadically shot at us but had no casualties. It was suspected that they were coming from the local village. One morning my tent maid gave me a gold Buddhist cross on a chain and said, "This so VC no kill you." I wasn't much for wearing jewelry, but figured if she thought it would keep me from being killed by the VC, I had nothing to lose by wearing it.

Later that day in the chow line with Chief Warrant Officer Bobbi Stanfill, I told him about the necklace. I said, "When the rockets come in today, I will be safe because of the cross." I had no sooner finished saying this when the rocket attack started. The two of us ran as fast as we could across the flight field to fox holes for safety. They probably were aiming more at aircraft than people. No injuries and not much damage. However, as we sat in the fox hole, Bobbi looked down and realized that shrapnel had hit his boot and ripped a hole in it. Jokingly I said it hit him and not me because I was wearing my good luck Buddhist cross. He didn't think that was funny and was pissed off that his shoe was no longer wearable.

Shortly after the "all-clear" a Special Forces guy, who apparently had overheard us talking about the cross in the mess tent, came over and wanted to know the name of the tent maid who had given me the cross. He had questions for her. As it turned out, all the tent maids had left the area about 30 minutes before the attack and had returned when it was over. How timely. That was the last day we had a tent maid on that operation.

Specialist Five Don Budlong,
Maintenance
February 68 – February 70

On 6 June 1969, we lost Staff Sergeant Victory Blake Sutton; he was the Bandit Platoon Sergeant.

On 18 June 1969, Private Timothy John Carolan, administrative clerk, died from non-hostile causes while on guard duty.

Delta crew at FOB

Rat Pack crew at FOB

HOW IN THE HELL DID WE DO THAT?

It was the day I believed I was going to die. We were working out of our FOB (Forward Operating Base) at Phu Bai. I had been assigned a team and would be responsible for getting the guys in and out of their recon zone safely. As with most Delta insertions, this one was at last light. The team leader had done a great job selecting the LZ (landing zone). There were no stumps, no trees, or short grass. It was large enough to get into without blade strikes. We were in and out in a matter of seconds. The team was on its way into the jungle, and we were on our way back to the FOB. All we had left to do was stand by and be ready to pick them up when they finished their mission.

Sometime in the early morning we got a message from the FAC (forward air controller), who had been in constant radio contact with the team. I got the dreaded "early phone call." The message was so unbelievable that I thought the other pilots were messing with my mind. While the team was settling in for the night, the men heard some noises. The next morning they discovered the sounds they had heard

159

were from an entire North Vietnamese Army battalion that had set up camp around them. The team wanted to get out ASAP, and it was my job to go get them. The 281st had performed hundreds of extractions and they were never routine. If the team was discovered by the bad guys, we got an immediate call to get them out before they were killed. This time, instead of a few bad guys, we were about to fly into a group of over 1000 of them! The crew and I normally wore 25 pound armored plates called chicken plates on our chests. I wasn't going to take any chances. I put on a flack vest first, then the chicken plate, finishing with another flack vest. I wrapped each leg with two flack vests and covered my forearms with flack vests. I was sitting in an armored seat and wore a ballistic helmet. I decided the only way they could get me was with a lucky shot in my face. When we took off, the aircraft had a significant list to the left!

Whatever Delta people wanted, Delta got. This mission called for some fighter support and extra gunships. By the time we arrived on station, the jet fighters had been there and worked over the area. Chances were good that most of the bad guys had been suppressed. The problem was there was a lot of smoke from exploded ordinance, and the last thing I needed was to go IFR (Instrument Flight Rules) into the landing zone. Things were all set. C&C (control and command) set me up for a straight in approach. At treetop level I couldn't see anything. I was at the mercy of the commander in the command and control helicopter. Two hundred meters out, one hundred meters out, 10 o'clock, slow down. I looked out to my left and saw the ground erupting. Wolf Pack gunships were walking me in with 40mm and rocket fire. I could almost feel the concussion from the explosions. I looked out to my right and saw a Cobra gunship helicopter flying straight at me firing rockets and mini guns. I wasn't sure whose side it was on. The gunner was firing under my skids and underneath my aircraft. There was a war going on out there, and I was right in the middle of it! This was insanity. If the enemy didn't get me, my own gun cover would! As we neared the LZ, the radio chatter exploded. C&C had gotten me to the LZ, and it was time for my crew to take over. The crew chief and door gunner talked me into the LZ, keeping my tail rotor and main rotor clear of the trees. The copilot was light on the controls with me, in case something happened to me, and he called out the instrument readings. The Special Forces belly man directed me over the team, putting me as close to them as I could get. The team leader was talking to the belly man. The gunships were coordinating their fire, and C&C was directing the fire. At any given time there were probably ten conversations going on. We were lucky with the LZ. It was clear enough to get into, and we could get close to the ground, so the team could scramble on board. All I needed was enough power to get us into the air and for the gunships to keep the bad guys down until we got out of Dodge. We had planned the mission well. Knowing the flight time to and from the AO (area of operations) and the estimated time on station, we had calculated that we would only need about 600 pounds of fuel. It worked; we were as light as we could possibly get. As we started our climb out, the world erupted again. The crew chief and door gunner opened up. I didn't know where Wolf Pack got all the ammo, but they were unloading with mini guns, rockets and 40 mm. Their door gunners and crew chiefs were covering us with their M-60s. If any bad guy had raised his head, he would have lost it! I pulled in power, nosed it over and gained airspeed. The red line for airspeed in the Huey was 120 knots, and I made sure I hit it as I low leveled out of the area. I wanted to get as far away as fast as I could. As soon as C&C cleared me for a climb out, I transferred the controls of the aircraft to the co-pilot, sat back in total exhaustion and wondered; "how in the hell did we do that?"

Chief Warrant Officer Brian Paine,
Aircraft Commander
Bandit 24

On 20 July 1969, Astronauts Neal Armstrong and Buzz Aldrin landed on the moon.

On 2 August 1969, Major George W. Little assumed command of the company

The following incident is an example of how quickly things could go bad while flying helicopters in South Vietnam without even engaging the enemy.

ALL IT TAKES IS JUST ONE SECOND

Part One

In August of 1969, I had been in country for ten months and was an AC (aircraft commander) in the 1st Platoon, the Rat Pack. During that month, the Rat Pack was on a mission with the 5th Special Forces Group, detachment B-52, Project Delta. Our FOB (forward operating base) was at Mai Loc in northern I Corps. That area, also known as First Corps, was the most northern section of South Vietnam.

As part of that mission, Delta planned to insert several recon teams in a single day into the mountains along the Laotian border, west of Mai Loc, beyond the abandoned marine fire base at Khe Sanh. North Vietnam and the Ho Chi Minh Trail were only a few miles away. I was assigned to be one of the pilots making the insertions that day.

The LZ (landing zone) selected for my insertion was an old bomb crater on a mountainside in a clearing surrounded by trees. When the day of the insertion arrived, the attempt to put the team off in that crater became the start of a very eventful afternoon. From the air, the LZ looked ideal but later proved to be less so.

There were three teams, I believe, to be inserted that day, and mine was to be the first one in. The operation consisted of a C&C (command and control ship) leading three lift ships, and a fire team from the gunship platoon, the "Wolf Pack," for cover.

SOP (standard operating procedure) on these operations was simple: as the formation flew by the site of the first insertion, the first ship would drop down to the LZ, and the remainder of the flight would continue toward the site of the next insertion. After off-loading the team, the first ship would climb back up and join the formation. Each ship, in turn, would follow the same procedure until all teams had been inserted.

****

We flew west from Mai Loc past Khe Sanh in a loose trail formation to the AO (area of operation). As the LZ came into sight, I circled down to it as planned, but once there realized I would have to land to a low hover rather than to the ground because of the terrain. The team would simply have to step from the skid to the ground, then move to the cover of the surrounding trees. While I hovered, my copilot, Warrant Officer John Korsbeck, along with the crew chief and door gunner, whose names I do not recall, made sure we were clear on all sides from any obstructions. In the few seconds it took the team to off load, the crew called out continuously to me via intercom, "You're clear left, Mr. Baker. You're clear right." There was no sound of any enemy ground fire or anything else out of the ordinary. I could not see the team exiting, but as each man stepped off the skid, I could feel the ship tip just slightly from the shift in weight. As the last man stepped off, and the crew chief said "Okay, they're all out," the ship suddenly began to shake. I remember thinking at the time, "Damn, that last guy must have really jumped hard onto the skid when he stepped off." I hesitated to let the ship settle down, but as I began to climb out, the shaking continued and I realized we had actually developed a heavy vibration. It was obvious something serious had happened. I checked the instruments, saw nothing unusual, and we had no warning lights. I heard nothing to indicate a mechanical problem. I asked John and the crew, "What happened?" Does anybody see anything?" They all reported they could not see anything wrong and did not know what had happened. Upon clearing the treetops, I leveled off and reduced power until I could figure out what was going on. I did not want to put any excess stress on the airframe or rotor system.

I radioed C&C to report our situation. After a brief pause they called back and told me to climb up and rejoin the formation. By this time I had decided that I wasn't climbing anywhere, much less up to altitude to rejoin the formation. There were no emergency procedures presented in flight school and nothing that I had learned while flying in Vietnam that prepared me

Warrant Officer Jim Baker inspecting broken tail rotor

162

for dealing with a sudden severe vibration in flight that had no apparent cause. I wanted to get on the ground as quickly as possible so we could figure out what had happened and decide what to do about it.

I replied to C&C that I intended to stay low and return immediately to Vandegrift Fire Base alone. Vandegrift was a marine fire base located between Khe Sanh and Mai Loc and was surrounded by mountains. In addition to artillery positions, it had an airstrip and a POL (petroleum, oil, and lubricants) point, and was the predetermined refueling point for our operation. I chose to return to Vandegrift since it was the closest secure location in the area. If we couldn't make it there and were forced to land somewhere else, a search operation could easily retrace our route of flight.

We made it to Vandegrift and shut down the aircraft. Almost immediately, a marine came running out to tell us they had been receiving intermittent mortar fire from the surrounding hills, and our ship would make an ideal target. We had no choice, however, and got out to examine the aircraft. We found the cause of our problem. The ship had sustained a hole, three to four inches in diameter, in one side of one of the tail rotor blades. While we were all gathered around the tail rotor trying to figure out what to do next, mortar fire started coming in on us. The marine immediately took off running in the direction from which he had come. The four of us, all aviation related personnel and unfamiliar with combat on the ground, took off after him. We followed him into an underground bunker, an amazingly secure and comfortable structure, with empty ammo boxes lining the walls and electric lights strung around inside. We waited there for a short time with the marine, and when he said it was safe, we went back to the aircraft. Almost immediately, the rest of the flight, having completed the remaining insertions, arrived to refuel. When I saw them coming, I quickly radioed about the mortar fire, but they elected to land anyway. Our company maintenance officer, Captain Jim (MOM) Torbert, was flying C&C that day, got out of his aircraft and came over to look at my tail rotor. We were discussing what had happened when once again the incoming mortar fire started. All the ships began to scramble to get off the ground, and we had to quickly decide what to do about mine. We could either fly it back like it was or leave it and jump into the C&C ship. Leaving my ship there meant it probably would be destroyed on the ground before we could get a recovery ship back for it. Jim said, "I'll fly it back. Will you go with me?" I said okay, and Jim took Korsbeck's seat in my ship while John took his seat in C&C. The crew went with John and rode back with him.

The flight from Vandegrift to the FOB was a very short one. Jim flew, and I don't think either of us spoke the entire time. The vibration was quite heavy, and I, for one, just hoped the aircraft would hold together long enough for us to make it back. It did, barely. We were the last ship in, and Jim made an abbreviated approach at an angle to land directly into what wind there was rather than land into a crosswind. We still had tail rotor control, which precluded the need for a running landing (the procedure for attempting to execute a landing with a tail rotor failure). On short final, at about 50 feet and 30/40 knots, the "chip detector" light, one of the segment panel warning lights on the instrument panel indicating a potential problem with the tail rotor system, came on. I immediately called that out to Jim even though I knew he had also

163

seen it. He replied with excited sarcasm something like, "I guess it is."

We landed to a hover, and Jim turned left and began hovering down the runway. Almost immediately, the whole segment warning light panel completely lit up as other lights came on, and the ship began to nose to the right. Instinctively recognizing complete tail rotor failure, Jim executed a perfect hovering autorotation, and we landed.

We had barely made it. We got out and found the tail rotor hanging by the drive chain from the top of the vertical fin. On a Huey, the tail rotor extends from the 90-degree gearbox, which is welded onto a metal base and mounted on the vertical fin. The vibration caused by the hole in the tail rotor blade was so severe that the base had finally snapped off and left the tail rotor and gearbox hanging. Had that happened on our final approach, there would have been nothing we could have done; we would have crashed and quite possibly not survived. More importantly, however, I'm glad I made the decision coming out of the LZ to not rejoin the flight. Had I done so, and the incident had happened in flight, I'm not sure if we could have survived. As it was, the four of us ended up coming home safely that day. None of us involved were ever able to figure out what caused the tail rotor damage. Something pierced the skin on one side of one of the blades but didn't go through to the other side. It had to be some sort of debris (foreign object damage) blown up by our rotor wash and into the blade. The crew chief and door gunner said they never saw us hit anything, and there was no enemy contact on the ground by the Delta team, so it wasn't hostile fire. One second everything was fine, and in the next second we had a major problem that led to a real exciting afternoon.

Chief Warrant Officer Jim Baker,
Rat Pack 15,
1968 - 1969

Part Two

As was the usual case on the insertion of the Project Delta teams, the senior officer on the flight operation flew the command and control (C&C) helicopter with the Delta command in the rear of the helicopter. I was the senior RLO (Real Live Officer) at Mai Loc, so the C&C responsibility went to me on this mission. With both commanders on the same helicopter, if any decision had to be made, it could be done right there on the spot. As the first team was being put in, I was watching very closely to make sure that everything went as planned before we flew on to the second insertion. I did notice a slight flash, more like just a change of color from dark to light, from the tail section of the helicopter, #460, in the hole as the team was jumping off. I radioed to ask if everything was okay, and Baker responded, "Yes, the team is off, and we are coming out."

Several seconds later I got the call that Baker and his crew wanted to return to Vandergrift immediately to check out the aircraft. I did not like the idea of one aircraft leaving and flying back alone, but knew that Jim Baker had been in country for a long time, was a great pilot, and would know what to do if he needed any additional support. I agreed to his request and said that on the return we had planned on a stop at Vandegrift to refuel. If he needed help, we could assist him at that time.

The other teams were put in without incident and the flight headed back to Mai Loc with the planned stop at Vandegrift for fuel. As we approached Vandegrift I was surprised to see aircraft #460 shut down on the pad. On our approach to the POL area (gas area) we were told that they had been experiencing incoming fire from the Viet Cong and that we might want to fly on to the next available POL location. I radioed back we all needed fuel and we would not stay for long.

As the flight was refueling, I ran across the pad to #460 where Jim and the rest of the crew were looking up at the tail rotor. I got a quick boost and stood up on the tail stinger to get a better view. It was very easy to see that one of the tail rotor blades had a puncture hole about the size of a quarter in the blade. I jumped down and I was trying to make a decision on the best course of action when Vandegrift once again began experiencing incoming rounds. I quickly reasoned there were several courses of action regarding #460: 1) Leave it there and get the crew and everyone else out of there. 2) Radio for a maintenance team to get a new tail rotor blade and have them flown out to Vandegrift to replace the damaged one. 3) Get a maintenance team out with a recovery rigging kit to get #460 ready for a sling load by a Chinook back to Mai Loc or Nha Trang. 4) Try to fly #460 on the short flight back to Mai Loc, even though the flight was over some dangerous mountainous areas.

****

Now, let me tell you a little bit about this decision. Right off I will say that we did not have multiple choice questions like this in flight school. We might have had some study like this in my ROTC classes, but I must have missed that day. The situation was kind of like those in the book about Vietnam, *What Now, Lieutenant?*, by my good friend Bob Babcock. His book deals with having to make split-second decisions. As a sidebar to this decision, I belong to an organization here in Atlanta called the AVVBA, the Atlanta Vietnam Veterans Business Association. We have close to 500 Vietnam Veterans from all services as members. One of my good friends in that organization is a marine who was in Vietnam in 1969 and was stationed at Vandegrift. He does not remember this specific date, but he said they hated it when a helicopter shut down on the pad, as it then became open season target practice for "Charlie" to try to hit the helicopter. He said they would really not have liked it if we had left #460 there for any length of time, certainly not overnight.

A second part of this decision rested on the fact that as well as a maintenance officer, I was also the recovery officer, and I had received training to be a test pilot. Consequently, I had multiple points of view regarding the above options, regardless of my choice. What now, Captain?

****

Broken tail rotor

I quickly jumped back up on the stinger to take another look at the tail rotor, and maybe it was the incoming shells, but suddenly the blade puncture did not look so bad. I said to Jim Baker, "I'll fly it back if you will go with me". Jim agreed; maybe he wasn't as smart as I thought he was. I told the crew and the other pilot, John Korsbeck, to get into the C&C bird and get the hell out of there. John grabbed his flight helmet and ran like hell to the other bird. I knew the crew chief wanted to talk to me about this being his helicopter and he was going to stay with it, regardless.

However, we didn't have time for that conversation. He went very reluctantly to the C&C bird and jumped in as they were pulling pitch and getting out of there.

Jim and I cranked up #460 and took off as the marines waved us good-by with the famous one finger salute. I do not remember the flight back as being real rough. However, remember, I was the unit test pilot and had flown some test flights with pretty bad vibrations. I decided to land on the runway at Mai Loc instead of on the pad, just in case. I still felt like we could land there instead of flying all the way to Quang Tri just to get a real airfield. Jim was with me all the way, calling power, fuel, and finally warning lights. We landed, and I began to hover and clear the runway when the tail rotor gave out. No problem. I did a hovering autorotation and put her down right there. Mission complete, teams inserted, and everyone home safe and sound.

Thanks, Jim, for hanging in there with me. If I had it to do over, I would have made the same decision, but I would have let the crew chief go with us to have the extra set of eyes and ears in the back to keep us straight.

After we returned from Vietnam we all kind of went our different ways. Like most of us, I kind of drifted away, and kept all of these memories buried in the back of my mind. After about 30 years I went looking on the web and found a 281st AHC web site. I looked around on the site, had some memories, and signed the visitor page. Several weeks later my wife told me that she had spent about an hour on the phone with a guy from Montana who said that I had saved his life in Vietnam. He had seen my name as a visitor to the site, and was calling to say "thank you." I asked my wife "Who was it?" She said "John Korsbeck." I said, "I do not know John Korsbeck." She gave me the details of the story which he had told her, and I said, "Oh, yeah, I remember that. I just don't remember John Korsbeck as being the new guy pilot." Well, what a treat to get reunited with John. For many years, I got to enjoy his phone calls (at all hours of the day or night) and his many stories on the web. Thank you, John, you will never be forgotten.

Captain Jim Torbert,
Intruder MOM
Maintenance Officer
1968-1969

WAITING, WONDERING AND WORRYING

I know the author of this book is writing about the men who went to war, their lives as soldiers, their combat, and even their deaths. It is a good thing for our children and grandchildren to know the story of the hardships endured by our men in South Vietnam. I do believe that since the time of the very first conflict or war, the wives waiting back home suffered as much or more, and in a very different way. We have a story too.

I watched as he walked up the ramp and into the airplane. I thought, "What a nice looking guy he is, looking so sharp and proud in his army uniform." My soldier husband was leaving me to go off to war. This was so completely new to me, so foreign and so painful. Yet I was so proud of him. I held our infant son close, watched as the small jet was pushed away from gate number 4, and just stared as it taxied away. He was on the plane sitting in seat number 27C. I was watching and could still feel his closeness as the twin-engine jet left the terminal and slowly made its way to the runway. I could still feel his presence as long as I could see the plane he was in. Then in a matter of minutes, the big jet was on its take off roll. It nosed up, and I watched as it climbed into the clouds and out of sight. I continued to stand there, looking at the clouds. For the first time in our marriage, I felt all alone.

I did not want to be a weeping wife, nor did I want to walk around in a daze feeling sorry for myself. I wanted to be positive, wanted to think positive things. I am not a complainer, but there was an empty feeling inside me. I made a promise to myself that I would overcome that. Besides, I had our son to take care of, to raise, never letting him forget that he had a father and mother who loved him dearly.

Earl was a helicopter crew chief, and I was always impressed that he knew so much about the "Huey," as he called it. He loved his job, loved flying, and I noticed numerous times he referred to the helicopter as HIS gun ship, as if he owned it, as if it belonged to him alone. I interpreted that as pride in his job, and I liked that about him.

I was now on my own, not close to a military base. Fort Polk was a good two hours away. If I needed any help or assistance from the military, I would have to make the four-hour round trip to the Polk and back. I had wonderful loving parents. Earl's parents were there for me also. I was one of the lucky wives, as I had the support most wives did not have. The only thing missing were other military wives. It would have been nice to have their company from time to time but I am not complaining.

Each day the evening news on our television set brought the war right into my living room. In most ways this was not a good thing. On one hand, I wanted to know about each unit, each battle and each location. On the other hand, it was a terrifying thing to see the horrors of war and to be in a constant state of fear that I might see my husband's face on the screen, his body injured or worse.

There were days that I just stood and stared out the window, days that I didn't want to do anything, days of waiting for a letter, worrying and wondering. There were days that I was not hungry, did not want to eat, and days when nothing tasted good when I did eat. Many times I needed to just get out by myself to walk, to sit and think.

All the days were long; the time moved slowly. It had been about six months since he had left me standing there in the small airport. Now it was my turn to go back to the same airport, board a jet plane and fly off on a wonderful and unforgettable trip. I was flying to Hawaii to spend a week, seven days, with the guy whom I loved more than anyone could ever imagine, my husband Earl. His leave had been approved. I was beside myself. I could hardly wait.

I arrived in Hawaii a day prior to his arrival from Vietnam. There were at least a hundred wives waiting for their husbands to arrive. The next morning we were all briefed, lined up and told what bus our guys would be on. Of course, Earl was on the last bus. I waited.

A carpet was laid out so they could make their way down the line of ladies and each find their partner. What a sight it was to watch as couples embraced. But, where was my Earl? If he was on the last bus he must have walked right by me because I had not seen him, for I had looked at each soldier as he made that walk. For about ten seconds I was terrified. Then after everyone had walked to the end of the line, I saw this handsome guy looking back and there he was. My, what a sight to see as we ran to each other and held on for what seemed like a long time. I was the happiest lady in the world. (Here I must say that I had lost a lot of weight and he also had lost weight, but I can't believe that I had not recognized him when he passed by).

We made up for that lost ten seconds over the next seven days. The time with him did me good, and he certainly needed some time away from the war. It was a wonderful time for both of us.

Watching him leave again was the hardest thing for me. Back home again, the waiting continued. I was counting the days until he would come back home. Then one day I saw an army car pull into our driveway. Two men in their dress uniforms got out and came to my front door. I almost fainted. The doorbell rang. I decided not to answer it. It rang again. I finally opened the door. There stood two men with a somber look on their faces, not smiling. I could hardly stand. I knew I could not keep my composure. I was turning into a wreck as they asked for a person who did not live there. I asked them to repeat the name. It was not me they were looking for. I told them who I was, and they apologized and apologized again before they left.

I finally got control of my emotions and was so thankful it was not me they had wanted to see, but I felt weak and so sad for the family they were looking for. The tears came flooding down my face, for I had come so close to hearing the saddest words that a wife could ever hear. It was not fair that these men came to my door by mistake, the wrong door, and had put me through the hardest agony a wife could ever go through. I had to stop thinking about myself, think about the family that they were looking for and the sad news they were about to hear.

From that day on, I got upset if I even saw a taxi driving slowly down the street, or an army car in the neighborhood or a soldier in a dress uniform. I was aware that bad news could be on the way to me or some other military family at any moment. I was waiting, wondering and worrying.

Marking the days off my calendar was a daily chore, as well as being thankful for all the blessings I was receiving. Best of all was a letter from Earl, letting me know what day he would be arriving back home.

Well, this is my story. I am proud to be a military wife, proud of my husband Earl, and proud of my country. Every year since I have wanted to go back to Hawaii to relive those wonderful seven days in paradise!

Darlene Broussard
Wife of Specialist Five Earl Brossard

On 2 September 1969, Ho Chi Minh died at age 79 in Hanoi.

THE GENERAL DIDN'T WANT TO KNOW, SO I DIDN'T TELL HIM!

I don't remember the exact date, but sometime late in October of 1969 enemy activity became so intense throughout the nights at Mai Loc, our base of operations, that the Delta Force Commander ordered me to evacuate the helicopters back to the marine base at Quang Tri after each day's mission. Late each evening after our mission situation seemed secure, we were to fly to Quang Tri, stay overnight and report back to Mai Loc early the next morning. On our first flight back to Quang Tri, we were flying in our normal travel formation, with the slicks leading and the gunships trailing. As we entered their airspace, I established communication with the tower, identifying the flight and requesting landing instructions. The flight tower cleared us for landing, and we came in low and slow, but on our down-wind approach, we began to receive automatic-weapon fire on our right. I immediately contacted the tower for permission to return fire, but was informed we were in a friendly no-fire zone, and I was denied permission to fire. We landed safely without anyone taking any hits. The second night was a repeat of the first night; again we were denied permission to return fire, and again we were able to land without any damage to our aircraft. After thinking the situation over, I decided a change was required. Before we departed Mai Loc on the third night, I briefed the flight crews, informing them we would depart in the same formation as the previous two nights. However, I wanted radio silence en route, and I wanted the gun ships to come forward and lead. Being the flight commander, I would be the one to contact the flight tower for landing instructions. Also, I briefed the gun platoon commander that if we were fired on, without any commands from me, they were to return fire so intense on those firing at us they would have no doubt as to who we were. Well, on this third night everything went pretty much as planned. When we started receiving ground fire, Wolf Pack blew the enemy away. Needless to say, this upset the marines. After we landed and were securing our helicopters, a marine officer came to my aircraft and seriously confronted me about what I had done. I kept a neutral face, but inside I was smiling. Wolf Pack had brought "Hell From Above," and lived up to its reputation of doing a great job.

A few days later Major General Burdett, First Aviation Brigade Commander, arrived at Mai Loc for an unexpected visit. I met his aircraft, reported to him, and he and I took an informal walk around our helicopter parking area. We shared general comments about conditions in Vietnam. As we approached his aircraft for his departure, he told me that he was not that familiar with our day-to-day operations, and because of the sensitivity of our mission, I should not discuss those activities with him. He said he didn't know what I had been doing, but whatever it was, I should just continue doing it. We said farewell, I saluted, and he departed. We were both smiling. We never again received ground fire in the traffic pattern at Quang Tri.

Major George Little,
Company Commander

JUST ANOTHER DAY AT THE OFFICE
WITH ANNIE, KATE AND SUSAN

In late October of 1969, the 5th Special Forces Detachment A-236 at Bu Prang came under siege by elements of the 28th and 66th regiments of the North Vietnamese Army (NVA). From 5 May through 29 June 1969, these NVA forces had besieged Ben Het and Dak To. Ben Het and Dak To were located along the border region north of Ban Me Thuot in the Pleiku area. Bu Prang, one of the southernmost in a series of A Camps situated along the Cambodian border in the II CTZ, was located south of Ban Me Thuot on the Cambodian Border. Strategically well located for intelligence purposes, the tactical setting seemed to me to be somewhat less than desirable. It was a typical A Camp configuration, situated less than five miles from the Cambodian-Republic of South Vietnam international border. The border ran generally north and south but occasionally would make a hook or turn. Bu Prang was located in one of these hooks. Flying from Ban Me Thuot down the "preferred route" along Hwy 14 to Duc Lap, the Camp would come into sight on the horizon, a 2,000 foot red dirt airstrip that gleamed in the morning sun like a beacon.

Continuing on a straight line course to the airstrip would take you directly over Cambodia and Camp Le Rolland, which was on the western side of the border. My "preferred route" was to circumnavigate the border and stay well east of highway 14 and approach from the east.

During the first part of the siege from 29 October through 3 November, I flew 46 hours of resupply and support for Detachment A-236 and its supported firebases, as well as spending many more hours on the ground waiting. These first six days were intense, and many lives were lost in addition to a Huey Gunship and its crew from the 48th Assault Helicopter Company. Firebases KATE, ANNIE and SUSAN were established around Camp Bu Prang by the 5th Battalion, 22nd Artillery. The security at these Fire Support Bases was provided by U.S. Special Forces from both Detachment A-236 and A-234 with rotating CIDG (Civilian Irregular Defense Group) forces composed mostly of Rhade Montagnards and Cambodes, who were fierce fighters and considered to be among the best warriors in the CIDG program.

By 3 November, the three firebases had suffered continued B-40 and recoilless rifle enemy fire and were pretty much beaten down. The NVA regulars that had worked their way south down the Ho Chi Minh Trail from the Tri-Border area of Laos, Cambodia and Republic of South Vietnam were not your garden variety VC. These troops fought to the death. The firebases were low on small arms ammo and water. Efforts to keep them resupplied had been repulsed by direct fire from enemy gunners. The Joker Gunship from the 48th Assault Helicopter Company was rumored to have been hit by a rocket propelled grenade (RPG). It broke up at altitude and exploded, killing the entire crew.

Early on the morning of 2 November, Chief Warrant Officer Jerry Badley and I, Warrant Officer Bob Mitchell, were flying resupply for A-236. We had made contact with the radio telephone operator (RTO) at Bu Prang and told him that we had his supplies, which had been loaded at the C Team at Ban Me Thuot. Naturally, he was glad to hear from us but told us not to land on the airstrip. He wanted us to make a low pass and throw the supplies off, so as not to become a magnet for enemy fire. Every time a helicopter landed, the compound was shelled. Well, we did not have to be told twice. We promptly set up an approach that would terminate at the middle of the strip near the camp entrance. Our intent was to fool the NVA gunners into believing we were landing at the touchdown threshold and then fly at low level down the strip below the tree line to the actual touchdown point. We received light small-arms fire on final and dropped below the tree line as planned. During our run down the length of the dirt strip, we could see the mortars hitting behind us. The NVA were not planning on a 100+ knot, low-level pass and could not keep up with us. We slowed just enough to push the cargo off and then pulled back up to altitude east of the camp. The troops recovered the supplies without incident.

We were about to head back to Ban Me Thuot when we received a call on FM from the radio operator at Bu Prang. He wanted to know if we could get some ammo and water into FB KATE, which was just southeast of Bu Prang. Jerry and I, both pilots in command with Jerry acting as Aircraft Commander, talked it over between ourselves and the crew and decided to give it a shot. Unknowingly, we assumed the worst part of this would be getting the ammo and water loaded at Bu Prang. Of course we had just came from there and managed to beat fate once already. The RTO gave us a frequency to contact for coordination.

The 155th was still working the area, trying to resupply the three fire bases. They had been successful in getting into and out of ANNIE and SUSAN, but KATE was left in dire need of 5.56, 7.62 ammo and water. Upon contact, we found three other UH-1Hs had tried unsuccessfully to get into KATE, which was surrounded by the NVA. The gunships had expended and were low on fuel, we were told, and could not cover us on our ingress and egress. Suddenly, this simple resupply was taking on another complexion. During the course of the radio conversation on VHF with the 155th C&C we got a call from call sign SPAD 05 on UHF Guard. Since Jerry was busy with the C&C, I responded to SPAD 05 and asked him to meet me on 241.0 UHF. SPAD 05 informed me he was an A1-E Skyraider and he could provide coverage for us to make a run on KATE. I immediately asked what he had in the way of armament and station time and if he could get slow enough to cover a Huey on a slow approach into a hot LZ. He quickly advised me that he had 20mm, 250 pounders, Napalm, and rockets and about three more hours of station time. I could not believe it. By this time Jerry had finished with C&C and had arranged for the pick up at Bu Prang. I told SPAD 05 we would meet him at SUSAN, and he could cover our approach into KATE after we made the pickup.

The pickup was flown much the same as the resupply about thirty minutes before. This time we came to a full stop, and the ground guys had us loaded in no time flat. The mortar rounds were making their way to our touch-down point as we flew out of the compound. Upon reaching SUSAN we hooked up with the Skyraider. This was the first time I had seen an A1-E, and obviously the first time I had ever had close support from one on a resupply. Jerry was at the controls, and I was operating the radios and monitoring our power. As we started our approach, things got crazy on the right side of our approach path, my side. The door gunner came hot and the noise was deafening. As we came through 40 knots, I looked out the right window and saw the Skyraider. It was a sight to behold. He had full flaps and was right beside us with the 20mm working out. The tree line was splintering from the massive amounts of HE steel being thrown out. With a few well-placed rockets from the Skyraider and excellent M-60 from our door gunner, we were in KATE. It did not take long to get rid of the cargo. We picked up two wounded in action (WIAs) and were on our way out in what seemed like a few seconds. The Skyraider (SPAD 05) was on his in-bound when we lifted off. I have never been involved in anything that worked so flawlessly under such difficult circumstances. We did not take a hit. The NVA obviously had a healthy respect for the awesome firepower that the A1-E Skyraider could provide, and they kept their heads down just long enough for us to get in and out. We were almost Bingo on fuel by this time and continued on to Ban Me Thuot to drop off the WIAs, refuel, and have a little lunch.

I returned to the Bu Prang area the next morning after leaving Nha Trang at first light. The mission was to support the CIDG camp just northeast of Bu Prang. When we arrived on station, I could not believe my eyes. The night before had been an eventful one for the guys at the firebases, Camp Bu Prang, and the CIDG camp. All three firebases had been abandoned, and the troops had escaped and evaded the NVA. The CIDG base had been overrun, and the Rhades had escaped into the jungle after a fierce fight. There were 20 to 30 NVA bodies hanging in the wire. We cruised the perimeter, checking for signs of life, but there were none. The camp was empty, save the bodies hanging in the wire surrounding the fortifications. We landed inside the wire and looked around for survivors or wounded but found none. I have no idea how many CIDG were killed or wounded that night, but the sight of the camp at first light is one that I will never forget.

During the siege of Bu Prang, officially from 28 October to 24 December, most of the casualties were among the ground troops involved, such as the U.S. Special Forces, which had one KIA, eighteen WIA; LLDB (Luc Luong Dac Biet) one KIA, two WIA; and CIDG with 25 KIA and 148 WIA. There were also two Australians WIA during the siege. Besides the ground troops, there was the early loss of the four-man crew from the Joker Gunship that exploded in mid air.

Warrant Officer Robert (Bob) Mitchell,
Bandit Pilot

Suggested reading, a very good book about fire base Kate:
Albrecht, W. and Wolf, M. J. (2015) _Abandoned in Hell: the Fight for Vietnam's Firebase Kate_. New York: NAL Caliber.

THE COST OF SURVIVAL

In November of 1969, as President Nixon announced to the nation his plan for withdrawing U.S. ground combat forces from South Vietnam, John Ware and I were making plans of our own. He and I were crew chiefs on UH-1H helicopters in the 281st Assault Helicopter Company assigned to the 5th Special Forces. For the past several months we had rotated between month-long field operations with the I and II Corps and the 5th Special Forces Headquarters in Nha Trang.

John was the top crew chief of the second platoon Bandits, to which I was assigned when I joined the unit. He soon became my mentor and taught me not only the technical part of helicopter combat and general survival skills, but also provided little helpful tips. An example would be attaching an empty pop can to the side of my M-60 machine gun, so the belt of ammunition would feed better into the gun. Another was to carry a machete in my ammo box to chop away the tangled ropes of a fowled McGuire rig.

While living in tents on our field operations, John devised a quasi-hot potato game, but instead of a potato we would ignite the end of one of our tracer bullets and toss it to each other. This small burning hot piece of lead kept our reflexes finely tuned and was always accompanied by nervous laughter and an occasional scream.

As in all combat units, each of us in the second platoon was part of a team that depended on one another. We depended on each other's combat skills while in flight and friendship/camaraderie skills on the ground. John was a real buddy. We all looked up to him, officers included.

Our company had three platoons, two "slick" platoons with twelve helicopters each and one gunship platoon with eight UH-1Cs. An insertion ship would fly into a landing zone to drop off and extract our reconnaissance or covert teams while two gunships, equipped with mini-guns, 2.75 inch rockets and M-60 machine guns, would fly our flanks giving us fire support when we needed it.

For a little variety, John wanted to switch from the lift platoon to the gunship platoon for the remainder of his tour. We were both getting short. John was going to extend his tour for a couple of months, so he could get an early out when he returned to the "World." I was a double digit midget (less than 100 days left on my tour of duty), scheduled to board a "Freedom Bird" back to the World in mid-December with 147 days left on my enlistment. Any E-5 non-commissioned officer (NCO) returning from Vietnam with less than 150 days was eligible for an early discharge.

John had gone through all the proper channels, and everything was approved for him to make the switch to gunships. He would be leaving his Huey, tail number 512, the best "hole ship" in the 281st Assault Helicopter Company. I had been bouncing from one ship to another since I had joined this special unit in April. I had worked my way up to crew chief and wanted #512 for my permanent ship. All of that was approved, and November 4 was the date set for the transfer to occur. We were at our base camp in Nha Trang, regularly flying daily support missions to small, remote, hill-top encampments in the Central Highlands.

The gentle hum of fans moving the hot humid air in our barracks was disrupted every morning at 0530 when we rolled out from our beds. November 4 began like every day began, by our heading to the bulletin board that posted our missions and chopper assignments for the day. But there was a mistake. John was still assigned to helicopter tail number 512 and scheduled for a mission to the Highlands. I was assigned to helicopter tail number 360 and headed to the Highlands as well. I woke John up.

The plan had been for him to have the day off to move from our barracks to the gun ship platoon barracks. We woke up our assistant platoon sergeant Ruiz and told him of the mess up. All three of us went next door to wake up our platoon sergeant and have him fix the mix up. He told us the duty officer must have forgotten to switch us that day, and he would take care of it later. He told us to fly our posted missions, and the transfer would take place the next day. At age 20 and being in the Army, there wasn't much more we could do to change things. With rifles in hand we grumbled our way to the mess hall, grabbed a bite to eat and a couple cups of coffee, and headed to the flight line as dawn began to color the eastern sky.

The ships had been fueled the night before, and mechanics worked through the night on any repairs before the duty officer assigned them for a mission. It was the crew chief's responsibility to inspect the ship to make sure all repairs were completed while the door gunner mounted the M-60 machine guns and loaded both ammo boxes. Our pilots also inspected the ship before we fired up.

The quiet morning stillness was shattered as our ship's turbines ignited and the whine of the engines increased. We all pulled on our helmets and went through radio checks. Thumbs up. John, in #512, was two revetments away, and as my chopper lifted straight up, I flashed a peace sign to him as we turned for the air strip and received permission from the air controller to take off. With our chopper's nose pointing down, we gained speed and altitude as we hit translational lift just over the concertina wire of our perimeter. The jungle below was still too dark to discern its true color, but the sky was glowing red, and the air began to cool as we headed west toward Duc My Pass, which lead into the Central Highlands.

By 0900 we had picked up Special Forces personnel and supplies in Ban Me Thuot and headed deeper into the Highlands to a hill-top A Camp near the Cambodian border. John and his crew on #512 were on a similar mission at another Special Forces camp in the Phu Khanh province just south of Ban Me Thuot.

The air in the Highlands was always much cooler than that of the coast. We always liked these missions to escape the intense humid heat. A weather front began building that afternoon and added freshness to the cool air. We finished our mission by early afternoon without being shot at a single time. It was a good day. After refueling at Ban Me Thuot, we headed home. The wind had picked up in the pass, and our ship was tossed around a bit, nothing too serious. Our crew had flown through gale force winds during the Monsoon season earlier in the summer.

Back at base camp, I remember checking out my ship as the sun began to creep into the clouds that were continuing to build in the west. I was checking out the rotor when one of the mechanics came over and said #512 had radioed that they were in trouble. The last radio transmission was from a new pilot, Warrant Officer Cavender. He said "Oh, my God, we're inverted!" and all went silent. We all knew helicopters cannot fly inverted.

It was 1920 hours. They were somewhere near Duc My Pass, and the storm and darkness were both building. First seat pilot Warrant Officer Terry Alford, the new in country Warrant Officer Jim Cavender, along with door gunner Jim Klimo, and John were missing.

We hung around the radio control room listening, hoping, praying. We wanted to fire up our ships and head out to find them, but we knew we had to wait until daylight. It was after 2200 when we headed to the Enlisted Men's Club to spread the word and have a couple of beers before turning in. The EM Club was our haven when we were at base camp. It was where we drank and found solace after defeating death each day. Drinking and laughing with buddies was strong therapy that helped blur the horrors of each day. On the evening of November 4, it was a gathering of men with concentrated hope for a positive outcome. We turned in, full of optimism.

Our whole platoon was up and ready to go before the first glimmer of the new day was apparent in the eastern sky. We had Green Beret "belly sergeants" for spotters; we had "sniffers" (mechanical devises that could smell smoke, fuel or even body odor). We had maps and assigned search areas. We had jungle hoists, rope ladders, and McGuire Rigs to pull them out of the tangled jungle vegetation. We had medics. And above all we had hope.

We searched, hoping the multi-layers of jungle canopies had softened their crash and that upon hearing our choppers, they would pop a smoke grenade to lead us to them. We looked for signs of broken vegetation, signs the chopper would have left as it crashed through the foliage. Nothing... All day we flew, stopping only to refuel and then search some more. And still nothing. After the second day without any results, I spoke with a couple of the Green Beret about going down on the ground to search below the jungle canopies. The request was denied. We searched for five long days without any sign, and then came the order "search efforts suspended." Our company had suffered losses like every other combat company fighting in a war.

We had zipped fallen comrades into body bags and carried wounded, bleeding men to our choppers. We were all too familiar with death and destruction. After several months of combat, we had become hardened by war, tempered by fear, and tuned by hope for survival. It was still possible that the crew of #512 could be out there, hurt, hungry and fleeing from the Cong. How could we suspend the search? Orders are orders, but every time we flew to the Highlands, it took us a bit longer to get there because we would fly low, straining our eyes as we desperately searched for any sign of the ship and our fallen comrades.

The life expectancy of a helicopter door gunner on a hole ship in a fire fight averaged seven seconds. Each of us lived every day to the fullest with that glum statistic looming over us. Being totally "in tune" with our senses, each of us outwardly mourned each time we lost members of our company. Deep down in secret recesses we were thankful it wasn't us that day. But discovering the circumstances involved with John's disappearance became deeply rooted in me.

The days and missions continued as my time in country grew shorter and shorter. The close calls increased: two blown-out engines in flight, an autorotation into a rice paddy after running out of fuel, two pilots wounded while extracting a team from a hot LZ, shrapnel from enemy artillery embedded in my ship, mortar fire striking the roof of a building I sat next to, a very near mid-air collision with a F-100 fighter jet, eight bullet holes within twelve inches of my head and four machine gun duels, all after John's disappearance. It was time for me to return to the "World."

On 12 December 1969, a big, beautiful silver "Freedom Bird" full of fellow survivors fell completely silent as its jet engines roared down the runway. As the wheels lifted off from hell, aka Vietnam, the cabin exploded with cheers and tears. We were really going home!

But home would never be the same. Christmas at home in Minnesota felt foreign. I was out of place. I was alive in the "World." and John, where was he? Should I be there instead of him? Without the focus of war, that reality started digging, clawing, tearing at my very being. No amount of alcohol or drugs diverted the guilt.

I ran across America, coast to coast, north to south, from Canada through Mexico. I hid, and I searched the depth of my soul while wandering in solitude in the Rocky Mountains of Colorado. Then I became invisible, an unknown wounded warrior in the bush of Alaska. Trying desperately to create my own healing therapy, I sought out intense experiences in life to layer over the guilt of being alive. I was searching for a reason to live when so many around me had died.

Years passed. And on my life's journey, I found a mountain woman who became my lover and a true friend in whom I could confide. We started a family together in an abandoned log cabin in interior Alaska, and a time of healing began.

On a trip back to my childhood home in Minnesota, I found John's home address in Oregon. In 1982 we routed our way through Hermiston, Oregon on our way to catch the ferry back to Alaska. We pulled off the highway, and I found Mr. and Mrs. Cecil Ware in the phone book. Judgment Day was at hand. I called the number and introduced myself as a friend and comrade of John's. I remember hoping with all my soul that a miracle had happened, and the voice would say John is alive and well. That didn't happen. Aileen, John's mom, invited me to their home, John's home. Aileen invited John's brother and nephew to come over, and I met the whole family. I brought pictures of John and myself to give them. After a while, I drew up all the courage I could muster and told them the whole story. The story that changed all of our lives. It was the tragic story of a forgetful duty officer posting the wrong mission assignments twelve years before that had caused them to lose their son. And it was the story of my daily struggles with that guilt. We all cried, and then they reached out from the depth of their loss and touched my troubled soul. Their goodness, understanding, caring and forgiveness lifted an intensely heavy mill stone from my neck. There is not a day that I live that I don't still think of John and thank him for my life. I have made it a point to live as full and happy a life as possible in tribute to John.

Aileen was very active in the MIA movement. In January 1987, she received copies of documents from the Department of Defense's Joint Casualty Resolution Center (JCRC) that shed the first light on John's disappearance.

A refugee fleeing Communist Vietnam was interviewed in Thailand by a JCRC officer. The refugee had been an enlisted man in the South Vietnam Regular Army on patrol in the forested region of Tuy Hoa/Nha Trang in 1969. The report reads: His patrol came across the wreckage of a US Huey helicopter concealed from the air by thick jungle

Specialist Mike Olsen and Sergeant John Ware

canopy. The aircraft had probably been shot down a few weeks earlier. They found the decaying bodies of four Americans amid the wreckage. He collected the four dog tags from the bodies as souvenirs. The "source" stated he assumed the incident was reported, and the U.S. would recover the bodies. He himself did not report it. The report goes on about how the source was subjected to a reeducation camp somewhere in North Vietnam after the South fell, and in 1979 he escaped. He eventually made his way to his sister's home in Thailand.

He stated that he sent his brother to the crash site. His brother found the site still untouched, recovered the remains of all four Americans, and returned to hide them near his home, somewhere in a hamlet near Nha Trang. This bizarre-sounding report has many blacked out sections and is difficult to read, but reportedly there was only one helicopter incident in that area in 1969. To my knowledge, no other contact was made with the source or his brother, as no further news followed that document.

More than 1,300 Americans are still listed as Missing In Action in Vietnam. The families and friends of **John Ware, Jim Klimo, Terry Alford and Jim Cavender** have no physical remains to emotionally bury their losses. I, for one, keep their memory alive.

John personally helped guide me through my first six months of combat in Vietnam, and subjectively, he has helped guide me through my last 30 years. His death has helped me to understand the greater meaning life.

Specialist Michael Olson,
Crew Chief
April 69 - December 69

THANKSGIVING DAY 1969

in Vietnam

"Death on Call" was the motto of the Wolf pack gunship platoon of the 281st Assault Helicopter Company.

In the fall of 1969, the North Vietnamese army held a large scale operation northwest of Ban Me Thuot in Central Vietnam. So pervasive was the operation that no U.S. army helicopters were allowed to fly in the area. That meant medevac and supply missions were also halted. The only U.S. helicopters permitted to operate were gunships. It was all top secret. Captain Jim Brown, our gunship platoon leader and aircraft commander; our copilot Ken Miller; Tubby Brudvig, the door gunner and myself, the crew chief; all were tasked with the mission of providing aerial support to the isolated outposts manned by U.S. personnel which were in imminent danger of being overrun. I asked Captain Brown how long we were going to be out on this mission and he replied, "If we make it for three days, then we will be relieved by another crew."

I vividly remember the trepidation and fear I felt about the mission, unlike any other mission I flew in Vietnam. If we got into trouble, we knew there would be no chance of rescue from medevac or any UH-1 helicopters in the area.

We made it to Bu Prang in the early hours of Thanksgiving Day, 1969. While Tubby and I were refueling our helicopter, the gunship we were relieving was refueling right next to us. While talking to their crew chief, he raised his shirt up to show us a bruise on his chest the size of a watermelon. He had taken a round earlier that day, and his chest protector had saved his life.

The outpost on top of a small volcano-like hill was manned by U.S. personnel who had been under intense attack from the North Vietnamese who were occupying the surrounding hilltops only a few hundred yards from their position. They were being attacked by mortars, rockets, etc. So intense was our engagement with the enemy we had to return to Ban Me Thuot twice to rearm and refuel. The personnel on the hill called in gunships and F4 phantom jets to suppress the enemy.

While refueling and rearming for the third time that day, we had our first crack at using flechette rockets. These were rockets with thousands of needles in the warhead which burst in the sky and sent them in a deadly spray over a vast area.

After the F4 phantom jets left, we headed into the volcano-like area at tree-top level, and all hell broke loose. Rounds were bursting through the floor of the helicopter between my legs. I immediately returned fire while hearing our copilot say, "May day, may day. We are going down." Glancing at the control panel, I saw that the lights were blinking red, indicating that we were crashing.

After a crash landing, we all managed to exit the aircraft. Tubby and I jumped out, taking as much ammunition as we could carry. We took up defensive positions around the helicopter and were immediately surrounded by the enemy force that we had been fighting most of the day. We were within hand-grenade range of numerous spider holes occupied by the North Vietnamese Army. An intense ground battle ensued for at least half an hour. We eliminated the enemy in the spider holes, but we were still receiving fire from the tree-line and surrounding enemy positions. Tubby and I left our defensive positions many times to return to the helicopter to get more ammunition since we had full mini gun trays sitting in the aircraft to use in our M-60 machine guns. Tubby was an expert with the M-60 and was doing his best to keep us alive.

Robert George, pilot; Larry Elam, crew chief; Jackie Keele, pilot; and Red Vandevender, gunner, were flying over us to protect us while we waited to be rescued. But no one was coming. George's mini guns were shot out, and he was running out of fuel. Realizing that no one was coming to rescue us, George landed a few yards away from us, just as the enemy was getting closer to our defensive positions. The four of us ran and jumped into his helicopter. So close was the enemy, the skid of the aircraft hit an enemy soldier in the chest when we took off. For our heroics that day, Bob George received a Silver Star, and the rest of us received a Bronze Star with a V Device for Valor.

Thirty-five years later, we found out the U.S. outpost we had been defending that day was overrun, and all personnel were killed.

There is not a Thanksgiving Day that each of us who are still alive does not think of the day that we were shot down and surrounded in a hopeless situation. Yet we made it back to our post to eat our Thanksgiving dinner out of a can. We had everything to be thankful for!

Daryl Evangelho,
Crew Chief
Wolf Pack

CAT DOCTOR

Working in maintenance, we normally didn't see the combat action that the flight crews saw. Being shot at was the exception rather than rule of the day for us. However, that didn't mean wrench bending was completely free from danger. After all, we never knew when some other mechanic, not paying attention to what he was doing, was going to drop a wrench on someone's head. And believe me, standing in the "hell hole" while adjusting the engine flight idle stop with the engine whining and rotors turning is no fun, especially when we all knew one small nudge on the cyclic stick could be a disaster for anyone in the hole. Although I spent most of my time on the ground, occasionally I was in the air.

Our test flights usually only had one test pilot, which meant someone from maintenance had to fly up front in the open seat. Our maintenance test pilots were absolutely the best, and they made sure whoever was flying up front with them knew enough about how to fly the aircraft if anything happened to them in flight, we at least had a remote chance of making it to the ground safely. They also liked having an engine man on board during test flights; not that we could do a damn thing if the engine failed in flight. As a result, I got a quite a bit of flying time and a fair amount of stick time too. I remember a very close call when I was in a helicopter.

There was a parts depot at Red Beach just north of us along the coast of the South China Sea that we had been to on a number of occasions. One morning we left on what we assumed would be a routine fifteen-minute run for parts and headed to Red Beach. The helipad at C-Team had a line of trees along one side. Once you cleared them, you could come back down and be right on the beach.

We left in one of the Wolf Pack's "C" models. Chief Warrant Officer Bobbi Stanfill was flying with his copilot. I was alone in the back.

We couldn't have been airborne for more than 30 seconds when the ship started to experience a very severe vertical vibration. The vibration was so bad that the seat belt left welts on my legs. Mr. Stanfill immediately dropped collective and put the ship safely down on the beach. I jumped out on the South China Sea side, only a few feet from the water. Looking up I saw smoke coming from the mast area. As the three of us stood outside the aircraft, another UH-1 landed on the beach. I swear he landed before our rotors stopped turning. Out from the other aircraft came a crusty old CW-4 who was known as the "Cat Doctor." He was the maintenance officer with the 282nd Black Cats in Da Nang. He must have heard Bobbi's distress call, and he came out immediately.

Wearing shorts and no shirt, the Cat Doctor strolled over, looked up at the mast which was still smoking, and informed us that it would have only been a matter of seconds, and we would have lost the mast, main rotor blades and probably our lives. Apparently the scissors and sleeve assembly was chaffing on the mast. I thanked God that Bobbi got us down safely. I'm not sure what we did next, but it probably involved going back to C-Team for a cold beer or two or three.

Specialist Five Don Budlong,
Engine Shop

TWO GUYS, THEN ONE

Being awarded a Purple Heart medal comes at a great cost. To earn it, a soldier has to suffer the pain of being wounded in battle. Many purple hearts were awarded posthumously, which was small comfort to the friends and families of the soldiers who were killed. Some soldiers would talk about getting that million-dollar wound, a wound that did not kill them but was severe enough to get them sent back to a state-side hospital to recover and then be given a discharge. The war would be over for them.

The commanders, the platoon leaders and every aircraft commander insisted all crew members wear as much protection as they could. A chicken plate, (chest protector) was provided, and most crew chiefs and door gunners wore a bullet-proof vest while flying. Most of the crew also wanted some protection underneath them in a helicopter while on a mission. This was to protect their bottom side, a very important part of their manhood, and rightly so.

A finger or a toe maybe, but there are some parts of a man's body that he cannot afford to lose, and at all times he would go to extremes to protect. It only takes one close call, or hearing a story of someone getting hit in the wrong place, to make the hair stand up, on the back of your neck.

Well, it can happen; you fail to keep your protection in place and then the bullet with your name comes your way.

In late 1969, while flying in support of Delta out of Mai Loc, a new captain showed up, Captain Jim Brown. He was going to be our platoon leader. I introduced myself, we chit-chatted, and Jim told me he had only about six months left. "Where have you been?" I asked. "In the hospital; I got shot," was his reply. "Where?" I asked, meaning where in Vietnam. "In my rear end." was his reply, an area of Vietnam I had not heard of. Jim had lost one entire testicle to the enemy, which, as he told me, was better than losing both guys.

I was selected to fly with him for his orientation flight and to familiarize him with our operations area. We did a complete by-the-book preflight. I introduced him to the crew chief and door gunner, and we were good to go. He was doing great. However, I had neglected to tell him my nickname was "Magnet Ass," but it was only a training flight. What could go wrong?

About a half hour into our flight there was a BOOM! A loud crack echoed through the cabin. I looked to my left and saw my new platoon leader flattened back in his seat with wide-open eyes. There was also a bullet hole in his greenhouse and, upon closer observation, one in the floor between Captain Brown's legs. He was mumbling, but I didn't understand much beyond something that sounded like "Ohmygoshwhatthehell. Canwegetoutofherenow"? I tried not to laugh but failed. Upon reflection, I wish I had stayed a few months more; I heard that Captain Jim Brown was one heck of a platoon leader.

Warrant Officer Jeff Murray,
Aircraft Commander

THE ENEMY

The enemy was not very smart when he fired at one of our choppers because within a minute his action would bring hell from above on his position. Most of us did not see a dead enemy soldier. When our enemies could, they would remove the bodies from the area, presumably so we could not tell how many of them were killed, but, more importantly, how many of them remained in the area.

For better or maybe worse, the measure of success in this war with no front lines became the number of casualties inflicted on either side. The body count was an important statistic; of course the higher-up commanders wanted a high enemy body count. In some cases, it was only an estimate. If we killed more than we lost we were winning. How could we actually know? Consequently, after a battle, the surviving enemy soldiers dragged their dead with them when they retreated. Usually the enemy buried them in a mass grave, which may have been prepared in advance by the enemy soldiers themselves. That had to be a bummer for them.

Over the course of our tour, we developed a healthy respect for the enemy. It seemed inconceivable to us they could hold up their end in battle against us. Well, in reality, they could not, but somehow they mustered the courage to stay in the battle, at least for a little while. They knew the area well and hit-and-run tactics worked well for them especially if they were outnumbered. Then they would fade away into the jungle.

The Viet Cong

The typical Viet Cong soldier we saw, usually post-mortem, wore only a pair of shorts, a button-down, short-sleeved shirt and thong sandals. Shoes were rarely worn by most of the Viet Cong. Some wore a conical straw hat. Many of them wore the familiar black pajamas and carried a small canvas backpack.

Usually there were three plastic bags tied to a belt. One contained about thirty rounds of ammunition for their AK-47, enough to reload their magazine. Another held a rice ball, the VC rations comparable to our C-Rations. The third bag held marijuana, which we understood the enemy smoked like American tobacco. Maybe the drug provided battlefield courage and possibly, as with our troops, a diversion from the stress of life in battle.

The North Vietnamese Army

Most of the regular soldiers in the North Vietnamese Army (NVA) wore olive-drab uniforms and were much better equipped than the Viet Cong soldiers. They carried more ammunition and usually had more access to mortar rounds, rocket-propelled grenades, (RPG) and hand grenades. They often had web gear with pockets to hold additional AK-47 magazines and other items. This equipment would not have been typical for Viet Cong soldiers. The NVA were well disciplined and brave, and they were a fierce enemy. They, in fact, looked like a military organization.

On average, Vietnamese people were small, the men weighing not much more than 110 pounds and standing around 5 feet tall. It was hard to fathom how these troops, with so little ammunition, equipment and poor living conditions could engage a much larger and better equipped force in combat. None of us would have ever traded places with them. These small people compensated for their inferior firepower and often lower numbers with cunning we would have admired had it not been used against us. They were the best at guerrilla fighting and the art of out-witting superior forces. Their strategy was to avoid knock-down-drag-out battles, which, of course, were to the advantage of the side with the most soldiers and better technological weapons; our side.

Their most common tactic was to hit hard and then run. Their objective was to inflict as much damage as possible in a short time and then fade away back into the jungle to wait for another opportunity to attack.

In addition to knowing the jungle so much better than we did, we faced an enemy that would never give up, no matter what the cost of lives lost. "You can kill ten of my men for every one we kill of yours, but even at those odds, you will lose and I will win," said Ho Chi Minh.

NEVER PEE INTO THE WIND

It was a busy day, we were flying admin runs called "ash and trash." We would fly to one location, then to another, pick up passengers, drop them off at another place, and even deliver mail, food and a number of other things to forward operating bases. If we stopped for any length of time, we would sit at flight idle. Ash and trash runs made for a long day of flying, stopping and refueling. We had just left a Special Forces forward operating base after delivering a sack of mail and other supplies that they needed. We were running late and needed to get back to home base before dark. It had been a very long day. The crew chief said we were good to go, clear on the left; the gunner then said, "Clear on the right." I increased pitch and departed into the wind. We were at about 150 feet and still climbing when the base radio operator called and said there was a guy dangling below our helicopter. I looked at the other pilot with that "what-the-hell" look on my face. I said, "What? Say that again." The radio operator repeated, "There is a guy hanging below your helicopter." I looked back and could see the crew chief right where he was supposed to be. However, when I looked to the other side, the door gunner was dangling by his monkey strap and swaying in the wind. I could not imagine what the heck was going on with this guy. I slowed down as he climbed back in. I could see that he was wet. I found out later that he had unhooked himself from his head set, so he could stand out on the skids to pee. He had not factored in the direction of the wind and had peed all over himself. He never said a word for the rest of the flight. I will not mention his name.

Jeff Murray
Warrant Officer

1970

THE YEAR OF THE DOG

By 1970 the 281st Assault Helicopter Company was into its fourth year of flying above the best and bravest, the 5th Special Forces Group of Green Berets. During those years the 281st had formed a special bond with the Green Berets, and each group knew they could count on one another, no matter what. No exceptions!

The 281st had also developed a healthy respect for the enemy. The North Vietnamese Army, joined by the Viet Cong, made a fierce enemy, an enemy that managed to hold its own in a battle against forces that obviously had superior equipment and firepower.

1970 began a new decade. It was the Chinese Year of the Dog. In Vietnam we never knew what to expect; there were no safe places. There was no reason to think 1970 would be any different from the previous years. It would be another tough year. When the American soldier is called to war to fight, to put his life on the line, he does so to win. He wants to win and believes that he can win. The 281st was still in the fight, and we were giving it everything we had. There was no letup. Each day on each mission the crews put their lives on the line for the men of the Green Berets.

The Wolf Pack gunship platoon was still flying the UH-1C and doing a great job. These gunslingers were always right in the middle of the action. It was a sight to see as they brought hell from above down on the enemy. The lift platoons were flying the more powerful UH-1H models. The talk was these crew members were doing even more, and the troops on the ground already thought they were the bravest men on earth. And they were.

Two Corps (II Corps) was the tactical zone of operations for the 281st Intruders, and it was rugged country. The Intruders flew missions from Phan Thiet, the most southern city in II corps, to as far as Kontum, in the northern part of II corps. The west side bordered Cambodia and Laos and the Ho Chi Minh Trail, and the east side had many miles of picturesque white sand beaches along the South China Sea. It was a beautiful sight from 3,000 feet. It was just too bad there was a war going on down there. The beauty vanished as our brave men gave their lives trying to save their fellow men.

The section from the sea to the mountains was seldom more than three miles wide. It was in this region that a majority of the rice crops were produced and harvested from four major planting sites. The coast was dotted by numerous small fishing villages and marked by five major cities: Phan Thiet, Phang Rang, Nha Trang, Tuy Hoa and Qui Nhon.

The centerline between the North and the South had a range of mountains with peaks from 3,000 to nearly 7,000 feet. These mountains were covered with a dense triple canopy jungle. The wildlife in those jungle-covered mountains was numerous because the jungle afforded an almost impenetrable preserve for tigers, elephants, wild boar, deer, bear, monkeys and a large assortment of colorful birds. And, of course, among the beasts was our enemy: The Viet Cong and the North Vietnamese Army.

The most western side of these mountains had a common border with Cambodia and Laos. When not cultivated, the low rolling hills of the region were covered with deep elephant grass which grew up to ten feet in height. The main agricultural pursuit of this region was tea and rubber with a few rice paddies around the populated area. The major cities in this region were Ban Me Thuot and Pleiku.

It was in the central highlands the Intruders earned their flight pay. It included an additional twenty dollars per month for combat pay. They were flying up and down the coast, over the mountains and along the western borders. The Ho Chi Minh Trail was really a good-sized road and was heavily traveled from the north with troops, supplies, tanks, trucks and heavily loaded bicycles.

New Year's Day was just another day. Besides the daily missions, there were troops in need of food, ammunition, general supplies and transportation for their sick and wounded, one day closer to going back home. The Intruders were busy supporting the Republic of Korea (ROK) Infantry Division, the 6/32nd Artillery, Recondo School, South Vietnamese Army, and Project Delta. The Gunship Platoon known as Wolf Pack had an opportunity to "work out." on sniffer missions and combat assaults, and they showed their usual smooth and accurate effectiveness.

SNIFFING

It was time for the boys to play. A new machine was developed which could detect traces of ammonia or smoke in the air. Flying low level over an area, the operator would be able to detect the chemical traces. Shortly after initiating the system, someone discovered the ammonia traces were not necessarily from enemy urine but sometimes from monkey pods in the jungle. Adjustments were made and the machine just detected smoke emanating from campsites.

The missions were composed of two slicks and a gunship. One ship flew as C&C and directed the other ship called the "hole ship" where to fly. C&C was responsible for keeping the hole ship flying over the desired areas and watching for any ridges or land obstacles the hole ship might not see. Once a hot spot was detected, Wolf Pack rolled in and shot the area up.

The hole ship was flying in the trees, 100 knots or more. It was like a roller coaster.

Total "seat of the pants" flying was the name of the game. This type of flying came to be known as NOE (nap of the earth) flying. Some of the guys returning to the states helped the Army write the instruction manual for NOE. The Army always had to have manuals.

The pilots would fight over the coveted hole ship position. In order to qualify, it was mandatory the machine operator in the back had to get airsick from all the motions. If the pilot didn't succeed, he was moved upstairs and flew the boring C&C spot. The missions were fun and a welcomed break from getting shot at while hovering in a hole.

We were on stand down with Delta but 5th Group was, by no means, going to let us rest. A sniffer mission was scheduled for the mountains west of Dong Ba Thin and Cam Ranh Bay. The area was relatively close to these secure areas so we were looking forward to an uneventful, fun mission. My hopes ran high for flying the hole ship until Buck Sorem said he was going to fly it. Buck was the platoon leader and the boss so I was relegated to the C&C position. I was not happy but Buck had the ability to give an order and you simply said "yes sir," with a smile. We flew out to the AO and Buck dropped down to do his thing. Up in the C&C I did my job well, keeping him informed of the flight path he was to fly. I was so engrossed with Buck's flying; I dropped down from the safe 1500' into the kill zone around 500'. With all the twisting and turning, I ended up overflying his flight path. I had no idea I woke up some bad guys but it was too late for them to hit me. Unfortunately, when Buck got to that spot, they were ready and unloaded on him. Dave Dolstein was flying in the right seat when a round came up through the bottom of the ship hitting the heel of his boot and spent right in front of his face. He reached down, picked up the bullet put it in his pocket and carries it around today. Buck reported taking fire and getting hit. I asked him how his instruments were and he said everything was green. "If everything is ok, let's finish the mission" I told him. He responded, "I'm going back to base and have things checked out." As he climbed out to head home I used an inordinate amount of expletives on him for giving up. (We were really good friends and I knew I could over step my bounds.) Once back at the maintenance hangar, the guys took off the floor panels and discovered the round had pierced the main control tube for the cyclic nearly severing it in half. Buck's decision to abort the mission avoided a crash and probably certain death for 5 guys. I went to dinner that night and ate a full plate of crow.

Chief Warrant Officer Brian Paine,
Bandit 24
Aircraft Commander

On 16 January 1970, Major Darryl M. "Steve" Stevens assumed command of the company.

According to The Army Times, on 26 January 1970, Navy Lieutenant Everett Alvarez Jr., an American prisoner of war, had been imprisoned in the Hanoi Hilton for 2,000 days. Unfortunately, he would remain there and continue to be tortured as a POW for another three plus years.

It appeared as if the NVA and the Viet Cong were reading our operations orders. No matter where we landed, the enemy was there. It seemed they knew where we were going and when we were returning. Where were they getting their information? Of course, we knew that the enemy was around us at all times.

From inside a helicopter, we could rarely hear the enemy shooting at us, but we could see the green tracers. They looked like basketballs coming straight at us. A .51 caliber coming at us looked like a large trash can that was on fire. Both scared the living dog out of us. A .51 caliber machine gun is a very powerful and dangerous weapon. The bad guys had them placed on just about every mountain top along the Ho Chi Minh Trail. On the 6th of February four of our good men were on a combat mission to help resupply the troops on the ground. Without warning the aircraft started taking fire; the .51 caliber was tearing up helicopter tail number 525. The crew chief, Specialist Five Alan H. Johnson, and door gunner, Specialist Frank M. Kaiser, returned fire with their M-60s. The aircraft was coming apart as the pilots tried to make a controlled crash landing in a rice paddy below the dense jungle. Aircraft Commander Warrant Officer Ron Lesonik and Warrant Officer Tarry T. O'Reilly used every skill available to fly it down to the ground, but there was just too much damage; the controls were shot up. Both pilots survived the crash, but four days later, **WO O'Reilly died of his wounds, in spite of the best medical help available.** That left WO Lesonik as the sole survivor, but with battle scars that would affect him for the rest of his life. Completely disfigured and missing both legs, Ron went to work at NASA working on the space programs. He's now retired from there and sailing his boat in the Caribbean somewhere. The 281st Assault Helicopter crews faced death every time they flew. **Alan Johnson, Frank Kaiser and Tarry O'Reilly gave their all and will never be forgotten.**

Only eight days later on the 14th of February, a crew of four plus two Special Forces soldiers aboard aircraft tail number 127 went down ten miles northwest of Dong Ba Thin while on a nighttime sniffer mission just a short way from Nha Trang. **Warrant Officer Eldon R. Payne, Warrant Officer Thomas A. Guenther, Crew Chief Michael A. Hughey, Door Gunner Staff Sergeant Bobbie H. Brewer and the two Special Forces men were killed, but never forgotten.**

The month of February started out tragically and ended the same way.

The year continued with the 281st very busy flying aviation support to the 4th Infantry Division, the Republic of Korea "White Horse" and "Capital" Divisions and also with ongoing aviation support for the MACV Recondo School. March included supporting nineteen different commands and accumulating 2645 accident free hours.

In addition to all the missions, the 281st never stopped training. If and when there was any free time, the pilots and crew underwent training, which included standardized check rides, in country orientation rides and more.

Extractions were always a scary thing, but saving a fellow soldier was the highlight of any mission and was what we were all about. However, sometimes it did not work out as planned. The hardest thing was going in to bring out our dead brothers, and no crew would ever consider leaving any of them behind. In most cases we did not carry body bags. The honored men we brought back were laid on the cabin floor and cared for with as much dignity as possible. The odor of death stayed in the helicopter and would cling to us as well. The blood soaked into the very pores of our being and seemed to never leave. It was something we never forget, but we continued to do it over and over again. Each crew member risked his life to bring home his brothers-in-arms. We were losing some really good men, and the year was just getting started.

THE MISSION

Part One

It's very early. My mind is working, and I wonder where I am. I feel my pistol next to me and am jolted back to reality. I lay there in the dark, muscles tense, never really sleeping, yet not awake. I think of the date: February 20, 1970. Then I remember the mission for today. It seems like I've been here forever, and this is only my fifth month. When will this end? Can I ever relax? Will I ever feel safe again? Somewhere I have a family waiting for me to return; I am never sure that I will see them again. Even if I do, I know my life will never be the same.

Slowly I push myself out of bed. It's still dark. As I dress, I go over the events from the night before, which gives rise to general thoughts about the patterns of my life.

Every night here seems the same: go to the club, drink too much, and check in with operations around 11 to see what missions we have for the next day. Fifth Special Forces Headquarters knows how to take care of their people. We have good chow, good clubs and tolerable living quarters. However, we are aviators, and when on a mission, most crews do not return in time to eat dinner at the mess hall. The only place to get food, unless we have some stored in our room, is the officer or NCO club. Most of the time our crews end up eating a sandwich in the club and drinking themselves into either a minor or major drunk, depending on the events of that day's mission.

Getting shot at is not an event that causes us to drink since that is almost an everyday occurrence. Some days your copilot, if he is a new guy, will pull some crazy stunt that might have killed us all, but due to skill, clearness of mind, swiftness on the controls, and mostly luck, the pilot saves the day. This would be the cause for drinking ourselves into oblivion: staying alive is a matter of luck, and who knows how long the luck will hold out. I'm sure that every one of the new guys is the cause of many an aircraft commander and crew getting up the next morning with gigantic hangovers because they cause so many unnecessary accidents. At this point in my tour, the loss of aircraft and crews, mostly due to enemy action, is a major contributing factor for my constant alcoholic fog.

The mission, the mission. Last night the operations officer and I accepted a mission to lead a combat assault into the mountains about 60 miles west of our compound in Nha Trang.

I volunteered for Vietnam, but since arriving here I've become wiser. I've been reluctant to volunteer for anything. However, our operations officer, Steve, is the persuasive type, and he convinced me this is the kind of mission two dashing, young captain aviators should lead. Besides, we will finish the mission by noon, in time to get out by the hooch to catch the rays and drink all afternoon. I think it will be cool to have a tan all over.

It is unusual for the commander to let his operations officer and new executive officer lead a combat assault in the same aircraft. I have just recently moved from 2nd Platoon leader (Bandits) to the company executive officer position. Normally, we fly in separate aircraft for obvious reasons. However, with so many missions and not enough time to rest the crews, we are giving some of the flight platoon aircraft commanders a day off.

After a long shower, I'm finally awake and ready to go. Flight helmet, survival kit, pistol, flight bag, map, and my M-16 with bandoleer of ammo. Although pilots are not issued M-16s, I have managed to get one. I figure the pistol is only to shoot myself with if I get in an unmanageable situation. With an M-16, I can put up a good fight.

It is still dark out as I come out of the officers' quarters, which are only about 200 feet from the flight line. I can make out the silhouettes of men moving about the aircraft, getting ready for today's troop insertion.

As I get to the aircraft, I see the crew chief is already there, and I begin to pre-flight. Not much talk early in the morning; besides, I'm not a morning person. The gunner arrives and starts mounting the machine guns. I notice that he has extra barrels and extra cans of ammo. I ask myself, "Where is Steve?" I have not seen him since we were in the latrine shaving. He was in his normal good mood, singing and talking like it was the middle of the day, not 0500 dark.

This is a new Huey with only about 200 hours. It is the old man's aircraft, and we need to be especially careful with it. Oh, no, this ship has a new gun system on the left side, a door-mounted recoilless .50 caliber. Never flown one with a 50 caliber. I'm sure this will be a unique experience. With the combat troops we will be carrying today, we have to be careful about the additional boxes of ammo. Plenty of 7.62 on one side but not enough .50, which takes up too much room and weight. Only have maybe 100 rounds of .50 and 1000 of M-60 ammo. Preflight is over. All crews meet in operations for an operations order and mission brief. Steve does the briefing:

"Our mission is to insert an infantry company of ROKs (Republic of Korea,) into an LZ in the mountains approximately 60 miles west of Nha Trang. This is a feint operation, with the remaining forces going into the mountains about five miles to the north. The platoon will be on VHF and UHF, with mission command on FM. The only recon of the LZ is by map, so it appears to be only a single or two-ship landing zone. Flight lead will determine that as we do the aerial recon for the insertion. No artillery support, only a light fire team of Jokers from the 48th Assault Helicopter Company to prep the LZ on final approach."

This is not good news. Artillery is a lifesaver, as I found out the hard way. Never, never go anywhere without artillery support. Steve continues:

"We do not expect to have any enemy activity. The pickup zone is about fifteen minutes to our northwest. We will be landing to the north. Stay in a trail formation. We will not shutdown. The troops will be broken down to six or seven per ship.

They will load from your left. Crew chiefs will watch them. We don't want anyone trying to go through the tail rotor. We will do two sorties. The main force will be approximately 5K to our north and will be inserting their troops about 15 minutes after us. Any questions?"

I can't help but think that the main force will get artillery support, but I keep my mouth shut. No one has questions, so Steve keeps giving us more information: "As for fuel, we should be able to do two insertions on one fuel load. Any problems, let me know. Clear weather is forecast. Everyone is pre-flighted and ready, so crank on me in 10. We will lineup on the taxi way in trail formation. Bandit 24, Bob Mitchell, will be chalk 2, and Marshall Hawkins, Bandit 26, will be trail. Others lineup as you come out of the revetments." The briefing is over.

Flights are ready, and the sun is trying to come up. What a beautiful morning, if there can be such a thing in Vietnam. We start taking off. There are no mechanical problems, and radios are working. This is going to be a good day.

I am flying. Steve is on the radios and has his map out. We arrive on time at the pickup zone (PZ) and load the troops with no problems. We are off the PZ and headed to the west with the troops. The Korean commander is on our ship and gets his map out too. Not sure what he is looking for since neither one of us have seen the LZ before. I can always tell who is in charge. He's the guy with the map and usually has a lost look in his eyes.

Short flight. Steve identifies a hilltop as the LZ. The gunships are on our left, only enough room for a single-ship insertion. I fly to the south and have the flight space out since we want one aircraft coming off the LZ as another is on short, short final. Need to be quick about this. Stay cool; the excitement is about to begin.

We are about to start our approach when I hear Steve say, "I've got the controls!" Steve is running the mission, and now he is going to fly the mission too. Steve can see the LZ better, and I will monitor the gauges and give him power readings.

The gunships are working the area; I hear mini guns and rockets. Our crew chief and gunner are on the M-60s and shooting. Short final, and power is good. Gunships are coming back around for more covering fire. We are in the LZ in elephant grass at a high hover; power good; crew chief and gunner are looking for the ground as we hover down in the thicket. Power good. Strong aircraft. I remind myself that this is the newest aircraft in our unit. We are a few feet from the ground, and the crew chief yells at the Koreans to get off. Everyone off, and we are coming out. Suddenly I hear weapons firing, and they are not ours. Sounds like an AK-47 firing somewhere close. Steve flies us out of the elephant grass and puts us in a fast climb, hauling ass. "That machine gun is still firing. Somebody take care of it!" I yell. We are maybe 200 feet off the LZ when our day goes to hell.

The whole aircraft shudders, and then we are vertical, looking straight up. Steve screams, "What the hell! I'm hit! I'm hit!" Instinctively I take over the controls. Just like we were taught in flight school, I level the aircraft and apply power. I think it's too late. The aircraft is shaking and vibrating like crazy. "Fly, damn you, fly," Why today? Why now? Dear God, I need help." Everything seems to be moving in slow motion. Steve is conscious but can hardly move. Hell, I'm settling with power. "Where am I going to crash this machine? Oh dear God, don't let us burn to death." I know that

Hueys usually burn on impact because the fuel tanks are almost full. "Steve, where are you hit?" He says that he can't feel his feet. I try to keep the rotor rpm up, so I will have power when I find a spot. If I get out of this, I promise to be a better son, father and husband. The ground is coming up quickly, and I see a bare area on a hillside to my right. I don't want to roll down the hill, don't want to burn. "Hold on, guys; we are about to crash." What is the rest of the flight doing? Steve is hit, and we are going down. Seems like I've been at this for a very long time, and we are still moving in slow motion. I hear my training commands in my mind: "Auto-rotate, flair and pull all the power you have." I guess we don't have much power at the end because we hit hard in a forward motion. I land on a wide, sloping spot on the hill. The nose of the aircraft is headed down the hill, but we stick to the hill.

The engine is running, and the rotor blades have taken out all the small trees and brush around us. Thank God we have not caught fire. Cut off the fuel, shut down the aircraft, leave battery on, so we can talk on the radio. I am still operating on instinct. I make radio contact. I report that we are all okay, but Steve is hit, conscious and talking.

We are still taking enemy fire. The crew chief gets on the fifty-caliber and returns fire. The concussion from the gun causes the door gunner to be knocked out of the aircraft. "Stop the shooting; we can't think or talk." He doesn't hear me. I unbuckle and am getting out when the concussion from the .50 cal. throws me out of the aircraft too. My head is really hurting. I had impacted the instrument panel when we crashed because my seat belt was not locked. A little blood is nothing to worry about. Gunner and crew chief do not have a scratch. The door gunner and I get back into the aircraft, and the three of us pull back Steve's seat and lay him out in the back of the ship. We cannot find any blood or figure out where he is hit. We pull off the chicken plate and see the wound. He has taken a round in his chest about an inch above the plate. The left side of the aircraft from the nose back has taken multiple hits, but the crew chief does not have a scratch. His lucky day so far.

Back on the radio, and Warrant Officer Pilot Bob Mitchell starts hovering down the hill from us. Can we get to him? I grab my M-16 and start down the hill to find him. I can hear the insertion still going on, and off in the distance I can hear Bob's aircraft. The trail down isn't too bad, but about 100 yards down the trail I am surprised by two Vietnamese coming out of the brush. Like in an old time movie, we all jump in fright and go in opposite directions. No time to shoot. I continue down the trail about another 50 yards when I came to an open area and see the helicopter hovering in a clearing about 100 yards further down the hill. Now that I know the location, I start back up the hill to get my crew.

When I get back to the helicopter, I am surprised and elated to see Sergeant Ron Lee, Mitchell's crew chief, helping get Steve off the aircraft. Lee had jumped off his ship and come up the trail to help us, even though he was unarmed. Somehow we missed each other on the trail.

It takes all four of us to carry Captain Bovio down the hill to the waiting aircraft. When we get to the aircraft, I realize Mitchell has not landed because of all the brush and has been hovering, I think, for a very long time. In order to get Bovio in the aircraft, Lee and my gunner grasp the skids and first pull themselves into the ship. The two of us on the ground hold Bovio above our heads while the two on the ship pull him in. We jump in and head to the nearest hospital at Nha Trang. On the way, Captain Bovio is conscious but unable to breathe on his own; we take turns giving him mouth-to-mouth resuscitation.

At the hospital we are taken to separate treatment rooms, and I can hear the doctors working on Steve. As soon as the medic treats me, I can no longer endure the hospital. I leave and walk back to my room in the officers' quarters. I am trying to figure out what happened, and I am very angry. When I get to my room, I keep going over the events. How could I have prevented this? Why Steve instead of me? Bad things have been happening for the past month. When does this end, or is this the end? I know that I should go to the club and be with people. I need to talk with someone, but there is no one. I'm alone.

A short time later, Major Stevens, the company commander, comes to my room and informs me that Captain Bovio is stable and is being transferred to Cam Ranh Bay. He asks how I am feeling. When I tell him that I am okay, he leaves.

The next couple of days are a blur. I go to the orderly room and to my office to work. The clerks are polite and offer words of encouragement. Each morning I start off with a vodka and orange juice with my coffee. I return to normal habits.

A few days after the incident, I am told by the commander that the following day I will be flying with aircraft commander Warrant Officer Bob Mitchell on a combat assault. I wonder if I can do this so soon, or if I should wait. Maybe I should wait. I don't.

The next morning it's the same old pattern. I start early, do preflight, do mission brief, brief crew and wait to crank. It is a ten-ship flight, but we will be part of a bigger assault. The location is Southwest of Cam Ranh Bay with artillery and gunship support.

The mission is going as planned; everyone is up, and we are out of the PZ and headed to our first LZ. A half mile from final, I see the artillery hitting our area. I'm on the controls, and Mitchell is watching me. The flight is tight, and the LZ is large enough to hold us. I'm sweating like crazy. I feel my knees and legs shaking. The gunships are working the LZ.

I don't want to do this. I don't want to be here. I'm scared but keep going. Short final, and the flight is progressing well. Mitchell is watching; I wonder if he can see my legs shake. Flight down, unload. Lead is coming out, and we are all doing great. For the next fourteen hours, we work that operation, and my knees and legs never shake again.

A few days later I get the bad news:

Captain Richard Stephen Bovio died on 27 February 1970, as a result of his wounds.

The company commander did me a favor when he sent me out on the next combat assault. For the rest of my tour, I knew I had the confidence and ability to survive as long as my luck held. And it did.

Captain Roger Green,
Executive Officer

Part Two

I was flying as Aircraft Commander that day with First Lieutenant Ned Heintz as my co-pilot, Specialist Five Ron Lee as my crew chief and Specialist Four Fred Howard as the door gunner. I was flying from the left seat with First Lieutenant Heintz in the right seat. Specialist Five Ron Lee was gunner on the left side, and Specialist Four Fred Howard was on the right.

This was a joint operation with the 281st Assault Helicopter Company UH-1H Slicks, whose call sign was Intruder, and the 48th AHC UH-1C Gunships, whose call sign was Joker. It was a 10th Combat Aviation Battalion assault mission. As I remember, the landing zone was large by our standards, and the intended touch down point was at the apex of a hill. There was a bomb or artillery crater at the intended touch down area. The LZ had been prepped by Artillery and/or Tac Air prior to the assault, and the Joker Gunships were providing cover on the assault. I was Chalk Two behind Captain Steve Bovio and Captain Roger Green. I remember discussing my position in the formation with Captain Green before the mission. I was a Senior Aircraft Commander and usually flew either lead or trail. Because Captain Green was about to be assigned as the Executive Officer, and Captain Bovio was about to become the Bandit Platoon Leader, Captain Green told me he wanted to lead the flight to give Captain Bovio the experience needed to do the job when he took over. I wound up number two, or Chalk Two, for this reason. I did not like to fly as number two because any aircraft in this position would usually take enemy fire first.

The aircraft were spaced at intervals so when one aircraft was on takeoff, the next was on short final. I was on final approach as Captain Green made his touchdown in the landing zone. The crew dropped their troops and moved forward to lift off. As they started their climb out, I was on very short final. I saw the lead aircraft yaw and pitch up to the left and then nose down to the right. Captain Green made a call; "Taking fire," followed by, "Going down." The aircraft disappeared below my line of sight before it crashed into the elephant grass on the down slope northeast of the intended LZ. I could see flying pieces of elephant grass and dust when the aircraft impacted. At this point in time I was committed to land and continued my approach into the LZ.

As we came closer to touch down in the LZ, we started taking light, small-arms fire on the left. We could not touch down in the LZ and came to a hover over the crater. Some of the troops jumped from the aircraft and crawled into the crater which was directly beneath my aircraft. Other troops stayed on the aircraft and had to be gently coaxed into leaving. My objective was to off-load the troops, get out of the hot LZ and move to the crash site. I called C&C (Command and Control), reported taking fire and told him my intentions. There was another aircraft near me in the LZ at this time, whose exact location I do not recall. The other aircraft in the assault aborted and began to orbit to the south. Things were happening pretty fast,

194

and decisions were made even faster. I directed Lee's fire to my 11 o'clock position, from which the small-arms fire was coming. The fire was very intense by that time, and we took a hit through the Green House above my head. The round passed in front of my face and directly in front of Heintz's face before exiting through his door window. We also took several hits along the left side of the aircraft fuselage and tail. We were not taking any fire from the right. The radio traffic was terrible. Lee and I discussed the possibility of his making his way to the downed aircraft to check on the crew. We decided that it was his call. He left the aircraft. Howard moved from his position to the left side of the aircraft. The M-60 on the left side began to fail due to excessive heat on the barrel. Howard removed the left M-60, moved back to the right and removed his M-60 to switch it to the left side of the aircraft. During this process the enemy fire increased as Howard was moving to the left side of the aircraft. He held the M-60 in his hands as he fired on the enemy gunner. He was standing directly behind the cockpit in the cabin area and firing out the left cargo door opening. This caused hot shell casings to fly all over the cabin and cockpit area. Lieutenant Heintz finally got Howard's attention and had him move toward the rear of the cabin area where he was closer to the left cargo-door opening. I had three radios blaring in my ears as I tried to communicate with Joker Lead (CW2 Gay, 48th AHC) on VHF, C&C on UHF and ground traffic on FM. I finally was able to pinpoint the location of the enemy gunner by following the tracers back to a muzzle flash. I then directed the Jokers in on the target. A pair of rockets took care of the enemy gunner, and there seemed to be a lull in the enemy fire. About this time, Lee had made his way back to our aircraft and briefed me on the situation with the downed helicopter. He explained Bovio was badly wounded and needed evacuation as soon as possible. During Lee's heroic sprint to the downed aircraft, he had run directly into an AK-47 carrying enemy soldier which caused both of them to fall to the ground. According to Lee both were surprised and stunned. They had both gotten up and continued to run in the direction they were initially heading. Once Lee was strapped in and the M-60s rearranged with a new barrel installed, I made the decision to reposition from our present location to that of the downed aircraft. I advised C&C of my intentions and moved my aircraft forward and to my right approximately 100 meters. I positioned my aircraft as near the downed aircraft as possible. The crew, both on the ground and in my aircraft, was directing me lower, but the elephant grass was too high. After a few seconds of trying to avoid hitting the grass, I lowered the aircraft over the downed aircraft, causing my main rotor blades to cut into the grass and brush.

The downed air crewmen were outside the aircraft as we hovered over as close as we could without making contact. Green and his door gunner and crew chief were on the ground outside the aircraft, pulling Captain Bovio out of his seat and repositioning him in the cargo area of the downed helicopter. Bovio had been hit in the left side by AK-47 fire and was paralyzed. I held my aircraft in a hover two to three feet above the downed aircraft. At this point Captain Green lifted the wounded Bovio, with help from the crewmen, and loaded him in the cargo area of my aircraft. After

Bovio was secured, Green and his crew came aboard. The small-arms fire had been suppressed by the Jokers by this time, so we were not taking fire during this phase of the flight. We flew out of the crash site to a higher altitude and proceeded toward Nha Trang.

After we cleared the area and were out of harm's way, I made radio calls to C&C and 281st Flight Operations advising them of my position and estimated time of arrival at 8th Field Hospital MEDEVAC Pad in Nha Trang. Flight Operations passed the information to the hospital. During the flight of 15 to 20 minutes, Bovio was bleeding profusely despite the efforts of Green and the other crewmen. Upon arrival at the hospital pad, the medics met us and helped off-load the wounded Bovio and other crewmen. To the best of my recollection, all of them went into the hospital to be checked. I flew back to the 281st area and shut down.

Post flight inspection revealed twelve bullet holes, both main rotor blades severely damaged and extreme stress to the airframe. Captain Green's aircraft had impacted the ground so hard the aircraft was severely damaged and declared a total loss. Both aircraft were sling-loaded by Chinook to Qui Nhon Army Aviation Maintenance Facility for further disposition.

The actions of Specialist Five Ron Lee and Specialist Four Fred Howard were truly outstanding, and without a doubt were pivotal in our success at extracting the crew of the downed aircraft. This was First Lieutenant Ned Heintz's first taste of combat, and he performed flawlessly in his role. Without these men working together as a team, there would have been two downed aircraft in that LZ on that morning. Specialist Five Ron Lee was awarded the Silver Star for heroism on this mission.

Chief Warrant Officer Mitchell's finger through the hole made by the bullet that just missed him.

Chief Warrant Officer Bob Mitchell,
Aircraft Commander

A JUMP FOR LIFE

On 27 April 1970, Chief Warrant Officer Bob Gardner had just returned from his extension leave. He was flying as aircraft commander on a mission for the 4th Infantry Division with his crew members on board. Warrant Officer Stan Miller was his co-pilot, Specialist Five George Tom was the Crew Chief and Specialist Four Gary Fields was the door gunner. They were flying north, deep into enemy territory, on a rescue mission through the An Khe pass when the aircraft was engaged on both sides by two deadly .51 caliber enemy machine guns. Bob took the brunt of the fire and slumped over the controls as the helicopter was coming apart. The controls were all shot up, there was no way Warrant Officer Stan Miller could control the aircraft as it nosed over. They were falling fast; all they could do was hold on.

Door gunner Specialist Gary Fields only had seconds to decide whether to ride it all the way to the ground and risk his chances of surviving an uncontrollable crash, or to jump. The helicopter was falling fast toward a rice field filled with water. At the very last moment, he made the decision to unbuckle his safety harness and jump for his life. Falling about 200 feet into a muddy rice patty, he hit hard. He was recovered by the crew of a 1st Cavalry Division helicopter that was flying in the vicinity of the crash. With life threatening injuries he was immediately flown to the nearest field hospital for treatment. There were no other survivors. Specialist Fields' injuries were so numerous he was evacuated first to Japan and then to a Veterans hospital in the states, where he remained in a coma for the first four months of his treatment. His luck changed when a very pretty nurse started checking on him every day, even on her days off. For the next two years the VA hospital was his home. He had good days and bad days, but slowly got better. Gary Fields had a very good reason to survive; he was falling in love.

After the second year, he was released from the hospital, and he took his nurse with him. They were married and moved to Springdale, Arkansas where they lived happily until his death on 31 October 2006.

He had survived the jump for life, and he had had a strong desire to live, yet he never fully recovered from that jump. For the rest of his life he lived with the pain from his war injuries, but he also lived with the love of a wonderful woman, his beautiful wife Tacara.

On 27 April 1970, the company lost three good men: Specialist Five George W. Tom, Warrant Officer Stanley J. Miller Jr. and Chief Warrant Officer Robert W. Gardner were shot down.

LONG DAYS AND HOT NIGHTS

The days were becoming hot and muggy, dusty and dirty. Malaria was common, so we all had to take large pills to prevent it. The pills had side effects, including diarrhea. Because of malaria or the diarrhea, there were times when some of the crew was grounded. However, the discomfort of diarrhea was so much better than coming down with malaria.

At home base in Nha Trang the chow was very good. The living conditions were good, and even though everyone was busy, generally speaking, life was good. When in support of Delta at the forward operating bases, (FOB) the food was mostly C-rations. We lived in tents, and when not on a mission, we filled sand bags to place around the tents for protection in case of a mortar or rocket attack. The maintenance people were busy and usually working out in the open: they kept the aircraft in great shape. Even in the hot, muggy, moist weather, the avionics men made sure each radio in each helicopter was working perfectly. It was everyone constantly working as a team that kept the morale up day after day. From the very beginning the 281st Assault Helicopter Company was known for its commitment to the troops on the ground. They always knew we would come get them when they got into trouble.

****

On 11 May 1970, the rocket sounded like a low-flying jet ripping through the air as it landed near two tents. With a thunderous explosion that shook the ground, it scattered huge chunks of jagged metal, which tore through anyone and anything in its kill radius. The communist 122mm rocket was particularly menacing. It weighed 112 pounds and had a range of ten miles, carrying an immense warhead of forty-two pounds. Although extremely inaccurate, it was a very loud and deadly weapon.

On 11 May 1970, Specialist Five Joseph W Cunningham, Specialist Five Scott Eugene Sutherland, Specialist Five Danny Joe Taulbee and Specialist Five Daniel Joseph Vaughan were killed in a rocket attack at Pleiku. Five days later Lieutenant Ned Heintz died from his wounds received from the same attack.

THE SOUNDS OF WAR

The loneliest sound was the fading whop, whop sound made by the helicopter as it flew away after the 281st Assault Helicopter crew had inserted me and my team into the dense jungles of South Vietnam. The sweetest sound I ever heard was the whop, whop sound of the 281st Assault Helicopter Company helicopters coming back to get us. They came in rain storms, dark of night and when we were surrounded by the bad guys. No matter what, they always came back.

Master Sergeant Arvin M. Briscoe,
U.S. Army Retired
5th Special Forces Group, Vietnam

The sound of an AK-47, which the enemy used against us, was quite different from the sounds of the M-14 and M-16 that our troops used. Almost everyone could tell by the sound whether there were incoming mortar rounds or outgoing rounds. After a few months in Vietnam, most of us could sleep through the sound of outgoing rounds, but the sound of the enemy's incoming mortars or rockets would wake us up, and we would dive for cover.

Each airplane had a different sound. Even the exploding bombs they dropped had a different sound. The weapons on each aircraft all had a different sound. When napalm was dropped, it made swishing sounds as it exploded, burning and sucking up the very air as it rolled and tumbled through the battlefield.

There were sounds that haunted us, never to be forgotten sounds:

> The sound of bullets hitting the helicopter. The thump, thump tic sound as each bullet tore holes in the skin of the helicopter, and the increase in volume when the bullets hit a component.

> The sound of the whispered voices of radio operator on the ground, when s team was about to be surrounded by the enemy and needed emergency evacuation.

> The sound of a desperate voice pleading over the radio for help.

> The sounds of wounded warriors suffering in pain in the back of the helicopter, while being flown from the battlefield to the nearest hospital for emergency medical attention

> The whistling sound a main rotor blade made when it had a bullet hole through it.

> The mind-numbing sight and sound when Puff the Magic Dragon lit up the night and saved your sorry butt.

> The absolute silence when the Magic Dragon was done.

> The sound of sadness in our voices when fewer ships came home than left that morning.

> The eerie sound of silence inside the helicopter when the whoop, whoop and whine stopped.

> The engine-crying sound when the jet engine started to burn the fuel cell sealant from the bottom of the tank just before it ran out of fuel.

The sounds of war were exciting, loud, scary and deadly. Over time these sounds had a destructive effect on the minds of those who heard them.

On 20 May 1970, Specialist Five Paul Bruce Lambertson and Specialist Five Arthur Gerald Qualls were killed in a helicopter accident. They were the last Intruders lost in the war.

All of the 281st, the clerk, supply sergeant, avionics, maintenance and every other member of the company, felt pain when we saw an empty bunk due to the loss of one of our own. War is hell. The life span of a flight crew member was very short in combat, yet I do not know of anyone, not even one man, who refused to go when he was needed.

Thousands of American Vietnam Veterans earned medals for bravery every day. A few were even awarded.

INTRUDERS WHO RECEIVED THEIR COUNTRY'S HIGHEST AWARDS FOR HEROES

DONALD B. McCOIG
Warrant Officer, Aviator
Donald B. McCoig was awarded the Distinguished Service Cross,
the second highest award for bravery in combat.

DONALD G. TORRINI
Warrant Officer, Aviator
Donald Torrini was recommended for the Congressional Medal of Honor,
he was awarded the Silver Star,
the third highest award for bravery in combat.

MAHLON E. BUCKALEW
Staff Sergeant, Wolf Pack Platoon Sergeant
Mahlon Buckalew was awarded the Silver Star,
the third highest award for bravery in combat.

ROBERT L. GEORGE
Chief Warrant Officer 2, Aviator
Robert George was awarded the Silver Star,
the third highest award for bravery in combat.

ROBIN K. HICKS
Warrant Officer, Aviator
Robin Hicks was awarded the Silver Star,
the third highest award for bravery in combat.

RONALD C. LEE
Specialist Five, Crew Chief
Ronald Lee was awarded the Silver Star,
the third highest award for bravery in combat.

LYLE BELTCH
First Lieutenant, Aviator
Lyle Beltch was awarded the Silver Star,
the third highest award for bravery in combat.

Warrant Officer Donald Bruce McCoig was 22 years, 2 months and 6 days old when he said, "I can," and in turn he gave his life for his fellow soldiers and his country. For his actions on 29 March 1968, WO McCoig was posthumously awarded the Distinguished Service Cross, The Distinguished Flying Cross, and The Air Medal. On 3 May 2000, the Headquarters Building of the 2nd Battalion, 10th Aviation Brigade located at Fort Drum, NY was officially named the McCoig Building in honor of Warrant Officer McCoig's sacrifice in the Vietnam War.

THOSE WHO WAIT ALSO SERVE

When your loved one is in Vietnam, a vigilant mindset of optimism is crucial. When the notification of injury or death arrives at your door, it is not entirely unexpected as it would be in the case of an auto accident or a crime. However, it is still a shock and takes you to your knees as the reality of war comes into your home.

When my husband, First Lieutenant Ned Heintz, was injured in May, 1970 in Nha Trang, South Vietnam while serving as a helicopter pilot with the 281st Assault Helicopter Company, the telegram delivery was reality. I knew what it meant: bad news. For the following five days we waited. Each day a new telegram was delivered as his condition worsened. We continued to wait and wait and wait.

On the fifth day, two U. S. Army officers, accompanied by the local Methodist minister, drove into my driveway. Again, I knew what that meant: really bad news. It could not have been easy for Army officers to deliver such bad news to those who were waiting. They handled it with extreme professionalism and compassion. The Army really does take care of its own. That same day, the phone calls began arriving from the Survivor Assistance Officer (SAO) to tell us he was coming the next day to make all the funeral arrangements and arrange for the transportation of "our hero." Again, extreme professionalism and compassion was shown; it was not just a routine task to be done. There were many details to be dealt with and a mountain of paperwork to be signed.

Then the process of waiting began again. For five days, we received daily reports on the progress of transporting Ned home and organizing the color guard and escorts from Fort Knox, Kentucky. We waited.

My in-laws and Ned's brother were somewhat overwhelmed with all the details and the Army way of doing things. As an Army wife, I had been "trained" as we had been briefed on several occasions as to our job.

The only dilemma that arose while working with the SAO was the 21-gun salute and playing of taps at the funeral. With tears in her eyes, my mother-in-law said, "No guns, no guns." The SAO assured her that it was how the Army honored their fallen hero, and it was needed for closure. After the funeral, she agreed that it had been appropriate.

There was not much information offered by the Army as to the incident. Again, we waited, but details never came. Sometimes, it still feels as if Ned went away and just didn't come back. When I think about him, he is still the tall, dark, and handsome man I had first met. He is gone, but never forgotten. I feel blessed that we shared our lives in many special ways. Memories do not fade. They become more vivid as time passes.

The 281st AHC have helped those of us left behind so much for so many years by providing details and remembrances of friendships formed. We can never thank them enough for not forgetting those brave men with whom they served. We truly are a military family. Keep the spirit alive!

Dr. Karen Heintz Forcht
Widow of First Lieutenant Ned Heintz

On 8 July 1970, Major Michael J. Wolfe assumed command of the company

THREE PHASES OF A TOUR

Statistically, you were more likely to meet your maker during your first sixty days in combat than during the next ten months of your twelve-month tour. During those twelve months, you went through three phases. The first few months, sixty days, was the new-guy phase. Being green as new grass, you had no idea what was going on. This learning phase was the most deadly. Learning what to do and, more importantly, what not to do required you to be a quick learner in order to survive. During the second phase you just did your job, doing what you were trained to do and listening to the old timers who had been there and done that. You were no longer a new guy, and what a relief that was. You did your time and tried not to think about all the "what ifs." If you were lucky, you reached the last phase; you were a short timer. A short timer was someone who had less than sixty days left in Vietnam. During this phase you became more paranoid, even more cautious, and your preflight took longer to perform. You made sure you had your act together, so to speak. You took more precautions when you were on a mission. You paid more attention to your surroundings; you noticed every little thing. Above all, you wanted to stay away from the new guys. Your most important possession was your short timer's calendar, where you checked off the days until the day you boarded the freedom bird going back to the good ol' USA.

RUMORS

The phone in flight operations was ringing constantly; every major unit in the II corps area wanted the 281st Assault Helicopter Company to help with their missions. In fact, there were fourteen major units requesting our services. For the last ten months the crews had been flying almost every day; this was one busy helicopter company. In October 1970, the 281st had flown 5,611.6 continuous accident free hours. No wonder they were in demand. The crews were performing at the highest level of proficiency and safety. The maintenance team kept the availability at 91.24 percent, an unheard of record in a combat zone.

The word was out; Secretary of State Henry Kissinger was holding secret peace talks with the North Vietnamese in Paris. How could it be a secret when it was all over the front page of the Army Times? We now knew the 5th Marine Division had departed Vietnam, and the 3rd brigade of the 9th Infantry had also left. What was going on?

There were always rumors about this and that. The most recent rumor was we were all going home and that the 281st would be no more. Every soldier certainly had his own opinion about the war, but the men of the 281st had their own special perspective of the war after flying all the secret and top secret Special Operation missions. They had their own special war far removed from others.

They wanted to win the war, and they knew they could. If there were peace talks it was okay, but they wanted peace with honor. Too many of our brave men had given the ultimate price; we could not just give up and walk away. The 281st had the best Army aviators, the best crew chiefs, and the best gunners. Flying the best kept helicopters, they made a winning team.

The rumors kept circulating throughout the month of October. If they were true, the future of the 281st Assault Helicopter Company was anyone's guess. Were they going to be reassigned, be given a change of name, sent back to stateside duty, disbanded or what? Toward the end of the month the 281st Intruders received word that on the 30th of October the company would begin a stand down of operations in preparation for deactivation.

This honored helicopter company had accomplished its mission; Project Delta had come to an end. The 5th Special Forces was assigned a different role. The war would continue during the peace talks while more troops departed. More men were wounded and scarred for life, and more men died. War was hell, but for the 281st to think they had fought in vain was worse. This was a proud company of soldiers. No matter what, they should all go home with their heads held high with pride. Some gave their all, and all gave their best. A promise was made never to forget those who gave up their lives, those men who went above and beyond the call of duty to save a fellow soldier.

Once an Intruder, always an Intruder.

The month of November marked the beginning of the end for the 281st Assault Helicopter Company. Most of the men could not believe it. In spite of being well-trained, well-disciplined, well-motivated and well-led, America's best were being reassigned; being sent to other units to serve out their time in Vietnam.

	Authorized	Assigned
Officers	19	17
Warrant officers	51	43
Enlisted men	219	171
Civilians	2	

A mission the men had never dreamed of performing was given to them; the task of preparing an inventory of the numerous items for turn-in or for transfer to other units. Flight operations was busy with pilots and crews from other units flying away our helicopters. It was unreal. Each passing day, the number of empty revetments increased, and by 7 November 1970, seventy-five per cent of the company's helicopters had been turned in. Other units were getting our well-maintained equipment. It was a sad thing to see them fly away with new crews at the controls.

The tempo increased daily, and trucks were lined up, loaded, and left in a convoy heading for Cam Ranh Bay carrying away our equipment.

Sergeant Gary Stagman had been the fourth man to sign in when the company was organized at Fort Benning, Georgia. He was a private first class. Almost five years later he was a noncommissioned officer. He was the only soldier to have played a part both at the beginning and at the end of this honored helicopter company.

The property books were closed, and everything was accounted for, except for what was most important. There were ten men, ten warriors, missing. How could we end this without accounting for those men? How could the books be closed without accounting for those soldiers? Where were they? How could we go home and leave them behind?

During the last few days I walked the flight lines, I checked the maintenance area and the motor pool. No more smell of JP-4, no whop, whop sounds of rotor blades. Everyone had left; the place was vacant. All the revetments were empty, the conex containers were empty, and everything had been taken away. I stood in the flight operations building, looking at a clean and completely empty area with not even a chair in sight. The sound of my combat boots echoed as I walked across the floor to the pilots' briefing room and back. There was an eerie feeling. I stood in the middle of that strangely quiet room and asked myself the old question "What if these walls could talk." I walked out, locked the doors and did not look back.

Captain Marshall Hawkins,
December, 1970

LAST DAYS

The green leadership tabs were pinned on my epaulettes as I became the last officer in charge of this honored 281st Assault Helicopter Company. I am now in command, if only for a short time. I am the only officer with the rank of captain to be its commander. I have been a flight platoon leader, flight operations officer, executive officer and now the company commander. The mission of the 5th Special Forces Group is changing. The Delta mission is over, and the war is taking a different course. The 281st Assault Helicopter Company is taking its place in the history books as the first Special Operations Helicopter Aviation Company to be attached to a Special Forces Group. I think we all stand proud to have served with so many brave men.

The handwriting is on the wall. It is over. Now it is up to me to make sure the ending goes smoothly, all the equipment is accounted for and properly signed for. It is my responsibility to make sure the process goes well and ends well. The equipment, from helicopters and vehicles, down to desks, filing cabinets and even the bunks in the barracks, has to be listed and then shipped out to other units and organizations.

It is an honor to be assigned to the 281st; an honor to have served and flown with some of America's best. I wish this Special Operations helicopter company could continue; could go on forever. Over the past four years we have made our mark in the history books. We are a proud band of men, soldiers and brothers. Our mission has been accomplished, and now it is time to close the books.

As I stand outside in the company area and look at the enlisted men's barracks, the orderly room, and the company headquarters, I think of all the decisions that have been made here over the past four and a half years, and I am filled with pride. A cool breeze on this December morning is blowing across the company area where our enlisted men stood so often in company formation. I remember seeing a similar scene in the old Wild West movies. The cowboy walked down the street, leaving town, as the wind blew the tumble weeds in front of the vacant buildings making up the ghost town. I think of him and compare myself to the last man leaving Dodge.

My duty of accounting for each item and making certain that the books balance is a challenge I have never performed before. With the help of good men we have accomplished the final mission. I make one last walk through the company area and turn out the lights.

Captain Nollie W. Wagers,
December, 1970

MISSION COMPLETED

ONE LAST LOOK

COMMANDERS AND FIRST SERGEANTS

July 65-June 66
Commander: Major Kevin Murphy (145, the 6th PL, and 2/171 before transition to the 281st AHC)

October 1965-June 66
Commander: Major Everdus H. Hackett
First Sergeant J. B. Cooley

June 66-11 February 67
Commander: Major William "Bill" P. Griffin
First Sergeant J. B. Cooley

11 February 67-9 September 67
Commander: Major Allen L. Junko
First Sergeant J. B. Cooley, May 1967,
followed by First Sergeant Edward Shortman

9 September 67-8 February 68
Commander: Major John W. Mayhew
First Sergeant Edward Shortman

8 February 68-July 68
Commander: Major Donald Ruskauff
First Sergeant Edward Shortman, May 68,
followed by First Sergeant Carl E. Bradershneider

August 68-17 February 69
Commander: Major Andrew J. Miller, Jr.
First Sergeant Carl E. Bradershneider

17 February 69-August 69
Commander: Major Ellie E. Lynn
First Sergeant Johnny C. Martin

2 August 69-15 January 70
Commander: Major George W. Little
First Sergeant Johnny C. Martin

16 January 70-7 July 70
Commander: Major Darryl M. Stevens
First Sergeant Vernon A. Erickson

8 July 70-14 December 70
Commander: Major Michael J. Wolfe
First Sergeant Vernon A. Erickson

14 December 70-1 March 71.
Captain Nollie N. "Woody" Wagers

Captain Wagers was the last Commanding Officer. He was in charge for 79 days after the departure of Major Wolfe. Captain Wagers closed out the unit and transferred the colors and guidon to the USAR on 1 March 1971.

281st Company Guidon

YOU ALWAYS CAME BACK

As with every Special Forces unit, we could be given any assignment at any time. In many cases the successful completion of a mission depended upon our ability to reach an objective quickly and get out of an extraction location even quicker. The unit that responded to our call in both of these situations was the 281st Assault Helicopter Company, our assigned aviation support unit. Assigned to support unique and dangerous Special Forces operations, they were a band of brothers so daring and courageous that they and their unit will, quite literally, go down in the pages of military history.

In my role as a Special Forces military advisor, I was witness to many bold, selfless acts by men of the 281st AHC. Not all of their missions or courage involved blazing, enemy ground fire. On one occasion, pilots and crew delivered desperately needed water to my large combat patrol by descending through a very small opening in a triple canopy jungle. We had used all of our demolitions to create a makeshift landing zone and could make it no larger. As helicopters came and went, their rotor blades clipped tree branches around the opening. An abrupt movement in any direction could have been instantly fatal to these brave airmen. When I cautioned them about the danger, each pilot responded in similar terms, "We're fine. Your water is coming down, but stay out of the way in case something does happen." This was just one of the many times that the 281st demonstrated their amazing flying skills and confidence.

On another occasion, the 281st volunteered to fly in support of a rescue that involved escaped Montagnard elders who were pleading for their village to be freed from enemy control and evacuated to a safe location. When advised of the mission and associated dangers inherent in such an operation, the response given to me by the 281st unit commander was for me to tell him where and when, and they would be there. As a result of the total support of the 281st AHC, our combined ground and air team was able to complete its mission, a mission that freed 165 men, women and children from the oppression that they had endured for years.

The rescue of the villagers might seem like a happy ending, but it was not.

Several members of my team and I stayed behind. We also had three American civilians with us. While our circumstances were tenuous, we knew we would be fine if our extraction was quick. Unfortunately, that didn't happen. A heavy storm had blown in off the South China Sea and grounded the 281st in Nha Trang while they were refueling. Regulations prevented the unit from flying in such weather conditions. To make the situation worse, the weather had restricted our radio communications. I was unable to reach our base camp or any other support unit. Our twelve-man combat team and three civilians were stranded in enemy territory in the middle of nowhere with absolutely no support available. The rescuers were now in need of rescue.

Fortunately for us, those who knew the 281st also knew that regulations were unlikely to prevent them from completing a mission. They always came back! The flight leader who extracted us was aware of our dangerous and life-threatening situation. After waiting as long as he felt he could, he directed his team of three helicopters to launch. Risking their own lives for ours, the three ships took off in a driving rain storm and headed in our direction.

Not knowing the 281st was on the way, we had begun to move off the LZ and down into the jungle with the intention of walking towards our nearest outpost, approximately 20 kilometers away. This was not what I wanted to do with three civilians in tow, but it seemed like the best of unfavorable alternatives. To return safely, we would have to carefully make our way through enemy-controlled territory.

We were almost in the jungle when my radio began to crackle. An olive-green gunship soon swooped down out of the clouds and hovered directly over our position. The 281st had arrived! As the gunship circled to provide cover for our extraction, one of the newsmen happily exclaimed, "It looks like a big, green angel to me!" We quickly boarded and left the area.

I personally witnessed many selfless and heroic deeds by men of the 281st. It can be noted that many Special Forces members involved in unique and sometimes secret operations are alive today because of bold and daring actions taken by the men of this unit.

Their friends, families and our country can be extremely proud of these men. I am proud to have served with them, and they made me very proud to be an American. It is likely that I am among those who owe their lives to these men who were unafraid to fly into the face of unknown dangers time and time again.

Even though it has been many, many years, I have never forgotten them. It always amazed me that these men constantly risked their lives to save the lives of others, and they did it nearly every day the unit served in South Vietnam. When I think about the 281st, it is with tremendous appreciation and admiration. It was their fearless actions in the face of unmistakable danger that earned the 281st the title of "God's Own Lunatics."

Major Thomas A. Ross,
U.S. Army Special Forces, Retired

THE SOUND THAT BINDS

Unique to all who served in Vietnam was the UH-1 helicopter. It was both devil and angel, and it served as both extremely well. Whether a LRRP, US or RVN, soldier or civilian, NVA, VC, Allied or civilian, it provided a sound and sense that lives with us all today. The memory of its sound immediately clears the clouds of time and refreshes the forgotten images within our mind. It will be the sound track of our last moments on earth. It was a simple machine with a single engine, a simple two-blade rotor system and a four-man crew. Like the Model T, it transformed us all and performed tasks the engineers and designers had never imagined. For soldiers, it was the worst and best of friends, and it was the binding material in the tapestry of a war of many pieces.

The smell was always hot, filled with JP-4 fumes and sharp drafts accentuated by gritty sand, laterite and anxious vibrations. It always held the spell of the unknown and the anxiety of learning what was next and what might be. It was an unavoidable magnet for the heavily-laden soldier who donkey-trotted to its squat, shaking shape through the haze and blast of dirt, stepped on the skid, turned and dropped his ruck on the cool aluminum deck. Reaching inside with his rifle or machine gun, a soldier would grasp a floor ring with a finger as an extra precaution of physics for those moments when the airborne bird would break into a sharp turn, revealing all ground or all sky to the helpless riders, all very mindful of the impeding weight on their backs. The relentless weight of the ruck combined with the stress of varying motion caused fingers and floor rings to bind almost as one. Constant was the vibration, smell of hydraulic fluid, flashes of visionary images and the occasional burst of a ground-fed odor of rotting fish, dank swampy heat, cordite or simply the continuous sinuous currents of Vietnam's weather, cold and driven mist in the northern monsoon or the wall of heated humidity in the southern dry season. Blotting it out and shading the effect was the constant sound of the rotating blades as they ate a piece of the air, struggling to overcome the momentary physics of the weather.

To divert anxiety, a soldier might reflect on his home away from home. The door gunners were usually calm, which was emotionally helpful. Each gun had a C-ration fruit can at the ammo box clip entrance to the feed mechanism of the machine gun. Cans of pears, apricots, apple sauce, and fruit cocktail all had just the right width to smoothly feed the belt into the gun, which was always a good thing. The gun had a large circular aiming sight, unlike the ground-pounder version. It gave the soldier the advantage of being able to fix on targets from the air considerably further than normal ground acquisition. Some gunners carried a large oil can, much like old locomotive engineers, to squeeze on the barrel to keep it cool. Usually this was accompanied by a large, olive-drab army towel or a khaki wound-pack bandage to allow a rubdown without a burned hand. Under the gunner's seat was usually a metal box filled with extra ammo, smoke grenades, water, a flare pistol, C-rations and a couple of well-worn paperbacks. The gun itself might be attached to the roof of the helicopter with a bungee cord and harness. This allowed the adventurous gunners to remove the gun from the fixed mount and fire it manually while standing on the skid with only the thinnest of connectivity to the bird. These were people you wanted near you, particularly on extractions.

The pilots were more mysterious. You only saw parts of them as they labored behind the armored seats. There would be an arm, a helmeted head and an occasional fingered hand as it moved across the dials and switches on the ceiling above. The armored side panels protected the pilot's upper torso; side, back, and seat, an advantage the passenger did not enjoy. Sometimes, a face shielded behind helmeted sunshades would turn around to impart a question with a glance or display a sense of anxiety with large, white-circled eyes. This was not a welcoming look, as the sounds of external issues fought to override the sounds of mechanics in flight. However, as a whole, the pilots got you there, took you back and kept you maintained. You never remembered their names, if you knew them at all; but you always remembered the ride and the sound.

Behind each pilot seat usually ran a stretch of wire or silk attaching belt. It would have held a variety of handy items for immediate use. Smoke grenades were the bulk of the attachment inventory, in various colors, and a couple of white phosphorous ones if a dramatic marking was needed. Trip flares or hand grenades would sometimes be included, depending on the location and mission. Hand grenades were a rare exception, as even pilots knew they exploded not always where intended. It was just a short, arm motion for a door gunner to pluck an inventory item off the string, pull the pin and pitch it, which was the point of the arrangement. You didn't want to be in a helicopter when such an act occurred as that usually meant there was an issue. Soldiers didn't like issues that involved them. It usually meant a long day or a very short one, neither of which was a good thing. Letting my mind focus on the past, this is the way it was.

The bird lifts off in a slow, struggling and shaking manner. Dust clouds obscure any view a soldier may have. Quickly, with a few subtle swings, the bird is above the dust and a cool, encompassing wind blows through. Sweat is quickly dried, eyes clear and a thousand feet of altitude shows the world below. Colors are muted, but objects are clear. Rows of wooden hootches, the airfield, local villages, an old B-52 bomber, the mottled trail left by a Ranch Hand, spray mission, and the open reflective water of a river or lake are crisp in sight. The initial anxiety of the flight or mission recedes as the constantly moving and soothing motion picture and soundtrack unfolds. In time, one is aware of the mass of UH-1s coalescing in a line in front of and behind you. Other strings of birds may be at one's left or right, all surging toward some small speck in the front, lost to view. Each is a mirror image of the other. There are two to three laden soldiers sitting on the edge looking at each other and at the other passengers all going to the same place with the same sense of anxiety and uncertainty but borne on a similar steed and sound.

In time, one senses the birds coalescing as they approach the objective. Perhaps a furtive glance or sweeping arc of flight reveals the landing zone. Smoke erupts in columns, initially visible as blue grey against the sky. The location is clearly discernible as a trembling spot surrounded by a vast, green carpet of flat jungle or the sharp point of a jutting ridge, As the bird gets closer, a soldier can now see the small FAC aircraft working well-below, the sudden sweeping curve of the bombing runs, and the small puffs as artillery impacts. A sense of immense loneliness can begin to obscure one's mind as the world's greatest theatre raises its curtain. Even closer now, with anxious eyes and short breath, a soldier can make out his destination. The smoke is now the dirty grey-black of munitions with only the slightest hint of orange upon ignition. No Hollywood effect is at work. Here, the physics of explosions are clearly evident as pressure and mass over light.

The pilot turns around to give a thumbs up or simply ignores his load as he struggles to maintain position with multiple birds dropping power through smoke swirls, uplifting newly created debris, sparks and flaming ash. The soldiers instinctively grasp their weapons tighter, look furtively between the upcoming ground and the pilot and mentally strain to find some anchor point for the next few seconds of life. If this is the first lift in, the door gunners are firing rapidly in sweeping motions of the gun, but this is largely unknown and unfelt to the soldiers. They are focused on the quickly approaching ground and the point where they will safely exit. Getting out is now very important. Suddenly, the gunners rapidly point to the ground and shout, "GO!" There is the jolt of the skids hitting the ground, and the soldiers instinctively lurch out of the bird, slam into the ground and focus on the very small part of the world they now can see. The empty birds, under full power, squeeze massive amounts of air and debris down on the exited soldiers, blinding them to the smallest view. Very quickly, there is a sudden shroud of silence as the birds retreat into the distance, and the soldiers begin their recovery into a cohesive organization, losing that sound.

On various occasions and weather dependent, the birds return. Some return to provide necessary logistics, command visits and some medevacs. On the rarest and best of occasions, they arrive to take a soldier home. Always they have the same sweet sound which resonates with every soldier who has ever heard it. It is the sound of life, hope for life and what may be. It is a sound that never will be forgotten. It is your sound and our sound.

Logistics is always a trial. Pilots don't like it; field soldiers need it; and weather is indiscriminate. Logistic flights also mean mail and a connection to home where real people live and live real lives. Here is an aberrant aspect of life which only that sound can relieve. Often there is no landing zone, or the area is so hot that a pilot's sense of purpose becomes blurred. Ground commanders beg and plead on the radio for support that is met with equivocations or insoluble issues. Rations are stretched from four to six days, cigarettes become serious barter items and soldiers begin to turn inward. In some cases, perhaps only minutes after landing, fire fights break out. The machine guns begin their carnivorous song. Rifle ammunition and grenades are expended with gargantuan appetites. The air is filled with an all-encompassing sound that shuts each soldier into his own small world of shooting, loading, shooting, loading, shooting, loading, until he has to quickly reach into the depth of his ruck, past the extra rations, past the extra rain poncho, past the spare paperback, to the eight M16 magazines forming the bottom of the load. He never thought he would need them. A resupply is desperately needed. In some time, a sound is heard over the din of battle. A steady whop, whop, whop that says, "The world is here. Help is on the way. Hang in there." The soldier turns back to the business at hand with a renewed confidence. Wind parts the canopy, and things begin to crash through the tree tops. Some cases have smoke grenades attached. These are the really important stuff: medical supplies, codes and maybe mail. The sound drifts off in the distance and things are better for the moment. The sound brings both a psychological and a material relief.

Wounds are hard to manage. The body is all soft flesh, integrated parts and an emotional burden for those who have to watch its deterioration. If the body is an engine, blood is the gasoline; when it runs out, so does the life. It's important that the parts get quickly fixed and the blood is restored to a useful level. If not, the soldier becomes another piece of battlefield detritus. A field medic has the ability to stop external blood flow, less so for the internal. He can replace blood with fluid, but it's not blood. He can treat for shock, but he can't always stop it. He is at the mercy of his ability and the nature of the wound. Bright red is surface bleeding, which he can manage, but dark red, almost tar-colored, is deep, visceral and beyond his ability to manage. Dark is the essence of the casualty's interior. He needs the help that only that sound can bring. If an LZ exists, it's wonderful and easy. If not, difficult options remain. The bird weaves back and forth above the canopy as the pilot struggles to find the location of the casualty. He begins a steady hover as he lowers the litter on a cable. The gunner or helicopter medic looks down at the small figures below and tries to wiggle the litter and cable through the tall canopy to the small up-reaching figures below. In time, the litter is filled, and the cable retreats, with the helicopter crew still carefully managing the cable as it winds skyward. The cable hits its anchor, the litter is pulled in, and the pilot pulls pitch and quickly disappears. However, the retreating sound is heard by all, accompanied by the silent universal thought "There but for the Grace of God go I, and it will be to that sound."

Cutting a landing zone is a standard soldier task. Often, to hear the helicopter's song, the impossible becomes a requirement and miracles abound. Sweat filled eyes, blood blistered hands, energy expended and with a breath of desperation and desire, soldiers attack a small space to carve out sufficient open air for the helicopter to land. It lands to bring in what's needed, take out what's not and to remind them that someone out there cares. Perhaps some explosives are used, usually for the bigger trees, but most often its soldiers and machetes or the side of an e-tool. Done under the pressure of an encroaching enemy, it's a combination of a high adrenalin rush and simple dumb luck: small bullet, big space. In time, an opening is made and the sky is revealed. A sound encroaches before a vision. Eyes turn toward the newly created void, and the bird appears. The blade tips seem so much larger than the newly-columned sky. Volumes of dirt, grass, leaves and twigs sweep upward and are then driven fiercely downward through the blades as the pilot struggles to do a completely vertical descent through the narrow column he has been provided. Below, the soldiers both cower and revel in the free-flowing air. The trash is blinding, but the moving air feels so great. Somehow, the pilot lands in a space that seems smaller than his blade radius. In reverse, the sound builds and then recedes into the distance. Always that sound bringing and taking away.

Extraction is the emotional highlight of any soldier's journey. Regardless of the austerity and issues of the home base, for that moment, it is a highly desired location and the focus of thought. It is provided by that familiar vehicle of sound. The pickup zone in the bush is relatively open or if on an established firebase or hilltop position, has a marked fixed location. The soldiers awaiting extraction, close to the location, undertake their assigned duties of security, formation alignment or LZ marking. Each is focused on the task at hand and tends to blot out other issues. As each soldier senses his moment of removal is about to arrive, his auditory sense becomes keen, and his visceral instinct searches for that single sweet song that only one instrument can play. When registered, his eyes look up, and he sees what his mind has imagined. He focuses on the sound and the sight, and both become larger as they fill his body. He quickly steps onto the skid and up into the aluminum cocoon. Turning outward now, he grasps his weapon with one hand and with the other holds the cargo ring on the floor, as he did when he first arrived at this location. Reversing the flow of travel, he approaches what he temporarily calls home. Landing again in a swirl of dust, aviation fuel and grinding sand, he offloads and trudges toward his assembly point. The sounds retreat in his ears, but he knows he will hear them again. He always will.

Colonel Keith Nightingale,
U.S. Army, Retired

Colonel Nightingale is a retired Army Colonel who served two tours in Vietnam with Airborne and Ranger (American and Vietnamese) units. He commanded airborne battalions in both the 509th Parachute Infantry Regiment and the 82nd Airborne Division. He later commanded the 1/75th Rangers and the 1st Ranger Training Brigade.

SO MANY WAYS TO DIE

Way too many American lives were lost in the small country of Vietnam. The Viet Cong used every method, both primitive and sophisticated, to kill as many of us as possible. The North Vietnamese Army was fearless and well disciplined; we lost a lot of good men in battle against them.

However, we lost more than our share to mechanical failure.

A number were lost trying to save their fellow men while flying in bad weather. Some were lost by pilot error. One of our commanders mentioned he used every tactic available to keep our crews from killing themselves. Safety was the name of the game.

The protests back in the USA fueled the enemy in many ways and indirectly caused more casualties. Politics was a major factor as it kept our commanders' hands tied.

There were so many ways to die in Vietnam. But the most disgusting way to die of all the possible ways was as a result of one of your own selling secret information to the enemy. John Anthony Walker, Jr. was a navy warrant officer who was responsible for the death of many, maybe more than the Viet Cong and North Vietnamese Army put together. Starting in the late 1960's he sold more than one million encrypted messages to the Soviets. He was the leader of the most damaging spy ring in our history. One of our congressmen on a trip to Russia mentioned to

Soviet Spy Chief Boris Solomatin, John Walker was "the spy of the decade." His response was, "Perhaps you are right."

UNFORGETTABLE CHARACTERS

There used to be a series of recurring articles in Readers Digest entitled "The Most Unforgettable Character I've Ever Met." I am sure most people have come across people in their lives who have made an impact, caused a moment of reflection, a series of unforgettable humorous events or who really aggravated us at one time. The 281st had more than its fair share of unforgettable characters.

Captain Stanley (Rudy) Morud

Rudy, as we knew him, was a real character from the first day he arrived in Nha Trang. Captain Stanley Morud, who had been a World War II fighter pilot, was a "do it now and do it right" leader with more combat flight time than most pilots. As the first commander of the 483rd Maintenance Detachment, he had the responsibility for developing a maintenance area, which would provide support to the newly formed 281st Assault Helicopter Company. True to Army procedures in Vietnam during that time period, Stan and his unit had no place to call home that was suitable for occupation or to conduct their mission. The first person Rudy approached was me, the unit aircraft maintenance officer. "How the hell does anyone expect us to do our job without equipment or the materials to fabricate our own area?" I couldn't answer his question because I had been scrounging support from the 339th Direct Support Maintenance Company based across the airfield in Nha Trang. I had known a number of the people assigned to the unit because I had been their unit commander at Fort Hood, Texas. I had been begging support for our unit for three months and had become quite successful at the task. Now we had our own support folks and a commander that wanted things set up correctly. I told Rudy we had requested support for construction of the helipads and taxi areas from the army engineers, but we were so low on the priority totem pole, not much was being done.

That seemed to trigger an explosion in Rudy's brain, and he stormed off to find my unit commander. Within a few days, the engineers arrived with a few dump trucks, a grader and a bulldozer and started initial preparation of the "new" maintenance area. The next day the dump trucks were gone, the grader and bulldozer were still at the edge of our helicopter parking area, but nothing else had happened. No dirt was moved, no sand bags filled for revetments, and no additional PSP (Perforated Steel Planking) had been put down. NOTHING!

By lunch time we were still working in rather primitive conditions when we heard the bulldozer start up. Looking up, I was startled to see Rudy at the controls of the olive-drab monster waiting for it to fully warm up before shifting the thing into gear and applying the throttle to get the dozer on its way. We couldn't believe what we were seeing, a senior army aviator piloting the bulldozer like he had been fully checked out on this heavy piece of equipment. Rudy eased his way between the rows of parked Hueys to "HIS" unit area and started rearranging the terrain to a more suitable configuration. In a short period of time, he had leveled an area for his maintenance tent. He then got the grader and really leveled things out. When the engineers returned a few days later, they were startled, to say the least. The spot where they intended to go to work was now the maintenance area for the 483rd with a maintenance tent set up and ready for business. Rudy's question for the engineers was, "Where the heck is the laterite paving and the rollers to compact the stuff into an acceptable hard surface aircraft ramp?" His antics were stuff of legend, but he was a real go-getter and one really outgoing person. I still have pictures of Rudy and that bulldozer snaking through the helicopter maintenance area. He was a man on a mission.

From fighter pilot to helicopter pilot to heavy equipment operator, he did it all! Rudy and his 97 men was the mainstay of the unit's support system, and thanks to their efforts it remained that way until deactivation. Rudy's boots were hard to fill.

MOM

Big Jim Torbert took care of everyone, and, wow, could he cook. As a result, everyone called him "Mom." I have no idea who affixed him with the moniker, but it was a perfect fit. His rank was never mentioned, but rank was often irrelevant in Vietnam. Mom had the coolest living quarters in the BOQ, with a balcony and a grill. If there had been such a thing as wine shipping back then, he would have been the resident oenophile. He was also one helluva pilot.

On one Delta mission a pilot peeled back a section of skin off of a tail rotor out in the middle of bad guy country. Mom arrived, declared the aircraft to be fit for a one-time flight, took the pilot's seat, and away he flew. It was not a long flight, maybe 15 minutes. A lot of us would have made the same decision and flown back. About three feet from touchdown, the 90-degree gearbox split apart. In spite of this, Mom landed the bird safely. I was impressed, but, remember, I said Mom was one helluva pilot. Fast forward to my last Delta rotation at Mai Loc, when someone nailed a deer. The Vietnamese want it, and that's fine, but we have enough meat to keep some for ourselves. Mom scours the local clubs, seeking some wine for a marinade. He cooks the venison to a fine T. For whatever reason, no one wants to join us, so Mom and I are the only ones at the feast and eat like kings. A few days later we're at Mai Loc again, and we take some incoming. Word comes down to evacuate the helicopters, and suddenly everyone wants to fly. And away they go; leaving behind a heavily unarmed "group" designated Task Force Mom: just myself and Mom. Period. It's a good thing we didn't get attacked that night because it would have just been the two of us taking on the enemy.

Jeff Murray

What can be said for an officer who out of great respect earns the title of "Mom"? James Torbett was a strong leader with outstanding flying skills. As the unit test pilot or the mission leader of a combat insertion, he was an individual who could be called on to professionally perform any task. His standards were high. As a result, the unit helicopter fleet was maintained in a manner that provided reliability to the young men who flew and crewed the aircraft in extremely hazardous combat conditions. He was a living example of how to always do the job right. On the ground Mom's talents as a leader were transferred into helping the young pilots of the unit gain confidence and learn team building rapport. His culinary skills were known throughout the unit, as he frequently organized and managed events that not only fed the troops but brought them together as a team while providing some of the comforts of home.

Jim Torbett is still very active in our organization. He is still "MOM" as he goes about his duties as the person in charge of our scholarship program. We appreciate his caring attitude and his hard work.

David L Bitle

Sergeant David Bitle joined the 145th Aviation Platoon in 1965 as a temporary duty door gunner, on loan from the 25th Infantry Division in Hawaii. David moved from "slicks" to the Wolf Pack as a door gunner, crew chief and platoon sergeant. He remained with the unit until 1969. His contributions to the unit and his leadership played a major role in its success. David was a "go to, can do" leader.

Louis J. (Lou) Lerda

Captain Lou Lerda was already "on the ground" when the 281st arrived in country. He had been transferred to the unit based on his prior assignments, his specialized training by the 6th Special Forces in the mission of the 281st prior to departing the States, as well as his organizational and maintenance management skills. His assignment was to develop a maintenance program that would be capable of maintaining the aircraft to the required high standards to support the unit's challenging mission. Captain Lerda's accomplishment of blending together the maintenance capabilities of five units into one was the foundation that kept the unit flying with the highest availability rate of any assault helicopter company in the war.

Gary L. Stagman

Gary was one of the first to sign in to the new company and to arrive in Nha Trang. Gary, flying as the crew chief, joined Rudy Morud to fly the first 281st helicopter off the ship and into Nha Trang. Over the next five years Gary went from crew chief to maintenance chief. Besides being one of the first in country, he was one of the last to leave when the company stood down. It was his skill as the NCOIC of the maintenance supply section that allowed the unit to maintain its outstanding aircraft availability rate.

Robert J. (Mo) Moberg

Mo was a soldier's soldier. Having been a Special Forces sergeant with experience in counterinsurgency, he had strong leadership skills. Mo was held in high esteem by his superiors and subordinates. He was probably the only US Army pilot and leader who, following the war, was remembered by name by the Chairman of the Joint Chiefs of Staff when he wrote of MO's outstanding service to his unit during the war. Mo served as the Bandit platoon leader, the officer in charge of the Project Delta task force and as the company executive officer. Those of us who knew and served with him knew him to be "Mr. 281st", as he set the standards of excellence in all aspects of the unit's mission.

Fredrick (Fred) Mentzer

Fred was a man of few words. A former officer serving with him once remarked that he could fly all day with Fred and not hear him say anything. In the air he was all business. Here is the author's personal note regarding Fred's reticence:

At my first association meeting in St. Louis, just by chance, I sat at the same table with Fred and his wife Karen during the Saturday night dinner. And, of course there was not much conversation going on. I finally said to Karen, "Fred and I had been in Vietnam at the same time." I mentioned to her, as the flight operations sergeant, I had observed Fred could lead his gunship platoon into battle, rain down hell from above on the enemy and bring all of them safely back, saying only a few words. She looked me in the eye and very quickly said, "You should try riding in a car from Oregon to St. Louis with him."

Fred assumed command of the Aerial Weapons Platoon when the former leader was seriously wounded, and he continued to train and develop the platoon, known as the Wolf Pack, to a level of performance marking it as one of the top gun platoons to serve in the war. More importantly, he and his unit were directly responsible for protecting the unit's crew members and the ground forces they supported. It was a job he and his Wolf Pack did extremely well. Many of us are alive today as a result of their skills and devotion to their duty.

Fred died suddenly 15 November 2014. RIP, Fred. A big thank you, to you and to all former Wolf Pack members for keeping us safe. You are truly above the best.

218

Donald G. Torrini

Donald Torrini was the only man in the unit to be recommended for the Congressional Medal of Honor. Don was another former Special Forces enlisted man who later, as a warrant officer pilot, raised the mark of excellence for performance of duty under fire. His skills as an Army Aviator were second to none, and his courage was beyond and above that normally expected. He was a "go to" pilot who could be counted on to perform the most difficult missions. There are numerous individuals who owe their lives to his actions under intense combat conditions. He set the standard for the very young pilots and crew members of the unit, and most of them lived up to those standards.

Robin K. Hicks

Robin Hicks was a hero in every sense of the word. Heroes are not born; they act when the situation requires them to do so. Robin saved the lives of his crew and passengers when his aircraft was hit by heavy fire, which instantly killed his fellow pilot. The aircraft immediately went out of control, and only by his quick and determined actions was able to land, although in an area where he and the crew came under heavy fire. He managed to get the crew into a bunker where they remained overnight. The next day he and the survivors, along with a South Vietnamese army unit marched all day through the jungle to reach a landing zone where his fellow Intruders could recover them. During that march, Robin, with the help of an USAF officer, carried the body of a fellow Intruder. When Warrant Officer Robin Hick handed the body of Warrant Officer Donald McCoig to the crew of the pick-up helicopter, he exemplified the Intruder creed which stated: We will leave no man behind.

MORNING REPORT

Abbott, William
Abney, Roy
Acevedo, Ramon, Jr.
Ada, Bob
Adams, Luther
Addis, Jack
Agnew, James, Jr.
Agustin, Reynaldo
Ahlborn, Richard
Aker, Billy
Akins, Luther
Albee, Craig
Albert, Robert
Alberts, John
Albright, Brent
Albright, Hugh
Alessi, Anthony
Alicie, Marvin, Jr.
Alipo, Anthony
Allen, Wayne
Allen, Wendell
Allen,. William, Jr.
Alford, Terry
Allison, Marvin
Alonzo, Terry
Althouse, Charles
Alvarado, Albert, Sr.
Alvarado, Zayas A.
Alvey, Richard
Amanzio, Anthony
Ament, Robert
Anderson, Joseph

Anderson, Kenneth
Anderson, Leonard
Anderson, Malcolm
Anderson, Raymond
Anderson, Roger
Anderson, Woodrow
Anderson, David
Andrews, Jeffrey
Archer, Lloyd
Armstrong, Dwight
Arnold, James
Asbury, Bobby
Ascenzo, David
Aschtgen, Ronald
Atkins, James
Atkinson, John
Attwood, Merton
Atwell, Raymond
Augustin, Renaldo
Autrey, E. L.
Avery, Pernell
Avery, Vincel, Jr.
Avica, Theodona
Avila, Theodore

Baderschneider, Carl
Badley, Jerry
Baglio, James
Bahre, Jared
Bailey, Donald
Bailey, James Jr.
Biley, William
Bainbridge, Waylmer
Baird, Rolando
Baker, Billy J.
Baker, Don
Baker Edward
Baker, George
Baker, James
Baker, Kenneth
Baker, Richard
Balcomb, Arthur

Baldwin, Joseph
Barker, Donald
Barlindal, George
Barnes, Kenneth
Barnes, O.
Barnes, Roger
Baromda, George
Barragan, Thomas
Barrett, Rick
Barron, Wallace
Basham, James
Bast, Worley
Bauer, William
Baugh, William
Beasley, Johnny
Beasley, William
Beck, Jerome
Beck, Anial, Jr.
Becker, Frank
Beech, Michael
Bell, Donald
Bell, Michael
Beltch, Lyle
Beltran, Daniel
Benfield, Terry
Benkowski, Douglas
Bennett, Donald
Bergantz, Denis
Berry, Bobbie
Bethany, Wesley
Bewley, Roy
Bierman, Curtis
Bigeck, Donald
Bilitzke, Joseph
Bindig, Ronald
Bingham, Robert
Birdsong Bobby
Bishop, Daniel
Bitle, David
Black, K.
Black, Lacy
Blackwell, Ken

Blackwell, Wallace
Blake, Jewell
Blazier, James
Blevens, Richard
Block, Richard
Bloodgood, Clarence
Blume, Norman
Bly, Frederick, Jr.
Boardley, Clark
Boarman, Joseph, Jr.
Bobo, Jerry
Bodrey, Jimmy
Bodzick, William
Boehle, Donald
Boisseau, Francis
Boling, Kenneth
Bood, Jerry
Booth, Patrick
Bouchard, James
Bouck, Richard
Boudreaux, Lee
Bovio, Richard
Bowley, Steven
Bowling, James
Boxley, Anthony
Boyd, Barclay
Boyd, Ronald
Boyington, John
Boyle, James
Boysen, Benny
Brack, Eldon, Jr.
Bradley, Louis
Bradshaw, James
Brafford, Robert
Brand, Leonard
Brannan, Elmer
Brannan, Ronald
Breen, Michael
Breisacher, Robert
Brendel, William
Brennan, William
Brewer, Bobbie
Brewer, Wilbur

Brewington, Jimmy
Bright, Donald
Brinkman, Richard
Brinkman, Robert
Brittain, Calvin
Brooks, Jerry
Brooks, Henry, III
Broons, Henry, III
Broussard, Earl
Brown, Arthur
Brown, Billy
Brown, Charles
Brown, Gerald
Brown, James
Brown, William
Brown, Jr. Robert
Bruce, James
Brudvig, Duane
Bryan
Buckalew, Mahlon, E
Buckley, Thomas
Budlong, Donald
Bullock, Robert
Burch, Elto, Jr.
Burden, George
Burgess, Cecil, Jr.
Bush, David
Butler, Allen
Butler, Bobby

Cabe, Charles
Carolan, Timothy
Caler, Earl
Callender, Weston
Cameron, Douglas
Cameron, William
Campbell, James C.
Campbell, James E.
Campbell, James L.
Canfield, Dennis
Capo, John, Jr.
Caporusso, Carmen, Jr.
Cardlan, Timothy

Carl, Robert
Carpenter, Michael
Carr, Thomas
Carson, Andrew
Carter, Bennie
Carter, William
Cartwright, Alvin
Casalett, Byron
Casteel, Jimmy
Castello, John
Cattron, Larry
Caudill, Michael
Cavender, Jim
Cavitt, William
Channey, Richard
Chase, Richard
Cheek, Earl
Chestnut, Danny
Chilton, Clarence
Chisholm, George
Chistianson, Robert
Christensen, Alan
Christensen, James
Christianson, Robert
Christy, Julius
Chudzik, Bernard
Church, Johnny
Clark, Charles
Clark, James
Clark, William
Clarkson, Walter
Clary, Thomas
Clay, Roger
Cleaver, Thomas
Clendenon, Jackie
Cline, Ben
Clinkenbeard, Larry
Clinton, Frank, Jr.
Clough, Richard
Cnota, William
Coe, William
Cofield, Jimmy
Coker, Michael

Colbert, Edward, III
Coleman, Lonie
Coleman, Lynn
Coleman, Richard
Coles, Alan
Coles, Lewis
Colon, Miguel
Colunga, Anthony
Colunga, Fred
Condrey, George
Condry, Robert
Cone, Jackie
Connell, David
Connell, Henry
Connolly, James
Conrad, Charles, Jr.
Conway, James
Cook, Michael
Cook, James, Jr.
Coolbourn, William
Coontz, John
Cooper, Alvin
Cooper, Richard
Cooper, Ronald
Cooper, Willie
Copenhaver, Philip
Corkran, Donald
Cornea
Cornelius, Darrel
Corney, Joseph, Sr.
Cortes-Perez, Pedro
Cotiguala, Billy
Cotlewalk, Robert
Cottrell, Jerry
Couch, Clyde
Counter, Fred
Cousins, Jerry
Cox, Marvin
Cox, Roger
Crabtree, Phillip
Craft, John
Craghead, Thomas
Cramer, Clarence

Crawford, Kenneth
Creed, Donald
Crosby, Hershel
Crosley, Thomas
Crossen, George
Crowe, Dennis
Crowe, Raymond, II
Cunningham, Joseph
Cunningham, Wayne
Cyran, John

Dagata, Joseph
Dahill, John
Dahm, James
Daniel, Ken
Darnell, Roddy
Davis, Allen
Davis, Darryl
Davis, Ernest
Davis, Joseph
Davis, Michael
Davis, Robert
Davis, Stanley
Davison, John, Jr.
Dayton, James
De Jesus, Antonio
Dean, David
Dean, Robert, Jr.
Deckard, Lloyd
Degener, David
DeHart, Vernon
Deisher, Gary
Deitz, Mark
Del Rio-Mendez, Jose
DeLeon, Ronald
Denmark, Allen
Dennis, Timothy
Denson, Richard
DeVere, David
DeVere, Don
Dewitt,
Dexter, Ronald
Dexter, Theodore

Dick, William
DiGenova, Daniel
DiJenova, Anthony
Dill, John
DiLullo, Dan
DiRienzo, James
Dlericuzio, Nichol
Dodd, Don
Dodd, George
Dodd, Robert
Dolen, Robert
Dollar, Victor
Dolstein, David
Donald, Kenneth
Donnell, Vic
Donohue, Michael
Dorn, Thomas
Dorr, Robert
Dosker, David
Dossett, George
Dostie, Armand
Douglas, Francis
Douglas, James
Downs, Harry
Doyle, Timothy
Draeger, Ray
Drapeau, Alfred
Draper, James
Dressler, Ronald
Driver, Leland, Jr.
Duclos, Michael
Duffy, James
Duggan, John
Duke, Edward
Dunbar, Dale
Duncan, Donald
Duncan, Louis
Duncan, Stuart
Duquette, James
Durham, Olden
Durtschi, Richard
Dustin, Gary
Dwan, Thomas

Easterwood, Jack
Edwards, Benson
Edwards, Justin
Edwards, Isaiah, Jr.
Eecj, Jerome
Elam, Larry
Elliff, Donald
Elliott, Max
Ellis, Larry
Elzie, Nepolis
Embrey, Kenneth
Emery, Charles
English, Phillip, III
Engro, Dewey
Erb, Douglas
Erbe, Russell
Erickson, Vernon
Esquilin, Francisco
Essenmacher, Sterling
Essig, Richard
Essor, Paul
Eubanks, Claude
Evangelho, Daryl
Evans, Roderick
Everett, Gerald
Ewton, Donald

Falco, John
Farley, Field
Farley, Robert
Farmer, Ernest, Jr.
Farrington, Kevin
Fayer, John
Feely, Michael
Fellenz, Michael
Felton, Ray
Ferguson, Davey
Ferguson, James
Ferguson, Joel
Fetty, Steven
Fields, Gary
Fields, Thomas

Fierro, Richard
Filmore, David M.
Fink, Frankie
Fiornia, Barry
Fisher, James
Fitzgerald, Michael
Flabbi, Gary
Flammini, Chester
Flanders, Leon
Fleming, Donald
Flemings, James
Flores, Peter
Fontanetta, Daniel
Foreman, Ronald
Forrester, Douglas
Forsythe, Harold
Fought, Harry, Jr.
Fowler, Ronald
Fox, Joe
Fox, William
Fraley, John
Franco, Daniel
Fraser, John
Frasher, Edward
Frazier, Peter
Fredricy, Charles
Freeman, Gary
Freeman, Ronald
French, Gary
French, George
French, George, Jr
Frisbie, Stephen
Frost, Jimmy
Fulgham, Jimmie
Funk, Frederick
Furcinite, Charles
Fuson, Sherman

Gachich, John
Gaddy, George
Galkiewicz, John
Gallagher, Arthur
Galloza, Gilberto

Galvagni, Gary
Gambino, Ross
Gangino,
Gallagher, Michael
Gant, Gordon
Garbina, Gregory
Gardner, Robert
Garland, David
Garner, Edgar
Garrett, Curtis
Garrett, Paul, Jr.
Garza, Arnoldo, Jr.
Garzaarza, Leonardo
Gasiorowski, Robert
Gauvain, Walter
Geeston, Clifton, Jr.
Gehling, David
Geltz, Kenneth
Gentry, Lloyd
George, Courtney
George, Larry
Ghezzi, James
Gibson, Cleaston
Gibson, John
Gibson, Leland
Gilbert, James
Gill, John
Gillette, Delbert
Gillette, James
Gilreath, Johnnie
Glaze, Ken
Gleson, John T.
Glidden, Warren
Glover, Louis
Glover, Daniel, Jr.
Goff, Glen
Goff, James
Golffredo, Michael
Golden, Gerald
Gomez, Joseph
Gonzales, Estephan
Gonzales, Manuel
Goode, Donal

Goodman, Michael
Goodman, Scott
Gordon, Walter
Gore, Julius, Jr.
Gott, Louie, Jr.
Gourley, Brent
Gow, David
Graham, Billy
Graham, Edgar
Grammer, Steven
Green, Charles
Green, Donald
Green, John, III
Green, Michael F.
Green, Roger, Jr.
Greiner, Paul
Grenier, Jon
Grice, John
Griffin, Darrel
Griffin, William
Grimes, Walter
Grogan, John G.
Grogan, Timothy
Grose, Ronnie
Gryfakis, Eftyhois
Guenther, Thomas
Gumbinger, Horst
Gutierrez, Manuel, Jr.

Haas, Edward, III
Hackett, Everdus
Habben, Dennis
Haddock, William
Halcomb, Roy
Hale, John
Hale, William
Hall, Forrest
Hall, Gary
Hall, George
Hall, Gerald
Hall, James
Hall, Robert
Hall, Ronald

Hall, William
Hallman, Gary, Sr.
Hallmark, Edward
Halsted, Alpha
Ham, Lance
Hamblin, Dennis
Hamilton, James
Hamilton, Karl
Hamilton, Kenneth
Hamlow, Fred
Haney, Donald
Hanie, Richard
Hannah, Lonnie
Hansen, Kirk
Hanson, David
Hardeman, Joel
Hardmon, Albert
Hare, John
Hargis, Michael
Harkless, Ronnie
Harms, Larry
Harris, Jeffrey
Harris, Lawrence
Harris, William
Harris, William
Harrison, Donald
Harrison, Johnny
Harrison, William
Harrop, Robert
Hart, Mike
Hart, Walter
Hartswick, Ronald
Hartzell, Kenneth
Hastings, Stephen
Haverly, Scott
Hawkins, Allan
Hawkins, Marshall
Hawn, Larry
Hayes, Jerry
Haynes Jessie
Hays, Michael
Hays, Rondoll
Hays, Jay

Hazel, Marcus
Hazzle, Bill
Head, Johnny
Heasley, Harold
Hebb, Gerald
Heck, William
Heh, Robert
Heintz, Ned
Heldt, Richard
Helms, William
Helpingstine, Bill
Helwig, Jerold
Henderson, James
Henderson, William
Hendricks, Clarence
Hendricks, Clifford J., Jr
Hendrix, Floyd, Jr.
Hendrix, Rodney
Hendry, Robert
Henrich, Ronald
Henry, Daniel
Henry, Samuel
Herman, Nelson
Herman, Ronald
Hernandez, Richard, Sr.
Herrman, Nelson
Hess, Charles
Hethcox, Larry
Hewlett, George
Hicks, Robin
High, Billie
Hillyer, Raymond
Himes, William
Hinds, Jack
Hiner, Harvey
Hines, Howard
Hinkle, Allen
Hinspater, Thomas
Hinton, Robert
Hobbs, Jimmie
Hobein, Joseph
Hodge, Henry
Hodges, Benjamin

Hodges, Jere
Hodges, Johnny
Hogan, Terrance
Holcomb, Manuel
Holcomb, Norland
Holloway, Floyd
Holmes, E, Jr.
Holt, James
Holt, William
Hood, Frank, Jr.
Hood, John, Jr.
Hook, Ronald
Hopkins, David
Hopkins, Larry
Hopper, John
Horton, William
Horwath, Joseph III
Hoskin, Donald
Hoskins, David
Houston, Richard
Howard, Fred
Howard, John
Howell, Harold
Howell, Ronald
Howlett, James
Hubbard, Clinton
Hubbard, Lawrence
Hudson, Johnnie
Huff, David
Hughes, Allen
Hughes, Johnny
Hughes, Ronald
Hughey, Michael
Hull, Paul
Humphreys, Corbin
Humphreys, Larry
Hunt, Jesse
Hunt, Lester
Hunt, Lestus
Hurd, David
Hutchins, Robert
Hutton, Wlliam
Hyatt, Bryan

Hyatt, John
Hyde, Steven
Hyden, John

Ifland, Kent
Ikerd, James
Interstein, Jack
Intreglia, Gregory
Isaacs, Russell
Isaacs, Wilfried
Ivey, James
Ivey, Roger
Iwasaki, Anthony

Jackson, Emanuel
Jackson, Henry
Jackson, Iverson
Jackson, James
Jackson, Paul
Jacobelli, James
James, Frank
James, Preston
James, Ralph
James, Tommy
James, William, Jr.
Jameson, Brian
Jaques, Douglas
Jaski, Joseph
Javins, Ronald
Jean, John
Jefferson, James
Jelsch, Timothy
Jenkins, Calvin
Jenne, Robert
Jensen, Allen
Jines, Lawrence
Jobes, William
Johansen, Peter
John, Shonnis
Johnson, Alan
Johnson, Curtis
Johnson, David
Johnson, Gregory

Johnson, Junior
Johnson, Kenneth
Johnson, Michael
Johnson, Rodney
Johnson, Thomas
Johnston, Gerald
Joiner, Jodie
Jones, Douglas
Jones, James
Jones, Johnnie
Jones, Michael
Jones, Richard
Jones, Timothy
Jones, Walter
Jones, Wendell
Jones, Walter, Jr.
Jordan, Charles
Jordan, Sidney
Juan, Don, Jr.
Junko, Allen
Jurecko, Daniel
Jutz, Donald

Kackmeister, Donald
Kaiser, Frank
Kallinen, Ronald
Kangas, Wayne
Kath, Robert
Kaufman, Norman
Keele, Jackie
Keeling, Phillip
Kelley, James, Jr.
Kelley, Leon
Kelly, Bobby
Kelly, Bruce
Kemble, Gene
Kennedy, Donnel
Kerns, James
Kerr, Rufus
Kersh, Willie
Kester, Duane
Keyes, William
Kimble, Gene

King, Buddy
King, Byron
King, Darnell
King, John
King, Joseph
King, Velter, Jr.
Kirby, Horace
Kirchmeier, Walter
Kisler, Donald
Kitchen, Dennis
Kitts, Lawrence
Klarner, Robert
Klimo, James
Knierim, Albert
Knight, David
Kolody, John
Komulainen, Wesley
Kopp, Arthur
Korsbeck, John
Kos, Darryl
Koshi, Joseph
Koshner, Alan
Koson, Clark
Krothe, Trubee
Kruck, Alan
Kull, Jack
Kunke, Kenneth
Kwedar, Edward

Labarbera, Gerard
LaCross, Gerald
Lacy, Joseph
Lacy, Frank, Jr.
Lagreca, Bartholomew
Lambert, Lester
Lambertson, Paul
Lamoreaux, James
Land, Thomas
Lang, William
Langevin, Jim
Laphan, Laurence J. S.
Larkins, Ernest
Lavender, James

Lawson, Howard
Lawson, Thomas
Lay, Robert
Laya, Robert
Leach, Edward
Leach, James
Ledford, Jimmy
Lee, Ralph
Lee, Ronald
Leeker, Lewis
Lefan, Warren
Leger, Raymond
Leonard, Grover
Leonard, Henry
Leonard, Paul
Lerda, Louis
Leske, Helmuth
Lesonik, Ronald
Leveille, James
Levell, Charles
Lewis, Clennon
Lewis, Frederick
Lewis, Larry
Lewis, Michael
Lewis, Timothy
Lewis, Matthew, Jr.
Lime, Michael
Lindamood, Mark
Lindberg, Gary
Line, Travis
Lint, Charles, Jr.
Lipa, Dennis
Little, Frank
Little, Daniel
Little, George
Little, Martin
Little, William, III
Loaiza, Gilbert
Lobin, Neal
Lobnbaugh, David L.
Lockhart, Roosevelt
Loflin, Michael
Loftin, Timothy

Lohman, Ronald
Lombardo, Frank
Long, Billy
Long, Dwight
Long, Robert
Long, William
Lopez, Frederico, Jr.
Lopez, Nick
Lopez, Ytiel
Losheaven, Davis
Loskbaugh, David
Loudin, Larry
Love, Leroy
Lovell, Ronald
Low, Gordon, Jr.
Lowry, Michael
Lubic, Richard
Ludwick, John
Ludwig, Richard
Lueck, Donald
Luinstra, Jerome
Lukason, John
Lulaks, Dennis
Lumsden, Jeffrey
Lundrigan, Thomas
Lutz, Danny
Luzio, Daniel, Jr.
Lynch, Ronnie
Lynn, Ellie
Lyons, Christopher
Lyons, James

Mac, Harg William
Mac Pherson, Frank
Macallister, G. R.
Macarty, Michael
MacPherson, Frank
Magiera, Daniel
Maioriello, Ralph
Malandro, David
Malay, Dennis
Malcom, Dennis
Maledy, Paul, Jr.

Mancy, Earl
Mangue, Edward
Mangus, Edgar
Manley, Earl, Jr.
Mannone, Dennis, Sr.
Markavich, William
Marler, Joseph
Marley, Roger
Marquette, Stanley
Marsch, Donald
Martin, Bruce
Martin, Daniel
Martin, Frank
Martin, Galen
Martin, Gary
Martin, Larry
Martinez, James
Martinez, Michael
Martinez, Peter
Martinez, Phillip
Marx, Darrel
Mason, Joseph
Massie, Dennis
Mathis, Jay
Matthews, Johnny
Matthews, Stephen
Mattioda, Larry
Matz, Robert
Mauldin, Howard
May, Robert
Mayhew, John
Maynard, Richard
Mayor, Cloyd
Mc Clure, Howard
Mc Farland, Joseph
Mc Laughlin, Leonard
McBroom, George
McCammon, Patrick
McCoig, Donald
McCollum, William
McCoullough, Robert
McCoy, Dan
McCoy, Gerald D.

McCoy, John
McCoy, Richard, Jr.
McCoy, John, Sr.
McDonald, George
McDonnell, Mike
McDougal, Calvin
McFarland, Dennis
McFarland, Joseph
McGee, Michael
McGoldrick, John
McGowan, Clyde
McGuire, Thomas
McKeegan, Thomas, Jr.
McKellar, Leonard
McKenzie, Michael
MCKillip, Kenneth
McKnight, Ernest
McLemore, Jimmy
McLendon, Alexander
Mcmahon, Larry
McMillan, James
McMillian, Robert
McMillin, Richard
McNeil, Kenneth
McPherson, Donald
McTaggert, Delmer
Meadows, John
Meadows, Phillip
Medeiros, John
Mehl, Theodore
Meints, Gene
Melvin, Michael
Menbourn, Kenneth
Mendez, Frank, Jr.
Mentzer, Fredrick
Metz, Robert
Meyer, Richard
Michael, David
Michaud, Edward
Mikle, Wesley
Millay, Charles
Miller, Charles, Jr.
Miller, Daniel, Jr.

Miller, Daryl
Miller, Delbert
Miller, George
Miller, James
Miller, Jere
Miller, Jerry
Miller, Johnny
Miller, Kenneth, Jr.
Miller, L.Z.
Miller, Richard
Miller, Ronald
Miller, Stanley
Miller, Thomas
Miller, Daniel, Jr.
Milligan, James
Milligan, Joseph
Mills, Terry
Millwee, Robert
Minock, John
Minogue, James
Minyard, Freddie
Mishler, Harold
Mitchell, Charles
Mitchell, David
Mitchell, Larry
Mitchell, Robert
Mitchell, Albert, Jr.
Moberg, Robert
Mohs, Duane
Moist, Alvin
Moller, Marc
Mondrinos, Vieron
Monsour, Frederick
Montoya, Jerome
Moore, Curtis
Moore, Donald
Moore, Rex
Morales, Marrerro
Morales-Santiago, Luis
Morasco, Joseph
Moreland, Charles
Moreno, Alonzo
Morgan, Donald

Morgan, Harry
Morris, Charles
Morris, Hubert
Morris, Raymond
Morsen, Lawrence
Morton, Charles
Morton, Dennis
Morton, Maurice
Morud, Stanley
Moss, John
Mousseau, Kerry
Mowrey, William
Mueslein, Robert
Munderback, Donald
Muray, Ken
Murphy, James
Murphy, Kevin
Murray, Donald
Murray, Jeffrey
Murray, Peter
Murry, Richard, Sr.
Musall, Richard
Muschweck, William
Myers, Alan
Myers, Norman, Jr.
Myers, Samuel

Naumczik, Gary
Nelson,
Nichols, James
Nichols, Michael
Nickerson, Eric
Nickles, Clarence
Nieckula, William
Nilssen, Theodore
Noble, Charles
Nordan, Larry
Noreault, Gerald
Northcutt, Gayl
Nowell, Jeffrey
Nueslein, Robert

O'Daniel, Charles

Obana, Norberto
O'Callaghan, Peter
O'Daniel, Charles
Odum,
Oeltjen, Da
Ogburn, John
O'Hare, William, Jr.
Ohmes, Robert
Oksa, Reino
Oleson, John, Sr.
Olson, Michael
Olson, Richard
Omdahl, Gary
Omer, Michael
Ore, David
O'Relly, Tarry
Osborne, Ernest
Outlaw, Wallace
Ouverson, Larry
Owen, Alva
Owen, Roy
Owen, Terry
Oxley, Donald

Pabst, Donald
Pace, James
Pagliarini, Thomas
Paine, Brian
Palascak, Ronald
Palmer, Arthur, Jr.
Palmerine, James
Pannell, John
Parden, James
Parenten, John
Parmiter, Larry
Parr, Daniel
Parrish, Larry
Parrish, Robert
Parrott, Dennis
Parziale, John
Pasco, Lawrence
Passmore, Edward
Patallos, Sam

Patek, Arthur
Patricelli, Clement
Patrick, Stephen
Pattat, Wayne
Patterson, Melvin
Payne, Eldon
Peacock, David
Pearce, Stuart
Pearson, Barry
Peck, George
Pedersen, Gary
Pederson, Randy
Pedone, Joseph
Peerce, William
Penn, William
Perez, Joe
Perrell, Jack
Perren, William
Perry, Edgar
Perry, Lester, Jr.
Peterman, Terrell
Peters, Art
Petersen, Stanley
Peterson, Bill
Peterson, Ernie
Peterson, Richard
Peterson, Dale, Jr.
Pethia, Paul
Petrevich, Denis
Petrie, Steven
Petty, Jack
Pfannenstein, John
Phillips, Benny
Phillips, Eddie
Phillips, Eugene
Phillips, Fred
Phillips, Harry
Phillips, Michael
Pierce, David
Pierce, Hjon
Pierce, Robert
Pike, Lon
Pikul, Walter

Pimental, Arthur
Pimentel, Hebert
Pine, Thomas
Pipkin, Butch
Pipkin, Travis
Pipkin, Glenn, Jr.
Plummer, Learnest
Poff, Glenn
Polk, Phillip
Pollak, Gary
Pollard, John
Pooker, Joseph
Porter, Jerald
Potter, Glen
Powell, Douglas
Powell, Jack
Powell, Steven
Prales, Charles
Prasky, Dale
Pratte, John
Price, Eugene
Price, Michael
Price, Robert
Proper, Lawrence
Prove, Robert
Pugh, Ellis
Pulliam, Lee
Pulse, Larry
Pummer, Thomas
Purdy, William
Purifoy, Roland
Pyle, Ernest

Qualls, Arthur
Quatman, John, Jr.
Quigley, James, Jr.
Quinlan, John

Rabik, Jerry
Ragans, David
Rahl, Timothy, Sr.
Raines, Donald
Rampone, Albert, II

Randall, Randy
Randolph, Edgar
Rannow, Michael
Ratliff, Cecil
Readinger, Frank, Jr.
Ream, Edward
Reaves, Johnny
Reblin, Paul
Redden, Gary
Reed, Richard
Reeder, Kenton
Reeves, Albert
Reid, William
Reignhardt, Cody
Reineke, Ronald
Reitz, Carl
Remd, Herbert
Renfrow, Ronald
Reyher, Sheldon
Reynolds, Eddie
Reynolds, Lawrence
Reynolds, Robert
Rhinehart, Roland
Rich, Aaron
Richardson, Gerald
Richer, Gerard
Richmond, Terry
Ridenhour, Thomas
Riley, Chris
Riley, Gary
Riley, Patrick
Rismiller, Harold
Rivenburg, Michael
Rivera, Jorge
Roark, Earl
Robb, Lovie, Jr.
Roberts, Talton, Jr.
Robertson, Steve
Robson Lawrence
Roche, Joseph
Rodgers, Clinton
Rodgers, Jack
Rodgers, James

Roesner, Dean
Roetter, Fred
Rogers, Clinton
Rogers, Douglas
Ronan, Patrick
Ronchetti, Raymond
Rose, Roger
Rose, Victor
Royster, George
Royster, Roy
Roza, Frank
Rozell, Gary
Ruiz, Mark
Runyon, Donald
Rush, Jay
Ruskauff, Donald
Russelburg, Cletus
Russell, Robert
Ryan, James

Saladin, James
Salas, Juan
Salzman, Jay
Salzman, Larry
Samples, Virgle
Sanchez-Alvarado, Angel
Sandoval, Joseph
Sanford, Bruce
Sangl, Rudolf
Santoya, Adolph
Sanve, Edwin
Sarris, Peter
Saunders, John
Savant, Lee
Savickas, Joesph
Schaedler, Ronald
Schemn, James
Schleher, Richard
Schmaltz, Joseph
Schmierer, Herbert
Schneider, Larry
Schors, Thomas
Schott, Douglas

Schrumpf, Michael
Schulke, Robert
Schuster, Wesley
Schwachenwald, Ronald
Schwanz, James
Schwartz, Barry
Schwartz, Ronald
Schwartz, Seymore
Schwendema, Richard
Schwerdtfeger, Donald
Schwuchow, Leroy
Scott, Gerald
Scott, James E.
Scott, James F.
Scout, Richard
Seago, Thomas
Seales, Charles
Sears, William
Seaton, Jimmy
Seaton, Neal, Jr.
Sebastian, Dennis
Seemann, Joseph
Sellers, Wayne
Sellick, Jack
Serafin, Alfred
Serig, Jack, Sr.
Sexauer, Louis
Shafer, George
Shaner, Gary
Shape, William
Sharp, Richard
Sharpe, Charles
Sharpe, Henry
Sharrow, Benjamin
Shaw, Hollis
Shaw, Robert
Shea, William
Sheley, Patrick
Shelton, Ronnie
Sheridan, Thomas
Sherrill, David
Shipe,s Franklin
Shipes, Joseph

Shirley, William
Shonnis, John
Shortman, Edward
Shows, Grady
Shumate, Richard
Simon, Andrew
Simon, Edward
Simpson, Douglas
Simpson, Frank
Sims, Robert
Sines, William
Sisk, Vaughn
Sisson, Charles
Sitz, Bruce
Skaar, Harold
Skogman, Roger
Slater, Arthur
Slaughter, Galen
Slone, Arie
Smith, Alfred
Smith, Charles
Smith, Daniel
Smith, Donald
Smith, Dwight,Jr.
Smith, Glen
Smith, John D.
Smith, John L.
Smith, Kenneth
Smith, Michael V.
Smith, Michael R.
Smith, Michael J.
Smith, Stephen
Smith, Thomas
Smith, Willis
Smith, Eldon, Jr.
Smyrl, Thomas
Sneed, Jimmy
Snyder, Terry
Soll, Keith
Soper, John
Sooper, Willie
Sorem, Robert
Southwell, Gary

Spahr, Lawrence
Spear, Michael
Spears, Garry
Spooner, Perry
Sprague, Neil
Squires, Mac
St. John, Otis
Staggs, Elbert
Stagman, Gary
Standley, Robert
Stanfield, Jerry
Stanfill, Bobbi
Stanley, James
Stanley, Walter
Stanley, James, Jr.
Stanton, Michael
Staples, Cal, Jr.
Staton, Shelby
Stebbins, Robert
Steele, Roger
Stenzel, David
Stephens, John
Stephens, Kit
Sterckx, Robin
Sterling, James
Stern, Joseph
Stevens, Raymond
Stevens, Danny
Stevens, Darryl
Stever, Raymond
Steverson, James
Stiles, Larry
Stinson, Glenn
Stitles, Robert
Stobe, Walter
Stockwell, Gene
Stokes, Walter
Storrs, Charles
Stowe, Douglas
Strange, Michael
Straw, Joseph
Strickland, Charles
Stump, Roger, Sr.

Stunda, T
Stunda, Thomas
Stutler, William
Suber, Carson
Sulander, Daniel
Sullivan, Billy
Sullivan, Gary
Sullivan, Joseph, Jr.
Sutherland, Scott
Sutton, Victor
Swigart, Ivan
Swol, Paul
Szulc, Albin
Szwed, Craig
Szymanski, Matthew

Tabb Billy,
Taggart, Thomas, III
Talbot, Stuart
Talley, Paul
Tanner, Charles, Jr.
Tatham, Jerry
Taulbee, Danny
Taylor, Bruce
Taylor, Edward
Taylor, Eugene
Taylor, Gregory
Taylor, Alpha, Jr.
Teague, Frank
Teague, John M.
Tellez, Eliseo
Terry, George
Terry, John
Testolin, John
Thacker, James
Theodore, John
Thieman, James
Thierry, Denogus
Thomas, Alan
Thomas, Jerry
Thomas, Milton
Thomas, Robert
Thompson, Robert

Thompson, Rodger
Thompson, Timothy
Thorn, Josef
Threatt, Robert
Thurston, Joe, Jr.
Tilton, Wesley
Timmerman, Robert
Tooker, Kenneth
Torbert, James
Tom, George
Torrini, Donald
Trammel, Robert
Troop, Donald
Trotter, Alexander
Trout, Hal
Troxel, Duane
Tucek, William
Tull James,
Turnblom, Thomas
Turner, Harold
Turner, Joseph
Turner, Ronald
Turnner, Roslen
Turpen, Gary
Tye, James
Tyler, Patrick

Ulakovic, James
Underhill, Peter
Urquhart, Robert

Van Alstine, David
Van Dyke, Michael
Van Fange, David
Vandevelde, Archie
Vandevender, Thomas
Varela, Lino
Vargas, Herman
Vargas, Maldenando
Vargas-Maldonado Esteian
Varner, Richard
Vasquez, Domingo

Vaughn, Daniel
Vaughn, Joe
Vereen, Agusta
Villaume, David
Vincent, Duane
Voga, Russell
Vogel, Douglas
Vogt, George
Von Fange, David
Voyles, Richard

Waas, Curtis
Wagers, Nollie
Wagner, Cletus
Wall, Daniel
Wall, Samuel
Walter, Robert
Walters, Franklin
Ward, Doyle
Ward, Jimmy
Ward, Joe, Sr.
Ward, William
Ware, John
Warren, James
Waters, Jackie
Waters, Rufus
Watkins, Randy
Webb, Larry
Wehr, John
Weigand, Edward
Weiman, Vernon
Weiss, Larry
Weitzel, Charles
Welch, Dennis
Welch, DuWayne
Welch, James
Welton, Robert, III
Wendle Wesley
Wesley, Lionel
West, Thomas
Wetmore, Paul
Wheelwright, Richard
Whisenant, Michael

Whisker, Jeffery
Whitaker, James
Whitaker, William
White, Ernest
White, James
White, Leslie, III
White, Ronald
Whitehead, Jack
Whitmore, James
Whitaker, GW
Whittaker, William
Wilkerson, Benjamin
Williams, Franklin
Williams, Glen
Williams, John
Williams, Joseph
Williams, Keith
Williams, Larry
Williams, Lawrence
Williams, Lawrence, Jr.
Williams, Richard
Williams, Robert
Williams, Russell
Williamson, Dale
Willis, George, Jr.
Willis, William
Wilson, Andrew
Wilson, Frank R.
Wilson, Kenneth
Wilson, Robert, Jr.
Wilson, Royce
Wilson, William A.
Wilson, William D.
Wilson, Willie
Wilz, Robert, Jr.
Winningham, Phillip
Winters, Walter
Wirkkunen, Roger
Wise, Martin
Witt, Frank
Witt, Lloyd
Wittel, James
Wittenberger, Lyle

Witzlstiner, Roger
Wolfe, James
Wolfe, Larry
Wolfe, Michael
Wood, Steven
Woody, David
Woody, Ronald
Working, Lisle
Workman, Billy
Wright, Henry
Wright, James, Jr.
Wright, Wayne
Wrigley, Joseph
Wrobleski, Walter
Wunderlick, Kim
Wylie, George

Yahiro, David
Yamamoto, James
Yancey, Leon
Yannuzzi, Robert
Yates, Harold
Yeater, Joseph
Yocham, Donell
Young, Benjamin
Young, Edgar
Young, James
Young, John
Young, Ralph, Jr.
Young, Roger, Jr.

Zara, Nickolas
Zarcone, Leslie
Zeglin, Thomas
Zepeda, John
Ziegler, Roy, II
Zuniga, Pedro

GLOSSARY

A-1E: Propeller driven, single-seat attack aircraft known as the Skyraider. It had a remarkable, long and successful career.

AC: Aircraft Commander.

Affirmative: Military term for yes or okay.

AG: Above ground level.

AK-47: Standard NVA assault rifle, Russian manufacture, 7.62mm, magazine-fed, shoulder-fired, automatic rifle.

Ammo: Ammunition.

AO: A unit's area of operations.

APC: An armored personnel carrier, a track vehicle used to transport troops or supplies and usually armed with a .50-caliber machine gun.

ARC Light: A B-52 bombing raid.

ARVN: Army of the Republic of Vietnam, South Vietnam's military force.

ASAP: Pronounced A-Sap. As soon as possible

Ash and Trash: All flights other than combat flights.

A-Team: Twelve-man Special Forces team. Each Green Beret had his own specialty.

Auto-rotation: A procedure for landing a helicopter without engine power. The weight of the falling helicopter creates a "pinwheel" effect that turns the blades. The pilot gets one chance to use the "pinwheel" effect to safely land the helicopter.

B-40 rockets: Enemy antitank weapon.

B-52: US Air Force high-altitude bomber.

Bandit: 281st call sign for the 2nd platoon slicks.

Base Camp: Where all our equipment was keep and where we flew from on missions. The 281st base camp was at Nha Trang.

Battalion: Military unit composed of a headquarters and two or more companies, batteries, or similar units.

Beaucoup: Pronounced [bow ku] French word for "many."

Beep-Beep: Indicated the bird was on the way home, like the cartoon character Roadrunner.

Bingo: When an insertion or extraction was successful, the pilot would say Bingo.

Bird: Any aircraft, usually a helicopter.

Body bag: Plastic bag used to transport dead bodies from the field.

BOQ: Bachelor Officers Quarters.

Bouncing Betty: A land mine that when triggered bounces waist-high and sprays shrapnel.

Brigade: A tactical and administrative military unit composed of a headquarters and one or more battalions of infantry or armor, with other supporting units.

Bunker: Cover protection against incoming explosives or bullets.

CA: Combat assault.

Cav.: Cavalry, shortened term for First Cavalry Division (Airmobile).

C&C: Command and control, sometimes called Charlie-Charlie.

CE: Crew chief.

Charlie: Name given to the Viet Cong and North Vietnamese soldiers by the American troops.

Central Highlands: A plateau area at the southern edge of the Truong Son Mountains, which was a strategically important region of South Vietnam throughout the 1960s and 1970s. It constituted most of I and II Corps Field Forces AO. Nearly one million people, primarily Montagnard tribesmen, lived in the 20,000 square miles of the Central Highlands in 1968.

Cherry: New, inexperienced soldier recently arrived in a combat area.

Chicken Plate: Chest protector, body armor, worn by helicopter pilots and crew, oftentimes the crew sat on an extra chicken plate to protect their other vital parts.

Chinese Hat: The button switch on top of the cyclic stick.

CIB: Combat infantryman badge.

CIDG: (pronounced "sidgee") Civilian Irregular Defense Group, often Montagnard or Vietnamese national guard types.

C-Model: UH-1C Huey gunship.

Chopper: Another term for the helicopter.

CO: Commanding officer.

Cobra: AH-1G attack two-passenger helicopter, also known as a gunship, armed with rockets and machine guns.

Collective: The left hand control that increases or decreases pitch in the blades of the helicopter.

Company: A military unit usually consisting of a headquarters and two or more platoons.

Concertina Wire: Roll of barbed wire for making a fence without using poles.

C-rations: Combat rations, canned meals for use in the field.

Cyclic: The right hand control that allows directional movement of the helicopter.

Daisy-Chain: A follow the leader circular pattern. Aircraft space themselves, so the target area is covered by one aircraft at all times.

DEROS: Date of estimated return from overseas. Military person's date of going back home

DFC: Distinguished Flying Cross.

DG: Door gunner.

D-model: Huey slick, troop-carrying helicopter with 1,100 horsepower turbine engine.

DMZ: Demilitarized Zone, the dividing line between North and South Vietnam established in 1954 by the Geneva Convention. It is very close to the 17th Parallel and the Ben Hai River, which runs primarily east and west. Five kilometers on each side was known as the DMZ and No Man's Land.

Donut Dolly: American Red Cross volunteer. Female namesake of the World War I counterpart to help the morale of the troops

Dustoff: Also known as "Medevac." Medical evacuation helicopter with a big red cross painted on the side.

E & E: Escape and evasion

EGT: Exhaust gas temperature, a turbojet engine thrust factor.

Elephant Grass: Tall, sharp-edged grass found in the highlands of Vietnam, often reaching six feet or more in height. It made judging where the ground was very difficult for helicopter pilots, or troops jumping out of the choppers. It also made booby traps placed in LZs very easy to conceal and difficult to spot.

EM: Enlisted member such as a private, specialist and sergeant.

Exfil, Exfiltrate, Exfiltration: To sneak out/pick up/extract ground personnel, or the point of exit from an AO.

Extraction: Withdrawal/removal by airmobile resources of troops from any AO.

Fast movers: Jet aircraft.

FAC: Forward air controller; airborne spotter who coordinates air strikes.

Fire Base: An artillery firing position usually secured by an infantry unit; also, fire support base.

Fire Team: Two or more gunships in attack formation

Flak Jacket: Heavy fiberglass-filled vest primarily worn for protection from light shrapnel. It was different from the "chicken plate" in that it was worn as a vest, and it was flexible, not rigid ceramic and metal.

Flak: Exploding antiaircraft shells.

Flying Formation: Two or more aircraft flying together

FOB: Forward Operating Base.

Freq.: Radio frequency.

Friendlies: U.S. troops, allies, ARVN, or anyone not on the enemy side.

Go-no go card: A checklist performed prior to first flight to see if the engine was up to snuff.

GPM: Gallons per minute fuel consumption.

Grease Gun: M3/M3A1 sub-machine gun, .45 caliber automatic weapon.

Grunt: The term used in Vietnam during the war to identify a line infantryman because of the sound he made when lifting an eighty-pound back pack prior to moving out. It is not a derogatory term.

Gunship: An armed helicopter.

Hanoi Hilton: Nickname American prisoners of war used to describe the Hoa Loa Prison in Hanoi, North Vietnam.

H-Model: Huey slick, a troop-carrying helicopter with a 1,300 horsepower turbine engine.

Hootch: A hut or simple Vietnamese dwelling usually made of thatched straw.

Hot LZ: A landing zone under enemy fire.

Huey: Nickname for the UH-1 series helicopters.

Hump: To carry something heavy like an M-60 machine gun when trudging on foot.

I Corps: (pronounced "eye core") the northernmost military region in South Vietnam, beginning near Da Nang and going to the

DMZ: The headquarters of I Corps was located in Da Nang.

II Corps: (pronounced "two core") the area of operations just south of I Corps from south of Da Nang to south of Cam Ranh Bay.

III Corps: (pronounced "three core") the area from south of Cam Ranh Bay to north of Saigon.

IV Corps: (pronounced "four core") the southern tip of South Vietnam from the Mekong River Delta to north of Saigon

IP: Instructor Pilot.

Jesus Nut: Main rotor retaining nut that holds the main rotor onto the rest of the rotor mast, so named because if it came off, only Jesus could help you survive

Jolly Green Giant: Air Force and Marine heavy, rescue helicopter.

JP-4: Jet fuel 50-50 mixture of gasoline and kerosene.

Jungle Penetrator: Metal cylinder with fold-out legs, attached by a steel cable to a helicopter mounted hoist, used to evacuate soldiers from thick jungle terrain.

KIA: Killed in action.

Klick, K: A kilometer, the U.S. military map metric measure equal to 1,000 meters or about six-tenths of a mile

Knots: Nautical miles per hour used for stating military aircraft airspeed. Ten knots is equal to 11.52 miles per hour.

LRRP: Long-Range Reconnaissance Patrol.

Lead: Lead gunship in a fire team.

LZ: Landing zone. A hot... LZ was either active with enemy fire, or expected fire.

LZ Prep: Prepare an LZ for landing aircraft and troops by suppressing enemy action through gunship rocket and machine gun fire, artillery bombardment, Air Force fighter jet heavy weapons, and even on rare occasions Navy ship bombardment.

M-16: The standard US military rifle used in Vietnam; successor to the M-14.

M-60: Standard lightweight machine gun used by US forces in Vietnam.

M-79: US military hand-held grenade launcher.

MACV: Military Assistance Command/Vietnam, the main American military command unit that had responsibility for and authority over all US military activities in Vietnam. It was based at Tan Son Nhut.

Medevac: Medical evacuation from the field by helicopter, also called dustoff.

MIA: Missing in action.

MSF or Mike Force: Mobile Strike Force; composed of US and indigenous troops, and used as a reaction or reinforcing unit.

Mini guns: Similar to Gatling guns. Operated by the co-pilot on gunships. They fired 6,000 rounds per minute.

Monkey Strap: Harness used for the crew chief and door gunner inside the helicopter

Montagnard: Indigenous mountain tribes, people of Southeast Asia (usually pronounced "mountain yard" by GIs). Shortened to "yards"

Mortar: A muzzle-loading cannon with a short tube in relation to its caliber that throws a projectile with low muzzle velocity at high angles.

MOS: Military occupational specialty.

MPC: Military payment certificate, used in lieu of cash or dollars in Vietnam, also referred to as "funny money."

Napalm: Highly flammable explosive used by Air Force fast-movers to burn up an area suspected of having enemy activity, or to lay down a barrier between friendlies and the enemy.

Negative: Means "no."

Nung: Chinese who had an excellent reputation as fighters and soldiers. It is this reputation that made them attractive to Special Forces.

NVA: North Vietnamese Army.

OD: Olive-drab color, standard Army issue green color. It also stood for Officer of the Day.

PAVN: People's Army of Vietnam, North Vietnam.

Peter Pilot: Copilot.

PIC: Pilot in command.

POL: Petroleum, oil and lubrication.

Pop smoke: To ignite a smoke grenade to signal an aircraft.

PSP: Perforated steel planking. It weighed 66 pounds, was 10 feet long and 15 inches wide. Made by Marsden Matting, it was used in construction, principally of runways and landing pads.

Pucker Factor: Gauge of the level of fear or anxiety in a combat situation

Puff the Magic Dragon: An Air Force C-47 aircraft fitted with side-firing mini guns and flares used to support night operations and defend fire bases from enemy attacks.

Purple Heart: U.S. military decoration awarded to any member of the armed forces wounded by enemy action.

PX: Post Exchange, military store.

PZ: Pick-up zone, area from which troops are extracted from combat.

Rat Pack: 281st radio call sign for the 1st platoon slicks.

R&R: Rest and relaxation, a three to seven-day vacation from the war for a soldier.

Recon: Reconnaissance, going out into the jungle to observe for the purpose of identifying enemy activity.

Recondo: The school that trained soldiers for tactical reconnaissance missions. The deadliest school in the Army

Revetment: A parking area for one helicopter that is surrounded by blast walls in the front and on one side. It was usually made of bags filled with sand about four to five feet high. The blast walls around a revetment were designed to channel any blast and damage upwards and outwards, away from neighboring aircraft.

RLO: Real live officer. Warrant Officers often referred to commissioned officers as RLOs

Road Runner Team: Team of about three or four ARVN Rangers that were a Top Secret unit, dressed as the enemy to infiltrate enemy ranks to gather intelligence.

ROK: Republic of Korea.

RPG: Rocket-propelled grenade, a Russian made anti-tank grenade launcher. It was also used to shoot down helicopters.

Satchel charge: A pack used by the enemy containing explosives that were dropped or thrown and were generally more powerful than a grenade.

Shrapnel: Pieces of metal sent flying by an explosion.

Silver Star: A US military decoration awarded for gallantry in action, third-highest award.

Slick: Troop-carrying helicopter.

Sniffer Missions: Slicks configured with a variety of sensory devices attached to the skids which would fly at low-level and very slowly above the canopy to detect high levels of ammonia from urine, and other indicators that enemy troops were, or had been in the area.

Snoopy Missions: Mission where one ship flew at tree-top level, trying to draw enemy fire from hidden troops. Gunships flew at higher elevation to locate the enemy, dive and attack.

SOG: Studies and Observations Group.

Sortie: One aircraft making one takeoff and one landing.

Special Forces: Green Berets.

Stars and Stripes: U.S. Military newspaper.

Tail boom: The back end of a Huey just behind the engine compartment.

Tet: Buddhist lunar New Year; Buddha's birthday.

Tet Offensive: A major uprising of Viet Cong, VC sympathizers, and NVA, characterized by a series of coordinated attacks against military installations and provincial villages throughout Vietnam. It occurred during the lunar New Year at the end of January, 1968.

Tiger Stripes: Black and green camouflaged fatigues.

Tracer: A round of ammunition chemically treated to glow or give off smoke so that its flight can be followed. Every fifth round fired is a tracer.

Translational Lift: The point at which a helicopter moves from a hover to forward flight.

Triple canopy: Thickest jungle with vegetation growing at 3 levels: ground level, intermediate and high levels.

VC: Victor Charlie, Viet Cong, the enemy.

VSI: Vertical Speed Indicator, an instrument that measures rate of climb and descent.

Wait-a-minute vines: A densely growing vine covered with thorns shaped like a fish hook

Warrant Officer: Military rank between commissioned and non-commissioned officers. Most Army helicopter pilots were warrant officers.

WIA: Wounded in action.

Wing: Second gunship in a fire team.

Wolf Pack: 281st Radio call sign for the third platoon gunships.

Yard: Short for "Montagnard," people who lived in the highlands. They belonged to a large number of ethnic minorities, most of whom had little love for the Vietnamese of the north or south.

OUR WAR

One time I heard a Special Forces medic say, "If you get hit, we can chopper you back to a base camp hospital in about fifteen or twenty minutes." He added, "If you get hit real badly, we will get you to Japan in about twelve hours." Finally he said, "If you get killed, we will have you home in a week."

None of that information was encouraging, to say the least.

We had a great appreciation for war: the glory, the horror, the sadness, the majesty and the courage. It is a sight to see, and once experienced, it is never forgotten. War is pure terror, yet believe it or not, it is exciting. War makes you a man; war brings you death, even when you do not die.

For most of us, this war would be our first and last, the only one we would endure. Even though we men of the 281st did not walk through the elephant grass, or the rice paddies, or the jungles carrying ninety pounds on our back, we did fly above the best into the valley of death. There was no safe place in Vietnam.

We considered ourselves fortunate to be assigned to the best helicopter company, and we were so honored to be among so many brave men. It was incredibly sad when one of our own did not make it back. We saw the empty bunk, witnessed the vacant place in the platoon, and always knew that it could have been any one of us. In just weeks, we grew up and became old men. Some of us could not recover, and some wanted more.

There was nothing more exciting than watching the fast movers on a bomb run. They dropped their deadly explosives, clearing the way for us. We saw the green tracers of the enemy unwinding through the dark. They looked as big as basketballs and each one, even though it missed us, appeared to be aimed right at us. Nothing was more satisfying than to see all the choppers return safely, but nothing was sadder than to have one missing, we of the 281st witnessed more than our share of sorrow.

Each of us who served in Vietnam has his own story. Some will tell it, some will write about it, and some will keep it inside, reliving it every day for the rest of their lives. We who witnessed our brothers die young also remember those who are still missing and those who were scarred for life with both visible and invisible wounds. We will never forget.

BACK HOME

Oddly enough, our folks back home knew more about the war than we did. They and everyone else in America received the "big picture" on the television set in their living rooms every night. Seated comfortably, our families watched as our wounded on stretchers and our dead in silver caskets were unloaded from the U.S. Air force C-141 Star lifters. They could observe our soldiers on patrols where they fought for their lives. They could watch fighter jets and B-52 bombers drop bombs. They could see helicopters loading and unloading troops, the wounded and those killed in action. The whop, whop sound of the Huey was in every living room. America had a front row seat to the Vietnam War. Most of us soldiers only saw a small part; we had no television, only The Army Times newspaper to keep us informed. Our area, our mission, was our war, and we thought that we were doing a pretty good job. We knew about the grunts out there in the jungle because we flew them out, and we were always ready to go back and get them, no matter what. This was our small world in Vietnam.

The people back home also saw a side of the war that we knew little about until we returned home. Antiwar activists and protesters were also making the front pages of newspapers and were being covered on the evening news. It was a shock for us when we arrived back home. The world we came back to was much different from the one we had left. Hippies were everywhere, some wearing old army field jackets with peace signs painted on the front and back. We thought that America had literately gone to pot. Veterans coming back from the war were confronted at airports with ugly insults and signs painted with BABY KILLER and HO CHI MINH IS GONNA WIN. Some of us were spit on, and rotten food and other items were thrown at us as we came off the airplanes. It was definitely a different America from the one we remembered before our tour. Some went to the airport bathroom to change out of their uniform as quickly as possible, but most of us wore our uniform proudly. The worst part was the disrespect shown to the disabled soldiers who came home without arms, legs and other injuries. We had done our duty. In most cases we did not give a rip what the protesters were saying or doing. We held our head high knowing that we had given our best. We were relieved to have made it home.

THE 281st U.S. ARMY RESERVE HELICOPTER COMPANY

After Vietnam

The Intruders of the 281st Assault Helicopter Company served five long, hard years in the Vietnam War and the reputation for excellence that they earned followed them home. In 1970 the unit and its supporting elements were deactivated and transferred to the U.S. Army Reserve. In the same year, the 281st was reactivated in Cahokia, Illinois across the river from Saint Louis. The 281st subsequently moved to Scott Air Force Base where it remained until 1988.

During this period many of the veterans from the Vietnam era continued to serve their country with the U.S. Army Reserves. The new 281st was home to one of the most outstanding Intruders to distinguish himself in combat: Donald Torrini; Captain Donald Torrini was originally assigned to the 281st as the maintenance officer. He was eventually recommended for the Congressional Medal of Honor for his service in Vietnam and was subsequently awarded the Silver Star for bravery, the nation's third highest award for bravery in combat. He is one of six Intruders to receive the award while serving with the 281st Assault Helicopter Company in Vietnam. Donald Torrini retired from the US Army Reserves with the rank of Colonel.

At the beginning of Operation Desert Storm, the unit was re-designated as the 7th Aviation Battalion of the 158th Aviation Regiment. The new unit was re-equipped with UH-60 Black Hawks and went on to serve in the Iraq War.

THE 281st AHC MEMORIAL SCHOLARSHIP PROGRAM

The 281st AHC Association provides scholarship support to the families of individuals who served with the unit in Vietnam. Scholarships are awarded annually to the descendants of the members of the 281st AHC by the scholarship committee who operates under a separate IRS approved 501© (3) non-profit organization.

Awards are made based on an individual's overall scholarship and citizenship merit. For complete details and application forms visit the members section of the 281st web-site; www.281st.com.

The fund is supported by contributions from the members of the association and our corporate sponsor, Human Resources Inc., a national staffing leasing corporation located in Crofton, Maryland. (http://www.hri-online.com) To make a tax-deductible contribution, please send your contribution to this address.

281st AHC Memorial Scholarship Fund
Attn: Walt Pikul, MBA, CPA, CFP ®
Treasurer
P. O. Box 41035
Fayetteville, NC 28309

EPILOGUE

This project started way back in 2000 when friends Jack Green, Bob Mitchell, Brian Paine and Jack Mayhew were thinking about writing a book about the company that we served with, the 281st Assault Helicopter Company, which provided combat aviation support to the 5th Special Forces Group for five years in Vietnam. We met several times to discuss finding an author and/or a company to take on the task. Jack Green started with his story, but just as he was working with a friend who was an author, he left us without getting permission. Following his death the three of us met with his author and found out that it would cost the association all of its money and more for him to write our story. We simply could not afford the expense. Then we decided that the three of us would write the book. However, that idea did not work out. Then we each evaluated our ability to do it solo, but, again, the idea did not work out.

We continued to talk about the book at our various meetings because we all wanted it to be written. There were so many stories of heroism to be told and so many great men to recognize. In fact, the whole company was staffed with some of the best men the army had. Our mission with the 5th Special Forces proved to be a one of a kind operation. Working with the Green Berets, our company performed beyond all expectations, for we flew above the best. We knew that we had an important story to tell. We just did not know how to get the project started.

Someone told us that we had an author in our association. In 2014 we asked him to take on the task of writing this book, and he reluctantly agreed. After so many years, we had someone to get us started. Finally, due to his commitment and tenacity and with the help of many of our Intruder brothers, the book is finished.

After reading this book you probably know just about everything you ever wanted to know about an Assault Helicopter Company that served in war time in the Republic of South Vietnam. You now know about the Huey that we flew, going into and out of holes in the jungle to insert and extract Special Forces recon teams, as well as providing aviation support where needed. You have read about danger, bravery, and tears. You may have cried too. A few stories probably made you laugh. All the stories are true; either told or written by the very men who experienced them. At the time, most were just kids, kids who became men in just a few short weeks. It is true that young men fight wars that old men start.

Some of these men loved the action, some hated it; some loved the Army, others definitely did not. For most men the war ended when they left Vietnam to go back home. For others, it has not ended. Some of our men still struggle with the memories of their years spent in Vietnam

The battles are refought. Our hearts go out to them. A grateful nation is finally starting to appreciate what all these brave men did when they were forced to change overnight from carefree kids to men facing death every day. Most of these men still say if they had to do it all over again they would want to do it with the 281st Assault

Helicopter Company, the U.S. Army's first special operations helicopter company.

We owe thanks to everyone who dug into his or her mind and files to contribute to the book. We know that for some this was a very difficult process. Besides those who shared their experiences, we thank several others for their contributions:

We give a special thank you to Joan Baker for her assistance and for creating the wonderful book cover. She is a very special person and an extremely talented friend of the 281st AHC.

Brian Paine, you made us all look good with the great pictures you provided. Your help with this project is much appreciated. We could not have finished it without you.

Marilyn Paine, who did the final editing of this, we all think you so very much for your time.

A special thanks to our author Will McCollum for the many months, years and long hours that he devoted to writing, collecting, organizing stories and information, then putting it all together to create this book. Will, we all owe you one.

In addition, we thank all the people who have read and will read our book. We hope you enjoy it.

The Intruder Book Committee

AFTERWORD

The 281st Assault Helicopter Company was deployed in the Vietnam War for five long years. During that time fifty-two men died or are still missing and presumed to be dead. Those who returned were destined to remember their experiences for the rest of their lives. Some suffered more than others, and today still carry the physical and mental scars of a horrific war. Others enjoy success in business and have built strong family relationships. One story in this book told of the generations of individuals that were the result of the brave actions of an Intruder crew in one situation. If one imagines the number of individuals who were born as a result of their father or grandfathers being rescued by the men of the 281st, the number would be astounding.

Thanks to the first US Army's Special Operations Helicopter Company, new tactics and equipment were developed to support our ground troops.

After the war the 281st returned to the active reserves while the men who flew and crewed their helicopters in war time went on to become members of almost all the professions that make up our society. Many continued their careers in the military, and at least fifteen members retired as colonels and/or command sergeant majors. One former Wolf Pack member retired from the U.S. Navy as a three-star admiral.

Over the years since the war, the men and wives of the 281st have formed a close bond and have established a formal association that meets annually to renew their friendships. These events are proof of the strong bonds that result from serving one's country in war time. You can learn more about these brave men at their website: 281st.com

1986

I was flying Cobras for the Washington Army National Guard. In October, on a trip from Yuma, Arizona to our base at Fort Lewis Washington, we stopped and spent a night in Reno, Nevada. The next morning the airport was closed for a few hours because President Reagan and Air Force One were in town, giving us time to do a leisurely pre¬flight inspection.

While I was reviewing the log book, one of the pilots of a civilian 727 parked next to us on the ramp wandered over and asked if he could check out my helicopter. "Sure, go right ahead." I told him. He looked around for a bit, and then mentioned that he had flown helicopters in Vietnam. We had the following conversation:

"What unit were you with?" I asked.

"The 281st Aviation," he answered. "In 1969, I flew slicks."

"That was my unit," I commented. "Were your missions as bad and as dangerous as ours were in 1966?" He got that faraway look you sometimes see when painful memories are being dredged up and said, "Yeah, the missions were bad. I was scared all the time." "Me too," I said. There was nothing more to add; we both understood what the other had been through. He took a few steps toward his airplane, stopped, turned and asked, "Do you ever dream of those days?" I paused for a few seconds before replying, "Oh, yes, I do."

Chief Warrant Officer Fred Phillips,
October 1986

MIA AND KIA

INTRUDERS WHO GAVE THEIR ALL

Fifty-two of the individuals assigned to the 145th Airlift Platoon, the 6th Airlift Platoon and the 281st Assault Helicopter Company either died while serving in Vietnam or are still missing and are presumed to be dead. Forty-two died, and ten are missing in action. The majority of these brave men were aircraft crew members. However, there were three who died in non-aviation related circumstances. The names of all fifty-two are listed on the Vietnam Wall. Additional details of their lives and of the circumstances surrounding their deaths can be found in the remembrance section of the 281st Association web site: 281st.com

MISSING IN ACTION

DANIEL ARTHUR SULANDER
Chief Warrant Officer
From MINNEAPOLIS, MINNESOTA
Aviator, 281st AHC
MIA as of December 2, 1966 in LAOS.
Helicopter 65-10088 was shot down.

ALTER FRANCIS WROBLESKI
Chief Warrant Officer
From FREEHOLD, NEW JERSEY
Aviator, 281st AHC
MIA as of May 21, 1967 in QUANG NAM.
Helicopter 65-09480 was shot down.

GEORGE THOMAS CONDREY III
Chief Warrant Officer-3
From ATLANTA, GEORGIA
Aviator 281st AHC
281st Assault Helicopter Company
MIA as of May 8, 1968 in QUANG NAM, South Vietnam.
Helicopter 64-14172 was shot down.

LESLIE DAYTON
Chief Warrant Officer
From GRANITE CITY, ILLINOIS
Aviator, 281st AHC
MIA as of May 8, 1968 in Quang Nam.
Helicopter 64-14172 was shot down.

ROBERT EARL JENNE
Specialist Four
From SALT LAKE CITY, UTAH
Door Gunner, 281st AHC
MIA as of May 8, 1968 in QUANG NAM.
Helicopter 64-14172 was shot down.

DANIEL EDWARD JURECKO
Sergeant
From CORPUS CHRISTI, TEXAS
Crew Chief, 281st AHC
MIA as of May 8, 1968 QUANG NAM.
Helicopter, 64-14172 was shot down.

TERRY LANIER ALFORD
Chief Warrant Officer-3
From PASADENA, TEXAS
Aviator, 281st AHC
MIA as of November 4, 1969 in KHANH HOA, South Vietnam
Helicopter 67-19512 was lost in flight.

JIM RAY CAVENDER
Chief Warrant Officer-3
From SANTA PAULA, CALIFORNIA
Aviator 281st AHC
MIA as of November 4, 1969 in KHANH HOA, South Vietnam
Helicopter 67-19512 was lost in flight.

JAMES ROBERT KLIMO
Sergeant First Class
From MUSKEGON, MICHIGAN
Door Gunner 281st AHC
MIA as of November 4, 1969 in KHANH HOA.
Helicopter 67-1952 was lost in flight.

JOHN ALLEN WARE
Staff Sergeant
From HERMISTON, OREGON
Crew Chief 281st AHC
MIA as of November 4, 1969 in KHANH HOA.
Helicopter 67-19512 was lost in flight.

KILLED IN ACTION

1966

LEON DARYIN FLANDERS
First Lieutenant
From FAIRFIELD, SOUTH CAROLINA
Aviator 281st AHC
KIA on June 17, 1966 in South Vietnam.
Mortar Fire
Lieutenant Flanders was the first 281st combat casualty.

WILLIAM RONALD BEASLEY
First Lieutenant
From BOISE, IDAHO
Aviator 281st AHC
Died on September 25, 1966 in South Vietnam.
Helicopter 65-07926 non-hostile accident

WILLIAM JOSEPH BODZICK
Specialist Four
From PETOSKEY, MICHIGAN
Crew Chief 281st AHC
KIA December 2, 1966 in Laos.
Helicopter 65-1088 was shot down.

LEE JOSEPH BOUDREAUX, JR.
Specialist Four
From NEW ORLEANS, LOUISIANA
Door Gunner 281st AHC
KIA on December 2, 1966 in Laos.
Helicopter 65-1088 was shot down.

DONALD HARRISON
Warrant Officer
From NEW YORK, NEW YORK
Aviator 281st AHC
KIA on December 2, 1966 in Laos.
Helicopter 65-1088 was shot down.

GARY BERNARD FLABBI
Private First Class
From BALTIMORE MARYLAND
Crew Chief 281st AHC
Died on October 26, 1966
Non-Hostile Ground Casualty.

HENRY THOMAS LEONARD
Staff Sergeant
From HENDERSON, NORTH CAROLINA
281st AHC Platoon Sergeant flying as the Door Gunner
KIA on November 11, 1966 in South Vietnam.

LAWRENCE WILLIAMS, JR.
Specialist Four
From NEW ORLEANS, LOUISIANA
Door Gunner 281st AHC
Died on September 25, 1966 in South Vietnam.
Helicopter 65-07926 non-hostile accident.

G. W. WHITAKER
Private
From OAKLAND CALIFORNIA
Communications Technician 483rd Transportation Detachment
Died on July 7, 1966, Heart Attack.

1967

MICHAEL PATRICK GALLAGHER
Private First Class
From DEARBORN HEIGHTS, MICHIGAN
Door Gunner, 281st AHC
KIA on May 21, 1967 in South Vietnam
While attempting the rescue of the
crew of a downed 281st AHC gun ship.

MICHAEL ANTHONY GOFFREDO
Private First Class
From GRIFFITH, INDIANA
Crew Chief, 281st AHC
KIA on August 6, 1967 in South Vietnam.
Killed in a USAF rescue attempt.

DARYL L. MILLER
Warrant Officer
From MUNCIE, INDIANA
Aviator, 281st AHC
KIA on August 6, 1967 in South Vietnam.
Killed in a USAF rescue attempt

JOHN CAMDEN SOPER
Private First Class
From STATEN ISLAND, NEW YORK
Door Gunner, 281st AHC
KIA on August 6, 1967 in South Vietnam.
Killed in a USAF rescue attempt.

LES HOWARD PASCHALL
Specialist Four
From CHICAGO, ILLINOIS
Door Gunner, 281st AHC
KIA on December 21, 1967 at Polei Kleng,
Helicopter accident at the Project Delta
forward operating base.

1968

DONALD BRUCE McCOIG
Warrant Officer
From VENTURA, CALIFORNIA
Aviator, 281st AHC
KIA on March 29, 1968 in THUA THIEN.

1969

TIMOTHY JOHN CAROLAN
Private
From CHICAGO, ILLINOIS
Administrative Clerk, 281st AHC
Died on June 18, 1969
Non-Hostile Casualty.

PATRICK JOSEPH RONAN
Sergeant
From PHILADELPHIA, PENNSYLVANIA
Crew Chief, 281st AHC
KIA on February 18, 1969 at PHU YEN.

VICTOR BLAKE SUTTON
Staff Sergeant
From HARTFORD, NORTH CAROLINA
Bandit Platoon Sergeant, 281st AHC
Died on June 6, 1969 at DARLAC.
Non-Hostile Casualty.

1970

RICHARD STEPHEN BOVIO
Captain
From GALVESTON, TEXAS
Aviator, 281st AHC
KIA on February 27, 1970 in KHANH HOA.
Helicopter was shot down.

BOBBIE HERALD BREWER
Staff Sergeant
From ATHENS, ALABAMA
Platoon Sergeant, 281st AHC
KIA on February 14, 1970 in KHANH HOA.
Helicopter crash.

JOSEPH W. CUNNINGHAM, JR
Specialist Five
From OCEANSIDE, CALIFORNIA
Crew Chief, 281st AHC
KIA on May 11, 1970 in PLEIKU.
Rocket Attack.

ROBERT WAYNE GARDNER
Chief Warrant Officer
From WHEATON, MARYLAND
Aviator, 281st AHC
KIA on April 27, 1970 in Pleiku.
Helicopter was shot down.

THOMAS ANDREW GUENTHER
Warrant Officer
From EGG HARBOR TOWNSHIP, NEW JERSEY
Aviator, 281st AHC
Died on February 14, 1970 in KHANH HOA.
Non-combat related helicopter crash.

NED RICHARD HEINTZ
First Lieutenant
From DE GRAFF, OHIO
Aviator, 281st AHC
Wounded in a rocket attack in PLEIKU.
Died of his wounds on May 16, 1970.

MICHAEL ALLEN HUGHEY
Specialist Five
From JACKSONVILLE, FLORIDA
Crew Chief, 281st AHC
Died on February 14, 1970 KHANH HOA.
Non-combat related helicopter crash.

ALAN HOWARD JOHNSON
Specialist Five
From SOUTH OZONE PARK, NEW YORK
Crew Chief, 281st AHC
KIA on February 6, 1970 at BINH DINH.
Helicopter was shot down.

FRANK MELVIN KAISER
Specialist Five
From MADISON, MINNESOTA
Crew Chief, 281st AHC
KIA on February 6, 1970 in BINH DINH.
Helicopter was shot down.

STANLEY JOSEPH MILLER, JR
Warrant Officer
From ELIZABETH, NEW JERSEY
Aviator, 281st AHC
KIA on April 27, 1970 in PLEIKU.
Helicopter was shot down.

TERRY THOMAS O'REILLY
Warrant Officer
From PLYMOUTH, MAINE
Aviator, 281st AHC
KIA on February 10, 1970 in BINH DINH.
Helicopter was shot down.

ELDON RAY PAYNE
Warrant Officer
From OKLAHOMA CITY, OKLAHOMA
Aviator, 281st AHC
Died on February 14, 1970 in KHANH HOA.
Non-combat related helicopter crash

SCOTT EUGENE SUTHERLAND
Specialist Five
From BREMERTON, WASHINGTON
Crew Chief. 281st AHC
KIA on May 11, 1970 in PLEIKU.
Rocket attack

DANNY JOE TAULBEE
Specialist Four
From LEE CITY, KENTUCKY
Crew Chief, 281st AHC
KIA on May 11, 1970 in PLEIKU.
Rocket attack.

GEORGE WILLIAM TOM
Specialist Five
From STANTON, TEXAS
Crew Chief, 281st AHC
KIA on April 27, 1970 in PLEIKU.
Helicopter was shot down.

DANIEL JOSEPH VAUGHAN
Specialist Five
from LOMPOC, CALIFORNIA
Crew Chief, 281st AHC
KIA on May 11, 1970 in PLEIKU.
Rocket attack

PAUL BRUCE LAMBERTSON
Specialist Five
From VAN NUYS, CALIFORNIA
Rotary Wing Mechanic flying as a
Door Gunner
Died on May 20, 1970 in BINH THUAN.
Non-combat helicopter crash.

ARTHUR GERALD QUALLS
Specialist Five
From MEMPHIS, TENNESSEE
Rotary wing mechanic flying as a crew chief
Died on May 20, 1970 in BINH THUAN.
Non-combat helicopter crash.

The mission of the 281st AHC was initially performed by the 6th and the 145th Aviation Platoons. These units were integrated into the 281st when it arrived in South Vietnam. Their brave men who gave their all are listed below:

GARY LYNN STEELE
Captain
6th Air Lift Platoon
KIA during the conduct of an airborne assault
mission south of Da Nang.

JOSEPH RALPH FOSS
Specialist Five
145th Air Lift Platoon
Aircraft number 63-08631 crashed on takeoff from Baun Briena Special Forces
Camp on April 5, 1965.

DANIEL EDWARD BISHOP
Warrant Officer
From NEWCASTLE, CALIFORNIA
Aviator, 145th Air Lift Platoon
KIA on April 19, 1965 in SOUTH VIETNAM.
Helicopter UH-1B 63-08632 was shot down.

JOSEF LOYD THORNE
First Lieutenant
From BROOKINGS, SOUTH DAKOTA
Aviator, 145th Air Lift Platoon
KIA on April 19, 1965 in SOUTH VIETNAM.
Helicopter UH-1B 63-08632 was shot down.

CHARLES F. MILLAY
Specialist Five
Crew Member, 145th Air Lift Platoon
KIA on April 19, 1965 in SOUTH VIETNAM.
Helicopter UH-1B 63-08632 was shot down.

TERRY W. MILLS
Specialist Four
Crew Member, 145th Air Lift Platoon
KIA on April 19, 1965 in SOUTH VIETNAM.
Helicopter UH-1B 63-08632 was shot down.

MISSING MAN TABLE

The "Missing Man Table" is set at every reunion of the 281st AHC to honor the men who are with us in spirit; never forgotten, they are our treasured guests.

Missing man table

The TABLE ..., set for one ..., is small – symbolizing the loneliness we feel without them.

The TABLE is round, to show our everlasting concern for our comrades killed in action and those still missing.

The TABLECLOTH is white ..., symbolizing the purity of their motives when answering the call to duty.

The single red ROSE, displayed in a vase, reminds us of the life of each of the missing, and the loved ones and friends of these Americans who keep the faith, especially those awaiting answers.

The vase is tied with a RED RIBBON, symbol of our continued determination to account for our missing.

The CANDLE is lit ..., symbolizing the upward reach of their unconquerable spirit.

A SLICE OF LEMON on the bread plate is to remind us of the bitter fate of those still missing in a foreign land.

There is SALT upon the bread plate too, symbolic of the tears shed by our missing brothers and their families and loved ones who still seek answers.

The GLASS is inverted ..., they cannot toast with us.

The CHAIR is empty ..., they are not here. Our lives are incomplete because they are not here to sit with us tonight. They were there for us ..., we are still here for them.

In honoring them ..., each of them ..., all of them ..., we stand and face their table ..., the table where they should be sitting with us tonight. We stand silently in their absence, and pray for success in our nation's effort to find our missing and bring them home.

Please raise your glass in a toast: "To the missing man, we will never forget your ultimate sacrifice."

UNIT RECOGNITIONS

MONUMENT MARKER

The 281st Assault Helicopter Company has been officially designated as the "first" US Army Special Operations Helicopter Company. This honor was commemorated with the placement of a monument at Fayetteville, NC, the home of Ft Bragg and the Special Operations Command.

The dedication ceremony for the 281st monument marker placement was held at the Airborne and Special Operations Museum (ASOM) in Fayetteville, NC on Saturday October 17, 2009. The ceremony began at 5:00PM at the monument, located at the front of the museum, and was followed by a private indoor banquet in the museum main entrance. At the conclusion of the banquet the museum exhibit section was opened for viewing by those attending the event.

This memorial stone was dedicated and placed in the Meadows Memorial Parade Field by the Special Forces Command at Fort Bragg, NC on Friday 7 October 2016. The stone was a gift to the US Army from the Intruders of the 281st Assault Helicopter Company. The dedication of the stone is the final step in identifying and recognizing the 281st as the Legacy unit for US Army special operations aviation units. The 281st stone was placed next to the Project Delta Memorial Stone and as such signifies the close working relations the two units developed in the Vietnam War.

ACKNOWLEDGMENTS

After being asked to write and organize these stories, I accepted and then heard, "Do not expect a lot of cooperation." The lack of cooperation rarely occurred, and it was counter balanced by all the assistance I received:

Retired Colonels John "Jack" Mayhew and Robert "Bob" Mitchell served as co-chairmen of the Book Committee. Their contributions throughout the whole process were immeasurable. Both of them contributed many of their own stories, as well as helping to edit the works of others.

Colonel Lou Lerda's excellent memory, advice and willingness to help with the beginning is so much appreciated.

Many, many thanks to all the writers who contributed stories; without their willingness to share their memories, this book could not have been written.

Thanks to Linda Lerda, Jim Baker, Marilyn Paine, Brian Paine, Dr. Karen Heintz Forcht and Don Budlong for their help and advice with proof reading and editing. I also want to thank my friends and neighbors Betty Winther, Kaye Steger and Greg Stammeyer for their help by reading and giving me great feedback.

Yvonne Gaudes for more than two years helped organize and edit each story. Thanks Yvonne.

Joan Baker is worth mentioning again for her cover design. If this book can be judged by its cover, it will be a top-ten seller.

Thanks again to Brian Paine for his help with photo editing. He was responsible for the restoration of the photos from his personal files and those of other members of the 281st.

Thanks to the folks at MindStir Media for printing and publishing this book.

The Author
December, 2015

On December 11, 2015, just as this manuscript was finished, Colonel Robert (Bob) Mitchell, who served as co-chairman on this project, died. His advice, enthusiasm, knowledge and experience, along with some of his own stories, made all this possible.

****

We all feel a great sense of loss when one of our members passes on to another and better life. Losing a member of our honored association gets harder and harder it seems. It is difficult to come to grips with the thought of our members getting older and we all dread thinking who will leave us next.

As I look back over the past few years, it seems like yesterday that Bob Ohmes, Tubby Brudvig, Fred Mentzer and Al Junko were sitting, talking and laughing at our reunion tables. For me, what a privilege it was being in the same room with them. Now, Bob Mitchell has left us to go be with his lovely wife Sherry. There is an empty feeling inside all of us. I try not to cry; I am a tough old Army sergeant but there are tears in my eyes as I write this.

Their names and stories, along with many others, are written in the pages of this book; they will never be forgotten.

I try to remember General George Patton's words, "It is foolish and wrong to mourn the men who died. Rather we should thank God that such men lived."

I miss them, we all miss them.
The Author

BINGO

BEEP BEEP

CPSIA information can be obtained
at www.ICGtesting.com
Printed in the USA
LVOW13*2221040318

568640LV00010B/66/P